The
Family
Inside

The
Family
Inside

*Working with
the Multiple*

**Doris Bryant
Judy Kessler
Lynda Shirar**

W. W. Norton & Company
New York   London

"Poem for Everyone" copyright 1974 by John Thomas Wood, Ph.D., Bainbridge Island, WA.

Printed in the United States of America.

First Edition

The text of this book was composed in Elante with display type in Souvenir. Composition by Bytheway Typesetting Services, Inc. Manufacturing by Haddon Craftsmen, Inc.
Book design by Justine Burkat Trubey

Library of Congress Cataloging-in-Publication Data

Bryant, Doris.
    The family inside : working with the multiple / Doris Bryant, Judy Kessler, and Lynda Shirar.
        p.   cm.
    Includes bibliographical references and index.
    ISBN 0-393-70142-5
    1. Multiple personality — Treatment.   2. Kessler, Judy, 1950-   —
Mental health.   I. Kessler, Judy, 1950-   .   II. Shirar, Lynda.
III. Title.
RC569.5.M8B79   1992   92-19219   CIP
616.85′236′0092 — dc20   [B]

W.W. Norton & Company, Inc., 500 Fifth Avenue, New York, N.Y. 10110

W.W. Norton & Company, Ltd., 10 Coptic Street, London WC1A 1PU

1 2 3 4 5 6 7 8 9 0

To the memory of Virginia Satir
1916–1988
Pioneer – Teacher – Mentor
Her light still shines with a universal glow.

Contents

vii

Preface

THIS BOOK IS THE culmination of six years of intense, exciting, and often exhausting work. The work had its beginning in June of 1985 when a young woman named Judy Kessler walked into my office. Her diagnosis was multiple personality disorder. I knew nothing about multiple personality disorder, but as I researched I found that not many people did. There was little information written on the subject at the time, no specific treatment, and even much disagreement among mental health professionals as to the validity of the diagnosis. Not without hope, I journeyed to a conference to hear a paper read on multiple personality disorder. The reading in no way added to my enlightenment, but the presenter did validate me and my work. He assured me that my findings would be of value in this new field, a field that needed "pioneers." Armed with that bit of encouragement I returned to my practice, free to create my own treatment plan. Fortunately, I had trained with another pioneer, Virginia Satir. Her concepts became the basic building blocks forming the foundation of that treatment plan.

As Judy and I worked together we began to see how effective these concepts were in her therapy. Believing what we learned would be helpful not only to therapists but to multiples as well, we began to write a book about our progress. At the same time, Lynda Shirar entered our lives. She too had studied with Satir, understood her concepts, and was willing to join with us in this endeavor. As co-therapist she brought with her another pair of eyes and ears, a keen intelligence that proved to be invaluable in the therapy sessions, and a real dedication to completing the book. In the past few years following Judy's integration, we three have continued to work together teaching and presenting at conferences, compiling information, and writing. This book is the result of that work. Each of us has played an integral part in its creation.

We hope this book will be helpful not only to therapists and students but to multiples and the general public as well. Another hope is that our readers will join with us in educating others about multiple personality disorder. MPD is too frequently sensationalized; when the truth about the causes of this disorder are presented, the effect is quite sobering. The facts are that the great majority of multiples are survivors of the most horrendous child abuse imaginable. While we, as a nation, acknowledge that children are our most precious and priceless commodity, child abuse continues to escalate. As a nation and as individuals, we must do more than acknowledge its existence. We must become advocates for children, for if there is no intervention, abusive family systems continue to perpetuate themselves and the tragedy of child abuse continues. For multiples the ultimate tragedy is to realize that if there had been no abuse they would not be multiples.

— Doris Bryant

Acknowledgments

Thanks

   To Jim Gunn for being an initial fellow pioneer.
   To Karen Bernstein, who was there from the beginning.
   To Susan Munro, our editor, for the opportunity she has given us.
   To those multiples whom we know and work with, who continue to
   teach us as they make their own difficult journeys.

In addition, Judy would like to thank her husband Lyndon, her son
Donovan, and her friends Jenny Ligon and Roger Bergeron; Dana
Myers for being a special help; Bobbie Curtis, R.N., for letting the
inner children be heard.

Lynda would like to acknowledge Doris as a mentor, a gifted therapist
whose teaching has always been accompanied by respect and loving
regard.

The
Family
Inside

Poem for Everyone

I will present you
parts
of
my
self
slowly
if you are patient and tender.
I will open drawers
that mostly stay closed
and bring out places and people and things
sounds and smells, loves and frustrations, hopes and
    sadnesses,
bits and pieces of three decades of life
that have been grabbed off
in chunks
and found lying in my hands.
they have eaten
their way into my memory,
carved their way into
my heart.
altogether—you or i will never see them—
they are me.
if you regard them lightly,
deny that they are important
or worse, judge them
i will quietly, slowly,
begin to wrap them up,
in small pieces of velvet,
like worn silver and gold jewelry,
tuck them away
in a small wooden chest of drawers

and close.

John T. Wood

chapter 1

Origins of MPD: Foundation for Treatment

DORIS: *"Imagine a childhood where, from infancy on, the child's experience of the world is one in which her needs are considered only in the most basic and minimal ways — many times, only enough to keep her alive and functioning. A world where the people to whom she is the most bonded, and on whom she depends for her life, respond to her baby cries with negative, punitive and abusive behaviors. A world where neglect, punishment, terror and pain are her constant companions. This is the real world for many multiples.*

"A child born into the world has no notion of what a 'family' is; she has no preformed ideas of what to expect or what life should be like. Her womb experience does not provide her with the coping skills she will need in the real world outside. That's what families are for: the family she is born into is her first social group, her teacher, and her guide. To a child there is no such thing as a 'normal' family; there is only the family she knows. Mother and father are her first 'gods,' possessing all the mystical qualities of gods — all-knowing, all-seeing and all-powerful. How her gods use or misuse their power will shape her life to a great degree. How her parents view the world and

1

themselves in the world will have been shaped by their own families and their own experiences, and that is the picture and the experience they will pass on to their children.

"A child born into an abusive family is not allowed to challenge that experience any more than her parents were able—for whatever reason—to challenge their own. They have accepted as 'normal' that which those of us who are more fortunate perceive as aberrant. The picture that a therapist attempts to challenge and help the multiple change is a generational one, one in which there were many lost childhoods and no concept of normalcy. Unlike many of us who enter therapy, a multiple has no solid foundation on which to begin her struggle toward wholeness; she must literally start from the very beginning. To help you better understand why this is so, here is Judy's own story of her childhood—a childhood not unlike that of other multiples."

Judy's Childhood Story

JUDY: *"I was born uncelebrated. I was not often held or nurtured. As a result, I lay in my crib most of the day, surrounded by the dismal iciness of gray walls. I was cold, hungry and dirty most of the time. In addition, I was not called by a name. I was an object that was discarded and dumped in the corner of a room, only to be used and abused for the pleasure of others. I did not know I existed.*

"From the time I was two years old and out of the crib until the age of five or six, I lived locked in my room, a prisoner isolated from the world outside. Only on special occasions was I taken from my room—to be used in rituals or pornographic movies.

"My room was located at the top of a staircase, and I could hear if anyone approached my bedroom door. Most of the day I strained to listen for the old wooden steps that creaked and cried with the footsteps of those invading my world. In my confusion, I believed that my abusers thought I liked their intrusions; I often heard them say, 'Are you ready for a little love?' Their love hurt.

"My days were filled with lonely play. I craved companionship. As my need to be with people increased, I created an inside friend called 'Little Judy'; she began to talk to me and I to her. I liked to

hear her voice, and I could play with her whenever I wanted. I felt so glad she was my friend; she made me feel good in my upside-down world. We were inseparable. My secluded and lonely world was now filled with laughter and hope. I knew better than to tell anyone of my secret friend, for they would take her away, just as they had taken away everything else.

"As the darkness of each night crept into my room and the light of day subsided, the shadows on the wall grew more monstrous. I hated the night. Often I would cry out for help, screaming, 'Do you know where I am?' It was not safe for a little girl to be alone at night in her room. I experienced the cries of other children inside my head as I sat in the corner of my room, terrified of the approaching darkness and straining to hear the footsteps of the invaders. When I heard their steps, and they reached the top of the stairs, my heart began to pump so hard I thought it would explode. Every breath was so hard; I gasped for air. I wheezed and shook as I heard the intruders unlatch my bedroom door. The doorway would then be filled with enormous, towering figures.

"Unable to cope any longer with the terror of the night, the rituals filled with sexual perversions and physical pain, I created more children inside to help me. Soon there were so many, I found that I could hide safely away inside, letting those I created survive what I no longer could. I did not experience pain, for it was held by my other selves. I did not experience anger, for it was kept firmly locked inside. I only experienced isolation as I 'flew' by myself above the room, watching below me as the invaders tortured the bodies of the other children I had created so that I could survive.

"Years went by during which I didn't know I was human, didn't know who I was. I lived in a world of silence, shattered only by the screaming voices of other personalities. The abusers raped my body, tortured me and took my body from me. They raped my soul and tried to take my spirit as well. They assaulted me with objects that pierced and cut and tore from me any belief I might have had that I was anything human. I was a thing, no better than a chair or a rock, or dirt. I was the filth that constantly covered my body. They had taken everything from me, including my 'self.' Thrown around like a rag doll that had no feelings, I was given to others to be used and I was carefully instructed to give them pleasure. I thought I was rotten and evil, that this could happen only to bad little girls. I was not sure

*of anything in this crazy world I lived in except that I was an awful
and ugly 'thing' and must deserve these awful, bad things that happened to me.*

*"I began school around the age of six or seven. School for me was
like an abstract dream running in slow motion. I tried so hard to
follow the rules at school. And, as instructed by the abusers, I never
talked about the abuse or said anything about my life at home. I
knew better than to tell the awful secrets. Almost daily I was sent
home from elementary school for not wearing panties (they hurt), or
for fighting with other kids on the playground, or for not listening in
class, or for lying, or for just not being 'a good girl.'*

*"I was not allowed to be involved in any outside activities other
than school and I was not allowed to have any friends. My isolation
continued, as did the secret abuse during the nights. From this time
on the lies were well hidden behind the false facades that the abusers
began to create. The abusers involved themselves in community
activities such as boy scouts and attended church on Sundays. They
were considered good upstanding people by others.*

*"Life was not real. I was not real. I was only this 'thing,' waking
each day so I could be used and abused each night. Time no longer
existed for me; I hid inside, covered by layer upon layer of created
personalities. I lay dormant inside myself, still and unformed. I was
not a person. I had no hope, no unity, no life at all. I felt ugly and
dead. I still to this day cannot comprehend how I survived, even
though I know it was my ability to dissociate that brought me
through."*

Dissociation: The Child's Defense

Judy's story is an excellent example of how a child is able to withstand
extreme and repeated abuses through dissociation and creation of multiple personalities. *Dissociation* is "an unconscious defense mechanism
in which a group of mental activities 'splits off' from the main stream of
consciousness and functions as a separate unit" (O'Regan, 1985, p. 22).

For Judy, as for most multiples, opportunities to pass through normal
childhood developmental stages were not available (see Chapter 3). Her
entire attention was focused on surviving each day, every day of her

life. Her initial creation of a playmate, Little Judy, was followed by the creation of the many personalities who would live her life for her. There is reason to believe that Judy used dissociation even as an infant in her crib.

Although dissociation is a common defense mechanism, and one used frequently by small children, not all children subjected to even severely traumatic abuse dissociate to the extent of splitting off autonomously functioning personalities. Why do some children become multiples? Richard Kluft (1986), theorizes that four factors are necessary to the formation of multiple personalities:

First, a child must have the (inborn) capacity to dissociate to that extent. Not all people do; and because there is evidence of generational multiple personality, the ability for dissociation may be partially a familial or hereditary trait (Braun, 1985).

Secondly, this child who has an extensive ability to dissociate is subjected to overwhelming and repeated trauma. Ninety-seven percent of multiples have a history of trauma that includes chronic and severe physical, emotional, and/or sexual abuse (Putnam, Guroff, Silberman, Barban, & Post, 1986). In some cases the trauma may have been non-abusive, such as a nearly fatal accident, death of a parent, etc. The definitive factor in trauma, whether abusive or nonabusive, is the presence of extreme and overwhelming anxiety in the child. The first successful use of dissociation to cope with such anxiety is followed by continued use of dissociation to cope with the subsequent hazards of life.

Third is a developmental factor, which includes the unique inborn personality and capabilities of the particular child, the time of life in which the trauma and dissociation occur, and the ongoing environmental dynamics.

Fourth, the child who becomes a multiple is without resources that could change the situation, provide safety and support, or give the child a chance to process the trauma or abuse. In the absence of safety and support, the child is forced to use the only coping skill at her disposal.

For Judy, as for other multiples, dissociation was the only way she could experience continued traumatization and survive. Because there were no outside resources she could turn to for help, she created a reliable helping system within herself. For many abusive events, Judy dissociated or "split off" four separate personalities: one to hold the pain, one the fear, one the anger, and one the memory. Other multiples may have fewer or more splits or personalities that can handle more than one abusive event; each multiple creates her own unique inner system. For Judy, the children created during each such event remained in that particular "cluster" behind an amnestic barrier, sealed off from awareness of the other personalities and their experiences. More personalities were created to deal with other aspects of Judy's life, such as attending church or school. These became the more dominant personalities.

Each of Judy's child parts was separate from the others and each had his/her own way of perceiving and relating to the environment. The child who was sent home for fighting at school was separate and different from the child who was too terrified to speak in class or the child who tried so hard to follow the rules. Each personality had a unique role or function. The child multiple was able to function in spite of the abuse she suffered by creating an inner "family" of parts that could perform their roles perfectly but out of the child's conscious awareness. As Judy grew older she continued to create other personalities to meet the daily challenges in her chaotic and abusive world. When she entered therapy she had over 60 separate personalities, who would eventually make their appearance.

Anyone who has survived such overwhelming and chronic abuse, and who has dissociated to this extent as a result, will be left with the monumental task of reconnecting all the separated parts. This she must do if she is ever to recover the lost "self," the child who was born into the world whole but who found that her only choice for survival was to give up that wholeness. Recovering and reintegrating the lost self become the task of therapy. For her and her therapist, the reconnecting of these dissociated parts will mean a long-term personal commitment and years of therapy.

Not every therapist will choose to work with multiples, not only because of the years of therapy and commitment involved but also because the tales that unfold about multiples' early childhood experiences are so painful that some therapists are unable to maintain their own emotional boundaries and either retreat or crumble under what feels like an onslaught of horror. The pictures we have seen as therapists and the lectures we have attended regarding child abuse do not prepare us to hear the enormity of the torture that some infants, children and adolescents experience. The statistics that we read concerning the degree of abuse suffered by a child who becomes a multiple take on new meaning when we hear the actual events recounted by a living human being. When we read that research indicates that 97% of those diagnosed as multiples grew up in extremely abusive families, we who work with these clients know what "extremely abusive" really means.

In this chapter, as we discuss our theoretical approach to treatment, it will help to remember that a multiple not only suffered abuse in her family system, but may also have suffered abuse as an adult at the hands of the mental health system in terms of misdiagnoses and inappropriate treatments. The client sitting in your office, now properly diagnosed, has most likely been in and out of treatment for years. If she appears skeptical about this new diagnosis of MPD there is good reason; she has met many "experts" in her time and has no reason to expect that you will be different from the rest. As you continue to work with her you will find yourself caught in a paradox.

First, the many questions she has had over the years about voices in her head, loss of time, etc., will begin to make sense with this new diagnosis of MPD, but the realization will clash head-on with powerful denial concerning the extent of her abuse and the culpability of her abusers. She will be torn between her need to know and her need not to know. This denial not only serves as a means of protection from and avoidance of painful memories, but is also validated by the larger society, whose own denial of the true extent of child abuse has helped to maintain abusive family systems.

Society, too, suffers from a need to know and a need not to know. It is only after centuries that the validity, extent, and reality of child abuse is being recognized, and only in the last 30 years is this reality beginning to gain acceptance. As that dark curtain of denial slowly lifts and the realization that healthy families create healthy children becomes more of a dynamic factor for social change than lip service to an ideal, there is hope that the generational cycle of abuse can be broken. It is here that therapists have an opportunity to implement theories that have proven to be most effective for change. Foremost among these is family systems theory.

When familial child abuse is taken into account, it becomes evident that the many personalities inside the client were not created in random fashion, but because of specific events and to allow the abused child to survive. In the adult multiple, these personalities do not coexist without relationship to each other. Rather, whether the personalities are acquainted with one another or not, they all together form a system that functions in the same ways as other systems. For this reason, we use a family systems approach to viewing and working with the personalities.

Family Systems Theory

DORIS: *"The concept of family systems has existed for decades, although the implementation of that notion as a powerful dynamic in therapy is fairly recent. Virginia Satir was one of a group of therapists at Stanford University in Palo Alto in the 1950s who began to define and use the systemic approach to treatment. She has since been called the 'mother' of family systems therapy. Since the majority of my training was with Satir, I have utilized her concepts in working with multiples.*

"One of Satir's major contributions to family therapy — one used today by all systems therapists — was the conceptualization of family members as a group or system. She saw each member as an integral and essential part of that system. Satir observed that order, sequence of events, and outcomes in families were determined by the actions, reactions, and interactions among the family members (Satir, 1988, p. 131). The essential parts (or family members) who made up the system had a certain order in the way they worked together, a particular kind of energy that kept the system functioning, and their own style of interacting with people outside the family. Using this concept, I have come to view a multiple not only as a part of the system in which she grew up, but also as someone who has created a system within herself, which I call her inner family."

Open and Closed Systems

Satir noticed that two main types of family systems exist: *open systems* and *closed systems* (Satir, 1988). In actuality, systems exist on a continuum from completely open to completely closed. While it is theoretically possible to have a completely open or closed family system, most are somewhere inbetween or toward one end of the continuum. For illustrative purposes, we will begin the discussion of open and closed families as if they existed at opposite ends of the scale.

Families, like most systems, exhibit certain characteristics in varying degrees that help to define the system as open or closed. To understand families as systems it is helpful to look at the following traits: (1) the rules that govern how the system operates; (2) the family's beliefs about itself and about the world; (3) boundaries; (4) contact or communication inside and outside the family; (5) how differences and similarities among members of the system and between systems are handled. These traits determine how relationships will exist and how power will be used and/or distributed in the family.

Rules and Beliefs

On close inspection, the processes of boundary-making, communicating, and relating in individual family systems reveal certain patterns of thinking and behaving. Systems therapists call these patterns the "rules" that govern how the system operates. The rules apply to how the family functions within itself and how it interacts with the outside world. Family rules are based on certain beliefs, often passed down from generation to generation. These family beliefs—as well as the rules—range from overt and openly discussed to unspoken or even covert, depending on what the family rules are about stating those rules. For example, a mother may be quite direct about passing on a rule and belief about table manners: "Don't talk while you're chewing your food—it's not polite." However, if this mother's pattern were to involve approaching many social behaviors with an *emphasis* on politeness, she might at the same time be passing on another powerful rule and belief: "You must always be polite, because what other people think of you is very important." Her manner and tone of voice may impart an even more powerful *nonverbal* message: "I (Mother) will be angry/hurt/ disappointed/disapproving of you if you (child) are not polite; for if others see you as impolite, they will think I am a bad mother." Possible embedded beliefs are: a child's job is to behave in a way that makes the parent feel good; a child is in charge of the parent's self-worth in the world.

The beliefs of a healthy family system lean toward the open end of the closed/open continuum:

1. "Self worth is primary; power and performance, secondary." (Satir, 1988, p. 132).
2. People have equal worth in relationships; differences are allowable because each person is unique.
3. "Change is welcomed and considered normal and desirable." (Satir, 1988, p. 133).

The beliefs of a family system that functions more at the closed end of the continuum tend to show more emphasis on power and control, leading to rules that are more rigid:

1. Control is important; "people are basically [bad] and must be continually controlled to be good." (Satir, 1988, p. 132).
2. "There is one right way, and the person with the most power has it. There is always someone who knows what is best for you." (Satir, 1988, p. 132).
3. Change is frightening; safety depends on maintaining the status quo.

The following sections discuss boundaries, communication and sameness/difference in family systems. As we talk about how each is different for open and closed systems, we will give examples of how both ends of the open/closed continuum would look, as well as how a healthy family system operates.

Boundaries

Boundaries exist both around the system and within the system. The figurative boundary around a family system is that which separates, protects, and defines the individual family from the outside world. In a family without an outer boundary (totally open), the family members might diffuse into the outside world to the point that there is no feeling of family unity or no protection from the outside world. Parents who fail to prevent a small child from running into a busy street are in a family system that is too open: it is without bounds. However, a boundary that offers safety and protection for a young child may be too constricting (closed) for an older child who needs the freedom to catch a runaway basketball or a teenager who wants a driver's license. In order to be healthy, the outer boundary of the family system must be in place, but permeable and flexible, to allow for the changing developmental needs of its members. A healthy outer boundary allows the family to take in information from the community and the surrounding culture as needed; it also allows its members the freedom to participate in outside community or social functions, to be a part of the world outside.

The inner boundaries of the family system deal with the issues of separation and protection versus enmeshment and endangerment. These inner system boundaries also help define the relationships between the people inside the system: how separate or connected and how safe or endangered are the family members from each other? Inner family boundaries, or lack thereof, affect the members' development of self. Overly defined boundaries around individual members in a family may prevent nurturing contact between members or the development of a sense of "family." Members may be physically safe from each other but too distanced within the system to develop trust in each other, which is a necessary foundation for developing a sense of self. Conversely, families with too few or too permeable inner boundaries between members may become incestuous or enmeshed. In this case connectedness oversteps the bounds into endangerment, prevents individual freedom of movement, and again precipitates loss of individual selfhood in the family system.

In a family system that is too closed, the adults believe that power and control are of primary importance (Satir, 1988). The outer boundaries may be sealed off, preventing an inflow of outside information that contradicts the family rules and beliefs and allowing those with the most power to maintain that power within the family. However, when a family has an extremely closed outer boundary, it does not necessarily mean that the inside boundaries between people are also closed. Where power and control are paramount, the inside boundaries between family members may be blurred if the one(s) in power demand the right to intrude on others' personal/body space in order to exercise that power. A family that places primary importance on the self-worth of each member will be more functional, as long as appropriate boundaries are in place. A healthy family system has an outer boundary that is open enough to allow contact with the outside world and inner boundaries that maintain the safety of each family member while allowing interpersonal contact.

Communication

A healthy family system allows direct contact or communication among members, as well as information exchange with the outside world through contacts such as school, work, friendships, books (reading), etc. Communication within a family may be open or closed. A healthy openness allows children to ask their parents questions and express feelings and vice versa. True contact permits honesty, allowing a child to ask and hear an honest answer to tough questions, such as, "Why does Mommy drink so much?" There are few secrets in such a family. True contact also means encouraging children to express their feelings—even negative ones such as anger—openly and appropriately (e.g., "I'm mad at you, Dad") without being punished or shamed. In the same way, adults in a healthy family system communicate honestly and directly with one another and with the children, sharing *their* feelings without using punishing, shaming, or abusive words and behaviors.

While it is perhaps easier to imagine how communication within a family system can be too closed or nonexistent, it is possible for it to be inappropriately open as well. For example, the mother who discusses her marital problems with a child crosses the parent-child boundary with inappropriate communication; such confidences place the child in a parenting role and may easily burden the child with feelings of responsibility for making mother happy. As a second example, parents who allow their children to express every feeling openly without setting limits on *behavioral* expressions (in the form of appropriate consequences, both positive and negative) run the risk of creating rather narcissistic adults who may have difficulty empathizing and developing intimacy in relationships with others. At this point one can see the importance of balance in the family system—and how difficult it can be to maintain.

In systems where power and control are primary, communication with the outside world or within the family itself may become too closed or censored as those in control set rules about talking that will maintain the hierarchy. Relationships may be regulated in such families by force and fear or by punishment and shame—and the development of each person's individuality and self-worth suffers in the process. Healthy family systems are open enough to allow a comfortable exchange between members and the outside world. Inside the healthy system, family members can interact without being overly dependent and are responsive and sensitive to one another.

Sameness versus Difference

A healthy family system acknowledges the importance of family identity, as well as personal growth and personal choice. In any family, members have both similarities and differences. How the system handles these affects each person's self-esteem. Families that rigidly require each member to be alike and negate or downgrade personal uniqueness in favor of fitting into an acceptable family mold are too closed. For example, parents whose stance is "In this family, everyone is intellectual and excels academically" may heap negative messages on the self-worth of a child who is artistically rather than scholastically inclined. On the other hand, parents who fail to distinguish between any of a child's behaviors with "this is acceptable" or "that is unacceptable" are too open; in this type of family the child receives no clear messages as to values or morals, becomes confused, and again finds it difficult to develop a sense of self because s/he lacks a solid foundation upon which to base self-worth.

Families that place priority on control in relationships focus on everyone being the same and on maintaining the status quo; they try to mold the members to fit the (only) "acceptable" rules and beliefs — which are determined by the family member who is in power. Any family member who disagrees strongly with the "ruling" party will definitely rock the family boat. In contrast, families that place priority on self-worth permit differences along with communicating clear moral boundaries; they endeavor to adjust the family shape to fit all the members.

Abusive Family Systems

Abusive families are often rigid closed systems. *This is the type of family system we will be referring to as a model for a multiple's family of origin, since it is the type of system that most often seems to occur in the childhood of multiples* (O'Regan, 1985). Not only are power and control priorities in this kind of family, but power is often used abusively to maintain control. In an abusive family system, members tend to live by a rigid set of rules where change and difference are rarely—if ever—permitted. There may be no boundaries at all within the family, while the outer boundary may be so impenetrable that it separates the family completely from outside interference. To more fully appreciate the extremes to which an *abusive* family incorporates a closed system, let us look at some common abusive beliefs that apply to children:

1. People are basically bad and must be continually controlled to make them good.
2. A child is bad if she expresses any needs that are contradictory to those of the abusers.
3. Severe punishment is the best method for control of a bad child.
4. Survival for the child depends on absolute obedience to the abusers.
5. A child has no rights.
6. A child is an object to be used for the pleasure and benefit of others in the family.

As explained above, not all closed systems are necessarily abusive. There is, for example, a healthy closed system that we've all experienced: the womb. There a child receives nourishment in a very safe environment.

If the baby is born into a healthy family system that exists on the more *open* side of the continuum, her experience will remain one of nourishment in a safe environment where she can ground herself while she ventures out into the world outside the family (see Figure 1.1). There will be acceptance of her uniqueness and support for her individuation from the family, and she will grow up with a healthy, positive view of herself and the world.

If the baby is born into a too *closed* family system, her experience may be quite different (see Figure 1.2). Her uniqueness may be disturbing to the parents, and she will be taught at a very early age that she must mold herself into the existing system—"for her own good," of course. This child's view of herself will be dictated by those who control the system. Individuation is difficult, for family approval will remain very important to whatever she does.

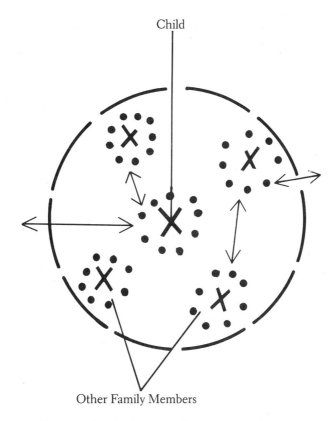

Child

Other Family Members

· Each family member controls own personal space.

· Family members have access to outer world and one another.

· Interaction with one another and outside world is encouraged.

FIGURE 1.1: Open family system.

If the child is born into this type of *closed abusive* family system, she becomes a captive of that system. Her experience is one of powerlessness and objectification, and she *must* learn how the system works in order to survive. There is no chance for individuation here; there is no escape.

Figure 1.2 is a metaphor for a closed abusive family system. The child is trapped in a womb-like situation, yet instead of healthy nourishment she receives poisonous messages about herself and the world.

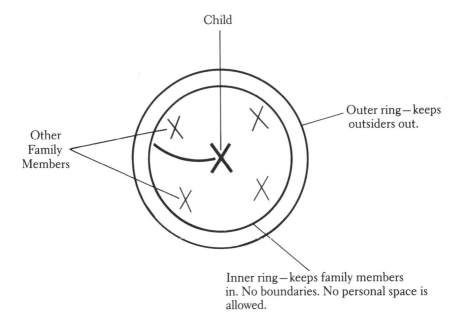

FIGURE 1.2: Closed/abusive family system.

Even when she separates from this family geographically, she takes with her those internalized messages: the rules and beliefs of her family of origin (see Figure 1.3).

The family of origin experience is so powerful for all of us that it colors our ability to see, hear, and feel. Even in adulthood it affects the way we think and behave. Because the abuse itself is so much a part of the family system in which the multiple grows up, the abuse and the abuser(s) often become "introjected" into her inside family of personalities. Following is a closer look at child abuse and its effects on the child in a typical rigid, abusive closed family.

Childhood Experience in the Abusive Closed Family System

The basic dynamics of any incestuous family are paralleled in the multiple's family of origin, except that for multiple personality victims the

Family of Origin   Adult Child/Multiple

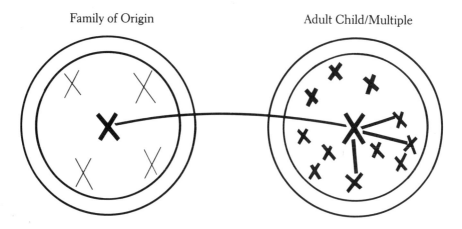

· Multiple physically separated from family of origin, but still has contact.

· Client receives abusive messages from both the family of origin and the *inner* family.

FIGURE 1.3: Geographical/physical separation from family of origin, with introjected messages.

family dynamics are intensified. The child's defenses of denial, repression, and dissociation are therefore necessarily more extreme. In the multiple's family of origin the parents often have rigid religious beliefs as well as the common abusive family beliefs listed earlier (O'Regan, 1985). The family may present itself as unified and upstanding when it is actually filled with fighting and violence. The parents may isolate themselves and the children from most community functions; usually at least one parenting figure has a severe pathology; and the family subjects the victimized child to contradictory and double bind communications on a regular basis (Braun & Sachs, 1985; O'Regan, 1985; Spiegel, 1986).

In severely abusive and incestuous families the dependent child is usually isolated in a rigidly structured, closed system, helpless to change that system or to remove herself from it. The only way she can survive is to *accommodate to it, assimilating the abuse into her life.* Characteristically, the multiple has survived overwhelmingly sadistic physical, sexual, and emotional abuse that has occurred repeatedly over a long period of time, often into adolescent years (Braun & Sachs,

1985). Magnify the factors of other abusive families about 100 times and you will come close to an accurate picture of the average childhood of many multiples.

Roland Summit (1983) identified five components of any victimized child's accommodation to incestuous abuse: secrecy, helplessness, entrapment, delayed disclosure, and retraction. These common elements are exaggerated in the child multiple's life.

Secrecy. A child depends on the adults in his/her life for the meaning assigned to the abusive experience. In the usual incestuous family, the adult's insistence on secrecy makes it clear that the experience is bad, no matter what the degree of the abuse. Secrecy becomes the "source of fear," as well as the only means of safety for the child (Summit, 1983, p. 181). For the multiple, the situation may be far more threatening. The child who is physically and sexually traumatized to the point of near death, over and over, has no safety even in silence. Revealing the abuse would mean even more severe punishment, and with it the increased possibility of actual death. When the abuse is truly life-threatening, secrecy is mandatory for survival.

For the multiple, secrecy also becomes part of a larger system of denial. The more horrible the abuse, the greater the need to believe it is *not* happening and did not happen. Dissociation allows the child to separate herself from experiencing what is truly too painful to bear in order to survive; continued dissociation throughout her life allows the multiple to disown the memories of what happened. The addition of the whole family's denial of the abusive events to the child's inner denial system causes the child to doubt his/her own knowledge and feelings at every turn, reinforcing the rigidity of the family's belief system and closure of intra- and interfamily communication.

Helplessness. In an "authoritarian" (rigidly closed) family system, children may be required to be obedient and loving toward the adults who take care of them (Summit, 1983, p. 182). While the adults may choose to leave a room when someone they don't like enters, can refuse a hug or touch, or otherwise demand that their own personal boundaries be respected, children in such families may *not* be given the same choices. In an abusively closed system, the parent, as the authority figure, is all-powerful. Children instinctively know that they are dependent on adults for their survival; they are not able to take care of themselves. We are all born little, and as children we are acutely aware of the size and power difference between adults and little people. When children, as helpless dependents, receive nurturing and safety from those powerful adults, they develop trust in others and in their environment.

For a multiple, that power differential has been twistedly abused; security and violence have been so intertwined that life itself may depend on the child's obedience. Trust has been destroyed in a process that would seem designed to drive a child crazy. In the absurdity of life in the multiple's family of origin, black is called white, and white is called black; good feelings are called bad, and bad feelings good. The victimized child is told again and again not to trust her own senses or her own self; she learns to trust the lie because that is all that is left.

The multiple is often scapegoated by the family, which means he or she may be singled out from other siblings for abuse and made to carry the burden of the whole family's tension and rage. This child then supposes there must be something singularly bad or wrong about herself in order for this special abusive treatment to be happening. When she is subjected to actual life-endangering violence or torture, her unmet needs for security and love are even more paramount. The child tries desperately to please or to "become good" in hopes of receiving what she needs from the people who abuse her. However, no matter what she does, in this rigidly closed system the rules and beliefs never change.

Entrapment. A "compulsive, addictive pattern" develops with incestuous abuse in families, which often continues until the child reaches an age of comparative independence in the teen years, or even later (Summit, 1983, p. 184). Therefore, if a child doesn't get immediate intervention from outside the family, his or her healthiest option is to learn to accept the situation and survive. *There is no way out.* Entrapment in an abusive closed system requires a child to make some intellectual accommodations, so that she can fit herself into its rules and structure in a way that makes sense to her. The dependent, helpless child has to have some sense of power and control in her life. She can't accept that the abuse is the perpetrator's fault, because that would mean that the parent who is supposed to love her and care for her is bad; the only acceptable option is to believe what her parents tell her: that she has caused the abuse. So the child begins to see *herself* as bad. Summit (1983) quotes from Shengold:

> If the very parent who abuses and is experienced as bad must be turned to for relief of the distress that the parent has caused, then

the child must, out of desperate need, register the parent — delusionally — as good. Only the mental image of a good parent can help the child deal with the terrifying intensity of fear and rage which is the effect of the tormenting experiences. The alternative — the maintenance of the overwhelming situation and the bad parental image — means annihilation of identity, of the feeling of the self. So the bad has to be registered as good. This is a mind-splitting or a mind fragmenting operation. (Shengold, 1979)

Young children are developmentally egocentric, that is, they believe that what happens to them is somehow connected to them and therefore under their control. Children younger than six or seven often have magical thinking, believing that they have the ability to make things happen to themselves and to others. When the adults in their lives reinforce these beliefs with such messages as, "What happened is your fault," or "You are bad, and I am doing this to make you good," children develop an exaggerated sense of responsibility for the abuse. The image of the self as "bad" stays with the child into adulthood. In other words, traumatic abuse changes a person's self-concept, the way she looks at the world, and her emotional capacities. The child must develop a way of thinking and feeling that fits the closed beliefs and rules and way of life in the family system. So first she learns to view herself as bad, the cause of the trauma.

Next, she reverses roles with the abusive parents. The child who blames herself for the abuse and is blamed by the family becomes responsible for the adults' behaviors and feelings. This sense of responsibility and self-blame is one that is confirmed by the parents. The child is also entrusted with the family secrets about the abuse, which if known would destroy the family. Being a closed system, this family is the only one the child has ever known and the one she depends on and must protect. Now "the child is given the power to destroy the family and the responsibility to keep it together" (Summit, 1983, p. 185). The family's anger and anxieties become the child's fault as well as her responsibility to ameliorate. In accepting the blame and the responsibility, she must find a place inside for her own feelings of pain, panic, rage, and invalidation; multiplicity is a way to do this. She becomes in a sense not only the family scapegoat but also the family sacrifice. In this family prison, the child multiple is required at *all* times to meet the needs of the parents, while almost none of her own physical or emotional needs are met.

The multiple's family of origin objectifies this child; that is, the child becomes a "thing" rather than a human being. A sense of not being a real person, which is common to multiples, can begin very, very early, sometimes as early as six months of age. The child's sense of what is real and unreal, true and untrue, becomes greatly distorted and is carried with her into adulthood. Multiples believe they caused their abuse and that they deserved to be punished and damaged.

Another major accommodation occurs in the child abuse victim's thinking. The child is forced to develop a splitting of reality regarding what is good and what is bad. In the multiple's family of origin the child has to structure her reality to protect the abusers, or she herself may die. Because the abuse for many children who become multiples begins under age five, before the child has developed a mature ego, the distortion of good and bad is enhanced. Multiples continue this polarization in their conceptualization of their inner selves: some parts are considered good, while others are seen as only bad.

When the child obeys the abuser and does what feels bad to her, she is told she is good; if she resists or tries to protect herself she is "bad." In addition, the child is put in a double bind by being told that the abuse would not happen to her unless she were bad, and that punishment makes her good. Later, she may even be told that the abuse never happened and that she is bad to say it did, compounding the trap. On top of this, the child's panic, rage, and sense of helplessness are not allowed expression; to express these feelings would mean more punishment. In this confusing abusive family system, it becomes impossible for the child even to decipher what the rules *are*, and any communication that might help is prohibited.

What is a traumatized human being to do in this kind of trap? The child victim believes she is intrinsically bad, worthless, and unlovable, and that she must be punished. For a multiple the feelings are at once so intense and so prohibited that they must be closed off from herself, disowned, and completely dissociated, along with many of the behaviors that express them. The multiple creates separate personalities to hold or to express pain, rage, shame, fear, aggression, and sexuality. Denial is the only feeling, thought, or behavioral mode that is acceptable to the family. When any of the negative feelings are expressed, fear of punishment and/or the need to punish herself may immediately follow, for these are feelings that were usually completely unacceptable in the original family system.

Delayed disclosure and retraction. Whenever a child discloses family abuse, she is likely to feel conflicted and to retract her disclosure at some point (Summit, 1983, p. 188). Telling means breaking a major rule of the abusive closed system: don't ever tell secrets. Delayed, conflicted, and unconvincing disclosure, along with retraction, bring the child's credibility into question in our culture. In addition to the developmental reasons that make it difficult for young children to pinpoint facts, traumatization itself can cause distortion in a child's thinking, while leaving the memory of the event intact (Goodwin, 1985). Distortions increase when the abuse has been caused by a family member, when the child has been required to join a conspiracy of silence, and when "a lifetime's experience has convinced the child that he or she is a second-class citizen without rights" (Goodwin, 1985, p. 12).

Additionally, if in an effort to maintain some inner stability and to support the family myth of normalcy and love, the victim tries to persuade herself that nothing really happened—just as the parents tell her—the child becomes even less credible to adults. The child herself fervently wishes that the abuse were not happening while it is happening and that it hadn't after it is over. The family reinforces that wish and makes it a belief by saying the abuse did not happen. Because of their ability to dissociate from memory and feelings—and from themselves—multiples have even more denial that abuse actually happened than do other victims. Memory is followed by disbelief, and re-remembering by denial, over and over. When the adult multiple reports past abuses, the magnitude of the types of abuses and numbers of perpetrators who were involved, along with the more bizarre-sounding and sadistic stories that the child personalities have to tell, horrify professionals. They may also defend themselves by disbelieving. This, of course, tends to reinforce the multiple's own disbelief, since this is what she heard in her family of origin.

It is easy to see how the confused and trapped child grows into the confused and still entrapped adult multiple, who carries with her the same beliefs she was taught as a child. When one or both of the child multiple's parents also has multiple personalities, the confusion may increase even more. It is a documented fact that many child abusers were abused themselves as children; in fact, without intervention, this kind of behavior may continue for generations.

Although the occurrence of abuse may be generational, not all children who are abused grow up to become abusers; nor do all multiples. However, a multiple who comes for treatment is likely to have one or more abusive personalities directly related to inner system maintenance or existing as introjects (see Chapter 4).

The Personalities as a Closed Inner System

Whether we like it or not, we all design our own families around the familiar patterns of our families of origin. In addition, all of us carry introjects within us, internalized messages from our parents, teachers, society, etc. Some of these messages are negative; some are positive. Satir says that when one of these early messages is introjected, we "swallow it whole" and it becomes something inside of ourselves that we live by, but which is not our own (Satir, 1986). For a multiple, introjects may become incorporated within punishing personalities.

Multiples, as they grow up in this very abusive closed family system, use the pattern that was modeled for them as children to create within themselves a closed family system of their own. If one of these inner family members is an introjected abusive personality, that personality will continue some form of abuse and in this way recapitulate the abusive pattern of childhood. Other punisher personalities may do the same. If there is continued contact with the abusers, the early poisonous messages may continue to be fed in from them also. So the multiple may receive negative messages from both the inside and the outside.

As in any rigidly closed family system, the multiple's inner family members are distrustful of outsiders as well as of each other. Communication is poor or nonexistent. There is continual conflict among inner family members as they seek ways to relieve discomfort and confusion. Some of the personalities may use drugs; some may try to reduce tension through self-abuse. This creates more discomfort and confusion for other inner family members, some of whom are doing their best to function in the outside world as members of the community.

As in any dysfunctional family, life for the multiple is lived in paradox. The different personalities play out their family roles with no understanding of the interconnectedness of their roles or of the part each one plays in maintaining the inner family system. And the introjected rules and beliefs from her family of origin maintain the dysfunction.

The following are common rules and beliefs from the family of origin that become internalized, stated in the way the multiple would phrase them to herself. In fact, she may hear these rules as instructions from voices of the personalities inside.

1. Don't trust.
   a. Don't trust yourself. I am not to be trusted because I am told by those more powerful than I that what I hear, see, feel, and experience isn't what I am hearing, seeing, feeling, and experiencing.
   b. Don't trust others. Other people are not to be trusted either, because when I trust I get hurt.
2. Be loyal.
   a. Protect the family. I must protect my family from outsiders, who cannot be trusted. Only members of my family can be trusted, because they told me this is true.
   b. Never tell family secrets. I must never tell the family secrets or something awful will happen to me or to someone else.
   c. Obey all family rules without question. Never disagree with authority, and never fight back. If I obey all the rules and don't ask questions, maybe I won't get hurt and maybe someday I'll do everything right—and then I won't be bad anymore and my family will love me.
3. Don't have needs.
   a. My needs don't count—because I'm bad and I don't have any rights. If I need something for myself, I am bad, and I make other people feel bad.
   b. I am here to meet others' needs. I make other people feel bad, so I am responsible for meeting their needs so they'll feel *good.*
4. Don't have bad feelings. Never show feelings of anger, fear or pain; these are bad feelings. If I have these bad feelings I am a bad person. When I show bad feelings, they make my family very upset, *so I must be punished so they will feel better.*
5. Stay in control. Be responsible, don't make mistakes. I am the cause of all the problems in the family so I must watch all the time to see if I can do the right thing and not make mistakes. If something goes wrong it is because I wasn't careful enough and it's my fault.

6. Don't act like a child (It's not OK to be who I am). I have to watch and listen carefully to what others say I should do and be, because it is bad for me to be what I am, *a child*—a child who has feelings and needs.
7. Don't be.
   a. When I do my best to be what others want me to be and to do what others want me to do, I don't know who I am. I am nothing.
   b. I have feelings, needs and wants, and I am a child; all my feelings, needs and wants are bad—it would be better if I didn't exist.

Within the abusive family of origin, the bond between people is tight, shutting out outsiders and keeping family members in. The message to the child in this family, which becomes the child's belief, is: "You can't survive outside the family." Yet for the child who is a multiple, survival *inside* the family is extremely difficult as well. Living every day in this family means obeying hurtful, restrictive rules, being hurt, and never, never being able to tell anyone. She believes herself to be ugly, bad, unlovable, stupid, and shameful. The abusers reinforce this belief by continued punishment "for her own good." It is within this framework that most multiples learn and internalize the family rules.

It would appear that the closed abusive family of origin is committed to systematically instilling within the abused child the *family's own powerful denial system*, the family's fears and way of viewing the world. Family members also project upon the child any feelings of guilt, blame, or shame they, the abusers, experience about their own extremely abusive behavior. When the child serves as the family container for guilt, blame and shame, the abusers can then deny and dissociate themselves from these feelings. The abused child is left to carry these disowned feelings, mirroring them back to the abusers and becoming a constant reminder of the bad feelings the abusers are trying to avoid. This can add to the "frenzy" of punishment abusers may inflict, for punishing the child may be a way the abusers attempt to get rid of feelings they themselves refuse to own.

The abusers' unspoken message, "I feel good when you feel bad" makes sense when this is taken into account, as does the message, "You are responsible for the way I feel." Severe abuse is known to be generational; destructively closed family systems breed other abusive closed family systems. In this type of family system, the feelings of powerlessness and rage the abusers felt as children may now be vented on someone who is even more powerless: their own child.

Here, however, is a paradox. As the abuse continues, the abused child becomes the *most powerful individual* in the family of origin, in that the other family members become dependent upon her to make *them* feel powerful. The child who is the receptacle of all the adults' unresolved issues is at the same time their redeemer. In punishing her, the abusers can exorcise those parts of themselves that are horrifying and heinous and that continue to haunt them, thereby gaining some sense of power or mastery over them. We believe that over time continuous denial and dissociation from their abusive behaviors and from their guilty feelings increase the abusers' ability to completely objectify the child.

As the family scapegoat, the child is powerless to protect herself; at the same time she accepts the responsibility for others' abusive behaviors because she is the "bad" one. The child is taught to believe that the abusive behavior is a result of what she did or didn't do. She never really knows. The inconsistency of the messages she receives from the abusers means she must be hypervigilant at all times. She searches for clues as to how she can change herself, or her behavior, so she won't get hurt. She believes the abusers are not responsible—she is; it is up to her to find the answers, to make the changes. In searching for answers she is her own detective, becoming very good at reading people. She becomes her own protector; she trusts no one.

The family bond, although negative, is very powerful. A multiple may find the bond very difficult to break. For an adult multiple who remains in contact with the abusive family of origin, all the old family injunctions and introjects are alive and well. There may be one personality who wants to continue to connect with the family. This will be a part who carries a great deal of denial, which will suit the family of origin well. Members of the family of origin usually continue to disown their projections and dissociate from their abusive behaviors, allowing them to live in a world of denial, the only world in which they feel comfortable. The rules about family loyalty and keeping family secrets will be in force, and the multiple, their grown-up child, is still considered the "problem."

In looking over the rules and beliefs a multiple lives by, it is easy to see where the therapist will encounter major road blocks. There will be issues in the client's inner family about trusting, which is from rule 1: Don't trust yourself, and don't trust others. There will be denial of past events and family involvement, from rule 2: Be loyal; protect the family, and never tell family secrets. She will have issues of self-worth, continually attempting to find out what kind of behavior is pleasing to the therapist and others, from rule 3: Don't have needs, don't have bad feelings — and always meet others' needs. She will dissociate from "bad" feelings: rule 4. She will use intellectualization, perfectionism, and protectionism, from rule 5: Stay in control, be responsible, and don't make mistakes. She will show loss of self, depression, suicidal thoughts, and behaviors, from Rules 6 and 7: Don't act like who you are, and don't be.

Patience on the part of the therapist is essential to the process of change for a multiple. It is not possible — nor would it be wise if it were possible — for the therapist to remove a system of defense that has literally kept her client alive all these years. To understand and use that system as an agent for change is the task of the therapist.

Remember that these old rules were formed and ingrained when the multiple was a child. Many of her personalities are fixated at the ages and developmental levels during which these survival rules originated. It will take caring patience to unravel these beliefs at every developmental level.

chapter 2

Symptomatology of Multiple Personality

What is MPD?

Multiple personality disorder (MPD) is the most severe of the dissociative disorders. We hate to use the word "disorder" with any client but especially with multiples; the dissociative skills they use and had to use as children seem to be the most normal, appropriate, and healthy way they could possibly have chosen to deal with monstrously horrible circumstances. If they had not become multiples, they could not have survived.

Dissociation is a phenomenon that exists on a continuum, from normal "spacing out," to denial, repression, depersonalization, amnesia, fugue states, and MPD at the extreme end. MPD may occur in clients having concurrent diagnoses such as depression, panic attacks, obsessive-compulsive disorders, and somatic complaints. However, MPD is commonly misdiagnosed, most often as borderline personality disorder or as schizophrenia. Multiples appear to be borderline because of what seem to be mood swings, identity disturbances, and self-mutilating behaviors; in addition, multiples may have a borderline part who is manipulative and demanding. The difference is that in a borderline client, the dependency and symptomatic behaviors seldom change, whereas in a multiple the picture *does* change depending on which personality is "out." One or more personalities may have borderline traits, and others won't.

MPD is misdiagnosed as schizophrenia as often as 50% of the time. Eugene Bliss, a noted psychiatrist who has studied MPD, found that in one psychiatric hospital ward he investigated, 57% of the patients who had been diagnosed as schizophrenic actually had MPD (Bliss, 1983). The main point of confusion is that in both schizophrenia and MPD the clients hear voices. However, in MPD the voices are almost always from within the head, rather than from outside. In schizophrenia, medication alleviates the hallucinated voices. In MPD, the voices are those of other personalities, who are necessary parts of the client, and medication does not help.

MPD is not usually easy to diagnose; to do so accurately one must learn to be, as Satir would say, a "detective," open to new ideas, open to the actual possibility of severely traumatic child abuse and to the horrific stories that unfold from the experience of the multiple. Any client who walks in your office with a history of severe child abuse may be dissociative or a candidate for MPD. With any client who comes in with panic attacks, obsessive-compulsive behaviors, unexplained physical symptoms, or depression, you need to check for child abuse in his/her background and consider the possibility of dissociative factors.

The *DSM-III-R* gives a rather rigid guideline for the diagnosis of multiple personality, which in reality may have little resemblance to the way adult MPD presents in your office. The two criteria listed in *DSM-III-R* are:

A. The existence within the person of two or more distinct personalities or personality states (each with its own relatively enduring pattern of perceiving, relating to, and thinking about the environment and self).

B. At least two of these personalities or personality states recurrently take full control of the person's behavior. (p. 272)

MPD clients don't always fit these criteria—especially B.—throughout the course of their history. For example, the personality who is "out" may be influenced by another inside, while a third personality looks out of the first one's eyes. In this case, the outside personality would not have full control of the person's behavior.

We have come to expect obvious, unconcealed MPD, with easily recognizable switching (A: "distinct"-ness), when the reverse is more frequently true. We have found that some multiples have one personality who is dominant for a long period of time, even years; this personality will show very little or no amnesia or time loss and give the therapist no hint of multiplicity. A multiple's symptoms are more often inconsistent, indistinct, and well-concealed.

According to Richard Kluft (1985, pp. 218–219), approximately 15% of adult multiples are diagnosed when they spontaneously dissociate in the clinician's presence; 40% show some subtle signs of MPD that could alert a therapist who was aware of the diagnosis and the indicators of MPD. Another 40% show no "classic signs" of MPD and may be discovered accidentally or by a therapist or client who really makes an effort to figure out what is going on. If you lump together the 40% of multiples who show only subtle signs of MPD and the 40% who show no obvious signs of MPD, 80% of multiples already in treatment will be very difficult to diagnose and very good at concealing their symptoms.

We believe with Kluft (1985) that the diagnosis of MPD requires "no more than the presence, within an individual, of more than one structured entity with a sense of its own existence." (p. 231). If we adhere strictly to the *DSM-III-R* criteria when we assess, we will continue to underdiagnose and misdiagnose clients with MPD.

Myths About MPD

Many clinicians, as well as the public, are skeptical of the diagnosis of MPD and downplay its validity and the numbers of people being discovered who have it (Dell, 1988). The skepticism leads to the circulation of myths concerning multiple personalities.

One myth about MPD is that it is simply a regression to a child state that occurs when the client is anxious. The literature is confusing about this, since even many current writers on MPD apply the term "regression" to multiples.

There is a difference between clincial regression and the dissociation that occurs in MPD; however, the difference is not always easy to distinguish. Regression can be defined as "a reversion to earlier behavior patterns or modes of thinking" (O'Regan, 1985, p. 22). In general, emotions, thoughts, perceptions, and behaviors mature as a person grows older. However, many people may regress to earlier emotions, thoughts, or behaviors when under stress or when in vulnerable situations. Normal regression exists on a continuum from mild to severe. Pathological regression occurs when a person stops attending to outside stimuli and becomes totally invested in himself and in his own body. Because of shutting out the "other," regression can be seen as a disturbance of (social) contact (Pruyser, 1981). MPD, in contrast, is a dissociative disorder—a disturbance in the *consciousness of the self.*

Pruyser (1981), borrowing from Karl Jaspers, lists four characteristics of an intact self. Two of these are lacking in MPD clients: (1) awareness of identity, the ability to say "I am the same one that I ever was and shall be;" and (2) awareness of oneness, the ability to say, "I am only one at each moment, for I have (or I am) an unity" (p. 228).

MPD usually begins in childhood in response to stress and abuse. The child encapsulates and organizes each part of herself, the resultant splits becoming personalities, each with its own life, history, feelings, and behaviors. The various personalities may also have verifiable differences in physiology, neurology, and immune system characteristics, which can be proven when the multiple switches.

Most people dissociate at times, and dissociation is very common in victims of child abuse; however, most of us do not dissociate *from our selves* the way multiples do. This type of dissociation allows a child to live through intense conflicting feelings and the severe physical pain of abuse. Each personality has his/her own role, function, etc., to play in the inner family that results.

Regression does not create separate parts, but rather allows the whole person to withdraw from a stressful situation. Multiples often do not remember switching from one personality to another, and the parts have varying degrees of awareness and intercommunication, which is different from regression. Multiples not only behave, feel, and think like children when they switch to a younger part, but *are* children when child parts are out.

In MPD personalities each (with the exception of some fragmentary parts) have their own history, which is associated with the time period of their creation and the lengths of time they have spent being "outside" in the world. In regression, the person involved continues to have and experience for himself only one life history.

A second myth about MPD is that clients and therapists can create

MPD in treatment. In particular, some have suggested that *hypnosis* can create multiples. The research shows that hypnosis does not create MPD (Bliss, 1983; Kluft, 1982; Putnam, Guroff, Silberman, Barban, & Post, 1986). Multiples are more susceptible to hypnotic inductions, and there is some research to indicate that multiples may have a genetic propensity to enter trance states (Braun, 1985)—a factor that may have saved their lives during child abuse. Hypnotically created "entities," however, "have no previous life history and serve no particular adaptive function" (Frischholz, 1985, p. 104); nor do they show any "psychophysiological involvement" when reliving memories (Braun, 1985, p. 131).

The literature shows that multiples also do not use autohypnosis— that is, they do not consciously self-induce trances to create MPD after learning hypnotic techniques from the therapist. The multiple's ability to go into trance is natural and spontaneous, an unpremeditated dissociation in response to life-threatening situations. The symptoms of MPD have been verified in patients who have never once been hypnotized (Bliss, 1983; Putnam et al., 1986).

We are very cautious about using hypnosis in the treatment of MPD, since multiples will use trance spontaneously and will bring each personality into sessions as needed when they feel ready to do so. Occasionally we do use hypnosis as we will discuss in Chapters 5 and 8.

Some professionals believe that multiples are clients who are "highly susceptible to the demand characteristics of a situation" and who create personalities to please a therapist (Putnam et al., 1986, p. 290). The fact is that multiples strive to conceal their multiplicity by every means available to them, rather than to please even a therapist who encourages them to reveal their personalities. Studies show that there is no difference in symptoms or number of personalities in multiples who spontaneously reveal their MPD to therapists versus those with therapists who suspected the MPD before it was revealed (Putnam et al., 1986).

If the above myths are false and spontaneous dissociation truly occurs, why have so many multiples been diagnosed only during the last five to ten years? MPD has been underdiagnosed because of the predominance of psychoanalytical theory, because of the resultant focus on repression rather than dissociation for so many years, and because of the more recent vogue of behavioral psychology.

Later, interest in schizophrenia developed as a new diagnosis, and it was applied to many clients who were multiples. Actually, MPD has had a definable symptomatology for the last 100 years. It was reported in the medical literature as early as the 18th century (O'Regan, 1985). MPD is not imaginary; nor is it created by clients or therapists in treatment. The usual cause for MPD is severe, prolonged child abuse. The enduring skepticism shows the resistance of our society to ac- knowledge its shadow side — the abuse we would rather not know about. Fortunately, this denial is gradually changing.

Although there is much individuality among multiples as to how they have created their inner families, the symptomatology, though varied, is basically the same. Below we discuss some of the major indica- tors, their causes and effects.

Voices

Hearing voices is one indicator of MPD and signifies the personalities' attempts to communicate with one another. Often the multiple experi- ences the continuing distraction of conflicting disturbing messages. In Judy's case, as with many other multiples, the internal talking was clearly the sound of voices, rather than merely thoughts. The noise they created was so loud and constant that Judy was not even aware of the other sounds around her. For instance, she had never heard the ticking of a clock. (See Figure 2.1).

During therapy, when the different personalities continue to emerge and the chaos increases, the arguing and the negative introjected mes- sages increase as well. The client may hear the sound of crying chil- dren. If the chaos is extreme, the sound of many voices may be heard, with people of all ages talking at once, each with a different agenda. It becomes increasingly difficult for the multiple to concentrate and ther- apy seems more of a trial than a help. Everything may seem to be getting out of control, and the chaos gets worse before it gets better.

Nightmares

As the work progresses, nightmares and insomnia increase. These nightmares can be reflections of actual events that occurred in a multi-

FIGURE 2.1: A clay sculpture portrays the voices of inner family members which Judy often heard.

ple's life. The dreams may indicate that the initial personality who experienced the event in the past and contained it within herself is now ready to release the memory and the feelings that go with that memory to the multiple. The client may not feel ready to receive either the memory or the feelings and may fight going to sleep in order to avoid dreaming. Exhaustion, however, only serves to weaken her defenses and the memories, long repressed, continue to break through into her dream world.

Nightmares may also be symbolic of the client's present journey in therapy and the conflicts that rage within as a ravaged psyche seeks to heal and renew itself. Reframing the dreams can be very helpful in therapy.

Panic Attacks

Panic attacks occur for some multiples on a daily basis. They can be triggered by a memory or by something heard or seen in the present that relates to events in the past. For instance, a man in an army uniform merely driving by in a truck may trigger an extreme anxiety attack in a multiple if someone in uniform took part in her abuse. She may not remember the abuse; she may not even know that the sight of a man in an army uniform was the trigger. All she may know is that she is experiencing an attack.

Panic attacks may also occur if the multiple believes she is about to be placed in a helpless, powerless state, one that is reminiscent of her past. For instance, a gynecological exam, where there are lights and touching that feels invasive, can be a trigger.

Another cause of panic attacks is the revelation of long-held secrets. The threat of death if these secrets are ever told has been imprinted at such a deep level in the multiple that to know intellectually that she will not die does not in any way diminish the terror she feels after the revelation. Awakened in the middle of the night by a nightmare, she experiences a dread that something horrendous is about to occur. She may not relate this to the revelation of a secret during a therapy session, for at that moment the feelings are so intense that she is completely immobilized by fear.

Depression

Depression, another symptom of MPD, is one of the ways a multiple unconsciously attempts to retreat from emotional pain that is overwhelming, to get away and gain respite from the internal and external chaos of a life that is out of her control. Her lifestyle leaves her feeling increasingly helpless and hopeless. As the depression deepens, she begins to obsess around the negative introjects she has carried since childhood, culminating in the one most destructive: "I am bad, I don't deserve to be."

Depression is particularly intense following the revelation of memories, when feelings about the memories and body sensations emerge and are experienced as if for the first time. The most difficult to deal with are the feelings of rage about the remembered traumatic events. The expression of anger on the part of the multiple was discouraged by the abusers. Through calculated forms of extreme punishment and threats, they managed to imprint in the child that anger is bad and its expression will have severe and painful consequences. This is such a powerful introjected belief that the initial feelings of rage about a memory are soon repressed and the adult multiple goes into deeper depression.

Feelings of shame over the objectification and abuse of her body and the introjected belief that she is the cause of all her pain and shame deepen the multiple's depression further. Agoraphobia may result as the multiple tries to hide her "ugliness" from the rest of the world. Suicide may seem a welcome release.

Antidepressants can be very helpful in dealing with the depressive state and in moderating the manic behavior a multiple may exhibit while attempting to maintain control over inner chaos. However, antidepressants must be carefully monitored.

The psychiatrist or physician who prescribes the medication and has knowledge of MPD will be aware that the multiple carries within her separate personalities and that these personalities can cover a wide age range. A range from infant to adult is common; this being the case, there will be a difference in how each personality responds to drugs. This is a unique factor found in multiples. Drugs that might be helpful to one adult personality may make a child personality sick or have absolutely no effect on another adult personality. This is one of the major reasons that any prescriber of medications for multiples needs to have a working knowledge of MPD.

Another reason is that, in order to do the work necessary for integration, all personalities must be available to the therapist and the multiple. This is not possible if some, such as the younger, smaller child parts, are so heavily drugged that they are unable to respond in therapy. Good communication and networking between doctor, therapist, and client are essential in achieving the proper balance.

Eating Disorders

Eating disorders are another symptom of MPD. A multiple may not be aware of when she ate, *if* she ate, or what she ate. If, when, and what she eats will depend on which personality is out, as well as on the age and the food preferences of that particular personality. If one of the dominant personalities decides she wants to go on a diet, for example, she may find that no matter how careful she is she doesn't lose weight; she may in fact gain weight. Without her knowledge and awareness, another personality may be snacking—perhaps a teenager who loves chocolate and soda. If the client finds candy wrappers and soda cans in her car or trash she can be sure of it. Sticking to a healthy diet when others are consuming junk food is impossible. Working on the diet per se will not be helpful.

For many multiples the abuses included the withholding of food as punishment, which becomes internalized as another introject: "When I'm bad I don't deserve to eat." In a depressed state this becomes: "I *am bad*, I don't deserve to eat." Anorexia can be the result. If food has been paired with abuse in such a way that the multiple can eat only if she participates in the abuse, the result can be an aversion to food—particularly to certain foods—and bulimic behavior may follow.

Obesity can also be a problem for multiples. Even when there is a desire to lose weight, fear of being "visible" remains strong. For a multiple there is always a correlation between visibility and abuse. Anorectic persons see themselves as fat no matter how thin they are; multiples see themselves as less visible even when, because of weight gain, they are more visible. They have dissociated themselves from their bodies to the degree they no longer feel attached to them, and they hide "inside." This is a metaphor for the workings of the inner family system.

Working on the eating disorder itself will not be successful. Communication between personalities and understanding leading to common goals must be established before change can occur.

Loss of Time

Over the years multiples grow accustomed to losing time—time measured in minutes, hours, days, months, or even years. The more dominant personalities may be able to stay around for years, but they are not able to remain in complete control. Time loss occurs when there are triggers that stimulate other personalities and these personalities emerge in confusion, not knowing how they "got there."

At an early age multiples learn to cover their confusion and cope with the unknown. Finding themselves in a place they have no memory of going to or being involved in a conversation with people they may not even know is "normal" for a multiple.

Length and variation of loss of time depend upon the strength of the multiple's inner family system. Is the system able to maintain the status quo or is it beginning to break down? Status quo can be maintained as long as dominant personalities are able to remain in control and there is some form of ongoing support, such as a nonabusive husband, wife, or friend. The breaking-down process can begin when a crisis occurs, when the external support system erodes, or when conflict among the dominant personalities results in a diminishment of their power to control the system. Therapy is a process that also breaks down this status quo. The result: chaos.

The therapist, upon meeting with the multiple, has an opportunity to witness this chaos. Dominant personalities still exist and are able to maintain their control in a rather consistent though constantly interrupted manner. Other personalities emerge, sometimes for a day, an hour, or a brief moment in session, and make their existence known. In this manner the therapist is introduced to the other family members, and the work toward integration begins.

Handwriting Differences

In the diagnosis of MPD one of the supporting indicators is the difference the therapist will find in the handwriting of this client, as opposed to that of other clients. Because of the wide variety of ages within a multiple, each represented by a different personality, there will also be a variety of handwriting styles.

Motor skills are not as well developed in the child personalities and differing educational levels will show. A journal page might consist of a very legible, articulate paragraph, a scrawled, misspelled entry, and a notation that appears to have been printed by a very small child. This would indicate to the therapist that the journal page was written by three different personalities, each at a different age and stage of development.

Physical Differences

Just as there are differences in handwriting that express the various ages and stages of the multiple's many personalities, there are also very apparent differences in body language, coordination, facial expression, vocabulary, voice tone, and pitch between some of the personalities.

One personality may curl up in a fetal position, eyes closed, sucking her thumb and making noises one would expect to hear from an infant. Then there is a switch and a young child takes the infant's place: the body uncurls, the child sits up. Her expression may be one of curiosity, fear, shyness, or a mixture of all three. If the child is one of the fearful personalities she may not make eye contact and may hold her body in a manner that clearly indicates a need to keep some distance from the therapist. She may sit very still, turn away, or begin picking at her clothes. She may answer questions in a childlike voice and leave the session (switch) immediately if she feels threatened.

Another child personality may be very curious and much less fearful. She may look around the office, glance at the therapist, smile, and respond more readily to the therapist's questions. Her voice will also be childlike and her coordination that of a small child as she picks up a crayon to draw a picture for the therapist.

Even when contained within a female body, male personalities will take on the voice and mannerisms of males. Vocal tones are lower, language style changes. Body movements are masculine, expressed by the way the client sits in the chair or walks across a room.

An adolescent personality will behave and look very much like any teenager in therapy. Depending upon the particular personality who appears in the therapy session, she may appear quiet, shy, guarded, or bored with the whole process. She may become verbally oppositional or indicate her distrust or anger about the therapy process in another way, such as by silence or a shrug of the shoulder when the therapist asks a question. She may appear restless, swing her feet, or slump down in a chair and look out the window. Her vocabulary is that of a teenager, as are her interests.

The more mature personalities differ also. There may be differences in dress that distinguish one from another. One may prefer polyester while another likes to wear jeans. There will be differences in language usage and tone. Where one may use slang terms and speak in a boisterous tone, another may speak precisely and quietly. The personality wearing jeans, casual in her manner of dress and speech, may also be casual about the way she sits in her chair or moves about the office, appearing more relaxed than the "polyester" personality, who is more controlled in body and manner of speaking.

A seductive personality's dress, speech, and body language will reflect her sexuality. She may be openly provocative, using her body and her language to communicate her presence, or she may present in a more covert way by being flirtatious.

When Judy was in therapy, there were similarities between some of the personalities, so it was difficult to always recognize the change from one to another. As we got to know Judy better, we could tell more easily who was out. Each one had a different manner of speaking, different tone and pitch in her voice, and different body language. The young children drew pictures with their left hand and the adults used their right hand. One personality needed glasses, others did not.

Body Memories

Body memories are physical reenactments of earlier physical trauma. The body has its own life and expresses its own memory of the abusive events. A multiple may experience body memories in a variety of ways. Asthma, hives, rashes, excruciating pain in various parts of the body, both internal and external, may occur—particularly in the genital and anal regions. Headaches, nausea (sometimes followed by vomiting), lumps that appear and disappear, welts and bruises are all common.

These body memories are very confusing to physicians who have no knowledge of MPD, for they can often find no physical cause for their patient's many discomforts. In an effort to ease the pain a multiple might request drugs which the physician may prescribe for a brief period of time while searching for the "real cause" of the patient's problem.

Drug therapy is often abandoned when it becomes apparent that drugs do not resolve the problem or when the doctor becomes concerned about addiction. The multiple is then left with her pain and no relief. Unless she is in therapy and has some knowledge of what body memory is, she will experience confusion, fear, and intense feelings of frustration and shame, all connected to the belief that she isn't doing something right. She concludes that it must be her fault that she hurts. The body memories will then continue unabated.

What Is it Like to Be a Multiple?

JUDY: *"Walking on the edge of life, never knowing when you may appear in a place you know nothing about or how you got there; being called by a name that is not yours; voices, broken families, suicide attempts, confusion, incongruent feelings of laughter and depression; unspeakable nightmares, cold chilling memories that don't belong to you; more voices, intense feelings of shame, guilt and anguish—this is what it's like to be a multiple. Life lacks continuity, strung along a time frame you have no control over; normal environmental stimuli are overwhelming, resulting in switching from personality to personality. And still there are the voices.*

"For a child, being a multiple is like giving life to an already dead thing, hidden away under the pressures of unspeakable tragedies: incest, beatings, emotional abuse, neglect, torture, paradoxical anger and love; tricks, always devious and cruel. These are demoralizing experiences that take away your childhood—forever.

"Growing up under truly intolerable circumstances, my feelings became too intense for me to bear, especially when the abusers warned against telling the 'secrets.' Their intensity grew as the abuse continued, all the way up to the age of 18. I began early to seal off from my awareness the child who experienced the pain of those horrendous experiences. I began to create personalities in my inner family who could serve as a means for me to survive. If I had not become a multiple, I would have either died or gone completely crazy. The struggle to survive the abuse was so overwhelming that the child-self hid away inside. Her existence was denied, and therefore she lived—but at a great psychological cost.

"In adulthood, my system of survival began to break down, and I became a prisoner of nightmares, memories, and pain. I felt dirty,

ashamed, self-destructive, and suicidal. I simply wanted to die at times when the chaos inside me became frightening and unbearable.

"I had trouble recognizing that I had feelings, and when I did I could not tell the difference between them. Expressing my feelings was so frightening to me that whenever I did my heart beat so hard I thought it would explode.

"I did not feel safe most of the time, but the nighttime was the worst, with nightmares, hallucinations, panic attacks and voices—so many voices. My body no longer belonged to me; it no longer felt attached to me, and I did not know it was there. Relationships were hard for me; it was almost impossible for me to connect with others. There was no way my personalities would allow outsiders into their world inside of me. My life seemed as if it were an open wound, oozing and infected. The unstable scab was continually broken, exposing the rotten flesh, tender and sore, unable to heal.

"As a multiple, I used denial and dissociation as tools to block the images of the abuse from my awareness. I learned how to deal with the voices I heard so that no one on the outside suspected I had many different parts. I learned how to protect my many parts from the outside world.

"I learned how to disguise the loss of time I experienced; in fact, I learned how to manipulate time and use it to accomplish life's everyday tasks. In almost every situation I learned how to maintain an outward appearance that everything in my life was great, even when chaos was running rampant on the inside. I learned not to show the pain which constantly pounded in my heart. But in reality there was not an ounce of my life that was not affected by the abuse which caused me to become a multiple; it permeated everything. I became even more trapped inside.

"My life as a multiple was like a piece of stained glass, broken apart by cold, heavy, dark lines. I was sure there was something important that was hidden in each piece, but I could not see the whole picture, only fragments of colored glass. Everywhere I turned, everywhere I looked, every feeling and thought I had as a person was experienced through the eyes of others, my personalities. Every thread of time in my life had been touched and was connected to my other selves, and I lived in constant chaos.

"When I began therapy the chaos became worse. Healing for a multiple is paradoxical. Remembering the abuse without feelings or being detached from the memories can bring no healing—only remembering. When I finally began to remember with feeling, my helplessness, terror, and physical pain were as real as if the memory was the actual experience. I felt at times as though I was being crushed, ripped open, and suffocated with the memories.

"Having to experience my feelings was one of the roughest parts of therapy. For years I had sealed off the very experiences which had caused me to become a multiple. Remembering meant having to survive these experiences twice, and it was worse the second time. I could no longer place the pain in depths beyond feeling. To heal, I had to go through the hell which I had fought so hard to survive the first time as a child.

"I had no control over the memories—they had control over me. I did not choose the time or place they surfaced, nor did I ever want another memory to emerge. I fought remembering, although I could not win. I paid the price with headaches, nightmares, and exhaustion. But I could not stop what was inevitable. Just when I felt that my life could be somewhat normal and I could put the memories of my childhood aside somewhat, I had another memory or picture that always seemed worse or more violent than the ones I had already seen, known, reexperienced and relived. I constantly wanted to be finished with therapy. I didn't want to remember anything more. And my resistance, as usual, made the remembering even more difficult.

"Reliving and owning the memories caused every part of my body to ache with pain. Large welts, bruises, or lumps would appear on my body during the night or in my therapy sessions. My back, legs, and arms were heavy with pain. It was hard to move any part of my body without the muscles inside aching as my body, too, remembered. My heart was so heavy, it seemed as if a large rock lay crushing my chest. I felt as though the weight of the grief would break my heart.

"I felt panic at night—total fear. I remember the fear, the terror, the horror, the shame, and the humiliation of those memories. I wanted to wash off the "dirt," feeling as if it were my fault. My tears flooded my world both inside and out. They helped wash off the dirt, but my shame filled a large part inside which I still keep in a secret place, not wanting anyone to know I have experienced Hell itself.

"This was my experience as a multiple, and I will always remember and honor the struggle and the courage of my inner family, who fought and helped me to become whole. For without them I could never have survived."

chapter 3

MPD and Lost Developmental Stages

As CHILDREN, MULTIPLES miss out on normal developmental stages, due to a combination of the family structure and the child's dissociation. Erik Erikson (1950) conceptualized human personality development as occurring in stages that normally coincide with specific ages. He saw psychosocial development as a process that begins in infancy and continues throughout the lifespan. Each stage of development contains a developmental task and a psychosocial crisis, from which the person emerges successfully or unsuccessfully. According to Erikson's theory, growth at each stage begins on a physiological level and progresses through social and psychological levels. While a person may be developing in parts of three stages at once, s/he is usually working mainly in one stage, and completion of more advanced stages is dependent on successful negotiation of previous developmental tasks. As we discuss Erikson's eight stages, you will see how multiples have either lost or been unable to progress through the stages of development. These lost or impaired developmental stages must be recognized by the therapist and regained by the multiple during her journey toward healing and wholeness of self.

44

Stage 1: Birth to One Year

At this age the baby depends on her primary caretakers; they are her main or only relationships. Developmentally, the baby's task or psychological conflict is to learn to trust her environment and to depend on others versus mistrusting and becoming pessimistic about trusting the environment. Many multiples in their first year of life suffer from extreme neglect; if there is no one in her life to pick her up when she cries, change her diaper when she is wet and cold, or feed her when she is hungry, the baby learns that she cannot trust her world, that it is a stark and lonely place. When parents hold and cuddle a baby, when they look at her and talk to her during that first year, they transmit a message to the baby that she exists, that she is loved — and lovable. Without that acknowledgment, a baby can lose awareness that s/he even exists as a human being. For a multiple, objectification may begin just this early.

Alice Miller (1981), borrowing from Heinz Kohut, D. W. Winnicott and Margaret Mahler, says that every child needs appropriate "mirroring" to develop a healthy self-concept. What parents normally do for a child from the day s/he is born is to metaphorically hold up a mirror that says: "See, you exist, and this is who you are. You really are human and you're important." The quality of care given an infant transmits a sense of meaning, as well as contributing to the development within the child of a sense of trust in an environment that validates her by responding to her needs in a congruent manner. She learns to trust her own responses and her own feelings by gazing into this parental mirror. In contrast, the mirror held up to a neglected and/or abused child is distorted. The message is, "Exist only when I want you to; you don't matter to me. Don't cry, don't bother me — neither you nor your needs are important to me." A baby raised in this manner can trust neither her environment nor her own responses, for they are never validated in a healthy way.

JUDY: *"In my case, I wasn't even called by my name as an infant. I didn't know that there was anyone there in my body — I didn't know there was a 'Judy.' No one said 'Judy . . . ' The people in my life just used the physical infant body for their pleasures; it was just an object. It wasn't until I saw my own hands as a baby (and I can*

TABLE 3.1
Normal Child Development and Development of MPD
(Columns 1–3 based on Erikson, 1950, and Clarke, 1978)

Age	Psychosocial Tasks	Healthy Parenting	Dysfunctional Parenting	Outcomes of Abuse for Child	MPD Development	Outcomes for MPD Adults
0–1	Trust in environment and caretakers Being taken care of	Meets infant's basic needs; allows infant to discover body boundaries. *Messages:* "You're human." "You're important." "Your needs are OK."	Neglect Abuse Objectification *Messages:* "Exist only when I want you." "Don't have needs."	Mistrust Anxiety *Messages to self:* "I'm not important." "My world is not safe."	Need for dissociation Infant may split off newly forming personality parts: wants, needs, feelings.	"I don't know where I end and you begin." "I can't trust anyone." "I have to take care of *myself*."
1–3	Autonomy Personal control of body Doing things "on your own"	Allows child to separate. *Messages:* "I am me; you are you." "You can have some control." "It's OK to do things." "You can think and feel."	Separateness is punished Engulfment or abandonment *Messages:* "I control you." "Control yourself." "You're doing it wrong." "Be the way I want." "Don't think, don't feel."	Shame and doubt Helplessness Anxiety Overcompliance vs. hyperactivity *Messages to self:* "I can't do it/I have to." "I feel out of control." "I am bad." "I won't feel."	Dissociation allows splitting off good vs. bad behavior and containment of "bad" feelings.	"I don't know what to think or feel." "I must always watch and see how others do things." "Wants and needs make me feel out of control." "I must be in control."

Age	Developmental task	Healthy caregiving	Abusive/neglectful caregiving	Effects		
3–5	Initiative Risking Exploring Separating real from not-real	Provides safety for exploration; defines real vs. not-real. *Messages:* "I will protect you." "You can do it." "You don't make bad things happen." "You can still have needs." "I will be here when you need me."	Constriction and/or neglect Confusion Double bind messages *Messages:* "If you risk/initiate, you'll get hurt." "If you get hurt or if I get hurt, it's your fault." "Don't trust yourself." "No one will protect you."	Guilt Anxiety Entrapment Role reversal Hypervigilance *Messages to self:* "I'm to blame." "I'm responsible for making others feel good." "It's my fault when I (or others) feel bad."	Increased use of fantasy and dissociation. Splitting of reality, moral values. Dissociation of personality states allows accommodation to double binds.	"If anything goes wrong it's my fault, and I must punish myself." "I still don't know what is good, bad, real, or true." "I can't trust myself."
6–12	Competence Intellectual and social skills Experimenting with ways of doing things	Allows further separation, with boundaries and support. *Messages:* "You can trust others." "The world is an interesting place." "You can use thinking and feeling to help you know."	Isolation *Messages:* "Don't tell our secrets." "The outside world will hurt you." "Home is the only safe place."	Inferiority Anxiety *Messages to self:* "I can't think/act for myself." "I'm stupid/ wrong." "If I fail it's my fault." "I'm a bad person." "I must try to look right."	Advanced dissociation allows encapsulation and disownment of abuse. "Created selves" perform as needed in outside world. Intellectualization, denial and copying increase as coping. Dominant personalities may begin to form.	"I have to conceal how or who I really am." "I must keep the secrets." "Nothing bad happened." "I must look OK."

(continued)

TABLE 3.1 (*Continued*)

Age	Psychosocial Tasks	Healthy Parenting	Dysfunctional Parenting	Outcomes of Abuse for Child	MPD Development	Outcomes for MPD Adults
13–18	Ego identity Belonging to a group Separation from home Developing sexuality	Sets boundaries, but allows limits to extend as child's responsibleness increases. Allows difference and disagreement. *Messages:* "We support you in your effort to discover yourself and be responsible for yourself." "We love you."	Constricting or nonexistent boundaries Symbiotic bond remains *Messages:* "I don't care what you do." "I'll tell you what to do." "Get lost/go away." "Don't leave." "You'll never make it on your own." "You can't trust anyone but us."	Anxiety Lack of identity or several identities among various social groups. Continued emotional enmeshment with abusers. Extreme fluctuations in behavior and moods or compulsive conformity and overachievement. Drug use. Sexual problems. Eating disorders.	Dissociation and denial become necessary to cope with intense internal chaos and conflicts between personalities. Amnestic barriers strengthen. Dominant personalities develop autonomy. Personality disorders may become encapsulated in personalities.	"I don't know who I am, how I feel, or what I do." "I want to be whole, but I don't know how."

remember this) that I even became aware of my own existence. There was one person who was there for a short period during my infancy, and for a time she did hold me and change and feed me. This was my only babyhood experience of nurturance. When that one person was taken away physically from my life it was a tremendous loss."

The contrast was so great between that one nurturing person's presence and her absence that her leaving made an impact Judy never forgot. Where there was nothing, that one person brought something; when she left, there was nothing again. Because the neglect was so severe, that one small contact was powerful enough that Judy incorporated this woman's nurturing into herself and made it her own. Her spiritual part was named after this person.

It would seem that, when abuse and objectification occur this early in life and when the infant's boundaries are constantly invaded negatively by others, the infant loses her chance to gain a sense of personal space or personal boundaries. At the same time, if the baby's physical movements are restricted to very small areas, such as a crib or a playpen, and if she is confined to these areas for hours at a time with no chance to crawl or explore, she learns that her physical boundaries are rigid and inflexible. Paradoxically, the child's "body boundaries" may be constantly invaded while a constricting environmental boundary prevents her from "invading" her surroundings to explore as babies normally do.

JUDY: *"In my case, I lay unattended for hours and sometimes days at a time with no interaction or stimulation from the outside world. There was no world outside my crib, only a cold, icy, gray wall."*

An abused infant does not get the chance to form her own boundaries—her boundaries are set by others. The baby is confused about where her own body ends and someone else begins; she is not allowed to find out that "This is me, this is what I want, this is what *my* body wants." In this tightly closed family system, the boundaries are controlled by the adults and can be changed at any time. When a baby is not allowed to find out where she ends and another person begins or leaves off, she has great difficulty developing a sense of self at all. It is possible that this type of abuse very early in babyhood may facilitate the splitting that creates multiplicity. The baby self, as yet unformed from birth, instead of becoming more defined as the baby is allowed personal boundaries, may stay fragmented or defused. As Judy stated in her story in Chapter 1: "I stayed inside, still and unformed."

If the baby has never "enclosed" herself in the sense of defining her body space or her wants, it may be easier—as well as necessary—to *split off* the newly forming personality parts: her wants, needs and feelings. In a sense she obtains and collects herself outside herself, encapsulating for safekeeping those wants, needs, and feelings. The extremely abusive family system may aid the creation of multiplicity when it refuses to allow the baby to enclose and define herself within her own body. The child learns to go beyond the body boundaries and to enclose her parts, her many selves, beyond even the reach of the abusers—she begins to create *personalities* who can contain the important parts of herself, splitting them "away" from her self and yet hiding them at the same time.

A multiple who has been this badly neglected has to develop and define all by herself a sense of who she is to pull from her family's distorted mirror the images of herself that will support her survival. The images created affect the child's second stage of development, in which, from age one to three years, the toddler struggles to gain a sense of autonomy versus shame and doubt.

Stage 2: Twelve Months to 36 Months

This is the time when a child begins to learn to be independent and to feel pride in her own sense of control. The toddler in effect says to herself, "See what I can do!" This "muscular-anal stage" is when the child learns to walk and talk and to control her own bowel movements. She wants to assert herself and exert some control in her world.

Stage 2 is one of personal *boundary-making*, the beginning of developing the self. For example, the child discovers: "I can make my own body move over here while my mother stays over there, and she can tell me 'Come here,' and I can say, NO." This is when the child first learns she is really not connected to mother and that she has a certain amount of independence of feeling, thought, and behavior. The child *should* begin to feel good about that. She is also free to find out what she does and doesn't like or want, how she feels, etc. If parental mirroring is appropriate, the message to the child is, "I'm glad you can do it yourself; you can have the control you want over yourself." If the parental mirror gives a picture that the child is bad to want some control, and the child is bad to want something *separate* from what the parent wants and does, the child develops shame and a profound sense of doubt in herself. A child abused in the previous developmental stage has already begun to doubt herself, which increases her vulnerability.

Multiples are often used as children for the benefit of their abusers, who are frequently parents; they are given the message that all their actions still have to be connected to and for the abuser. And they are usually told that, whatever they are doing, they are doing it wrong. The abusers teach their children that they do *not* have control, that they are not human beings with needs or wants, that they do *not* have personal boundaries. Punishment is a common consequence of the child's expressing separate wants and needs. The abused child who is in this second developmental stage learns not a sense of autonomy and control, but a sense of helplessness and being OUT-of-control. The child who becomes a multiple learns that control, rather than being a positive, means danger.

The adult multiple still has a difficult time knowing what another person's boundaries are or knowing where she ends and another person begins. Having only what has looked appropriate in the past to go on, as an adult she still needs always to check to see how other people set boundaries. At the same time, being in any adult relationship will require the multiple to deal with her own feelings, because in childhood closeness (relationship) *always* meant pain. For an adult multiple who experienced such confusing messages about trust and boundaries from infancy on, the very awareness "I want something from you" in an adult relationship with any other person—including a therapist—might cause feelings of terror and being out-of-control. The multiple doesn't even know *how* to want something of her own that is different from what another person wants, or how to get close to someone in a healthy way. She is even inexperienced in how to get *away* from someone, other than through dissociation, because she was always engulfed as a child.

Although the multiple is so afraid of wanting, as well as afraid of pain in relationships, she bonds herself intensely to a therapist. Why is this? The adult who was so abused as a child has yet to complete the first two stages of development; it is as if she still, like the baby, perceives herself as tied to the parenting figure by the umbilical cord. She doesn't know where mother (therapist) ends and she herself begins; she has always been engulfed, just as she was in the womb. She does not know about being powerful in her own body as a separate person; she has not had enough opportunity to learn that. Transference, therefore, will be strong, as will countertransference, because the therapist will find herself in a parenting role. (This will be discussed further in Chapter 8.)

The adult multiple who comes to therapy may be an extremely intelligent person who knows as much about psychology and its vocabulary as anyone—yet she is an adult with infant needs and two-year-old needs, and so on. Even a person who has grown up in a "normal" family and has had an opportunity to grow through all the developmental stages is likely to have received some confusing messages about herself and to lack little pieces of each different stage. A multiple will lack pieces of each developmental task as well, but the void in her experience, and therefore in her repertoire of behaviors, will be much more pronounced. In something like pseudo-development, the child multiple develops by watching and copying how someone else did things. Developmental successes are not made her own.

> JUDY: *"I remember when I went to kindergarten. All of a sudden I found myself in the school cafeteria at lunchtime. I thought to myself, 'What do I do?' It was scary not knowing what to do, since I had never been allowed to be in any social situation before going to school. So I copied the other kids, whoever was in front of me in the food line; I took whatever food that child took, moved my arm and hand the same way, etc. It was a way to make it work and not be noticed. I have heard other survivors say that the only way they, too, learned all these social skills throughout their lives was to mirror other people. When I had to go out to dinner, I mimicked others' behaviors so I would look passable. I would do anything not to be noticed, so I wouldn't get in trouble and be punished. I found that was the best method to teach myself about things I didn't know."*

For the child who must mirror others, rather than be mirrored herself, there is no sense that *she* is doing the behavior; rather than "I want this," or "I'm doing this," she is doing simply what must be done. There can be no "self" attached to the "I" in learning and doing this way, nothing that can grow into a sense of personhood. The child only learns the mechanics of making the body move in a way that looks right from others' point of view. And she learns that she had better do it right or she's going to "get it." A multiple learns to look like everyone else in order not to feel stupid or make mistakes; to make a mistake may mean punishment or even the threat of death. Foremost in the child's mind is the thought, "I have to do it right — exactly right."

Paradoxically, while the child who is becoming a multiple feels controlled by forces outside herself and feels herself to be out-of-control, she must often develop nearly total *self-control* of her wants, her feelings, her mouth, her body movements, her thoughts. And she must maintain this self-control at all times to avoid punishment, hoping she can control the behavior of the adults by her own behavior. In addition, she must learn this self-control without modeling; she must teach it to herself. In fact, all her learning, inside and outside her family, depends on her own quickness and ability to achieve immediate self-control.

Because of the accommodating she must do to cope with abuse, a multiple never successfully completes developmental tasks for herself. After a certain age, if splitting has become a way of life, there is not even one personality whole enough to experience life and develop completely, although each personality learns a bit from being out in the world for a time. By the time the multiple reaches adulthood, she has personalities of many different ages in varying stages of development and partial development. For example, one eight-year-old part may show some signs of healthy two-year-old development, but another eight-year-old part may not — because she didn't have the life experiences to complete certain developmental learning.

When the multiple becomes a client, the therapist may see a four-year-old part who will be afraid to take a crayon, afraid to make her own hand do what she wants it to, without the therapist's express permission. There may be a two-year-old part who has not been allowed to say "no" even though she should have been. And there may be another two-year-old who did have a chance to do that in life, and *can* say "no." Both parts may be the same age, but they have had separate and different life experiences depending on what they were created for and when they were out in the world. (See Figure 3.1.)

Stage 3: Three to Six Years

According to Erikson, in stage 3 the child struggles with initiative versus guilt and shame. Here again the child learns within the context of the family system. In stage 3 she learns either that it is OK to take the

FIGURE 3.1: A crayon drawing by several of Judy's child personalities, showing different developmental stages.

initiative, to try new things, to have her own sense of direction about life, to be (a boy or) a girl; or she learns that she must instead wait to be told what to do and think and feel, and she feels guilty if she takes initiative herself.

This is the age of magical thinking and fantasizing, when the child is still egocentric. Children between ages three and six or seven believe they can make things happen, both good and bad—sometimes just by wishing it. Most children, for example, think to themselves at times something like: "I wish Daddy wasn't here to make me sit in the corner," or "I wish Mommy would fall and break her leg so she couldn't take me to the dentist." So if the child believes that by thinking she can make things happen—especially "bad" things—and then something bad *does* happen to Mommy or Daddy, the child feels guilty and at fault.

Many children between ages three and five create an imaginary playmate. Having an imaginary playmate is a natural thing for children at this stage; they talk to this friend, even see and hear him. The imaginary friend is quite real for the child. For the child growing up in an extremely and chronically abusive family, however, this type of fantasizing can become a coping mechanism.

> JUDY: *"When I was three years old I had a toy box in my room. It was empty, but I had one crayon that I had stolen. I drew a circle on the toy box and then imagined the circle was a ball. With the natural ability to fantasize, I went one step further and created a child personality to play with that ball. I was able to make something not real become real. As another example, I saw another child leave my house and go outside and play, because although I wasn't allowed out to play, I saw that child on the swing set from the window of my room. And I could imagine a child who could play on the swings with him; I could make that happen."*

In a healthy family system, the parents help their preschool child to understand what is real and what isn't, what she *can* cause and what she cannot. But when abuse is happening in a closed family at this age, the child does not receive corrective mirroring about what is real and not real; she is told that she can and does make "bad" things happen, not only to herself but also to others in the family. This type of family overtly or covertly reinforces the child's egocentric belief that she is "bad" and blameworthy when bad things happen. At the same time, the child is often given the conflicting message that what is real *isn't* real (e.g., "Your dad didn't do that—you're lying").

At the age of three years or so, the child multiple's world may begin to seem upside down: the confusion about what is real and unreal begins here and continues to adulthood. If parents or other authority figures continually tell the child that upside down is right side up, then the child believes it. In a healthy family system, when the normal child says in her egocentric way, "I think I am responsible for everybody's feelings and I make bad things happen," then the adults hold the mirror right side up, telling their child, "No, you didn't make that bad thing happen and you are not bad." But in the abusive family system the adults feed back to the child a quite different message: "You are bad, and you made that bad thing happen. And what you see is not what you are seeing, and what you feel is not what you are feeling — except when I say it is." Here the adults turn the mirror back and forth, upside down, sideways and backward. The mirror is never consistent, but ever changing — and the abused child doesn't know which way the mirror goes, what she is seeing, or how to look at it.

> JUDY: *"When I was taken downstairs from my room to be abused, I believed I was making these people abuse me because I was bad. I thought I deserved what I got because there was something about my way of being or doing things that made them want to hurt me. When my abusers would say, 'Well, do you want a little love right now?' I thought I had given them the idea that abuse was the way I liked love — so it was my fault. I also remember that during a film-making session, one of the other children involved was hurt, and I was blamed for it. The abuser told me, 'See what you did? This child got hurt because of what you did.' At the same time, I was told and believed that because a movie was being made, that what happened wasn't real; they told me that anything I saw was not true. On one hand I was told that it* was *happening, and on the other that it didn't happen at all, that they were just making a movie."*

How is a three-year-old or a five-year-old, who is just learning to discriminate between what is real and what is imaginary, to discover the truth? It isn't possible. And within the majority of adult multiples there is a three- to five-year-old child part. The confusion about what is true and real and what isn't is almost always an issue for a multiple — and with it the belief that she must be punished for the bad things for which she is responsible. The guilt and shame that come from that belief begin during this developmental stage. If the child does not receive a positive sense of being able to be self-directive, to go ahead and act on her own initiative, if she does not have appropriate boundaries from a parent who tells her, "Your initiative is okay because I am setting the limits so you *cannot* hurt yourself or me," then the child feels guilty about what she wants to do and what she does initiate, because she hears that it hurts other people.

At this age, when children are particularly sensitive to feedback on their exploring or initiating behaviors, even doing something that does *not* hurt others, *if it is forbidden,* may produce feelings of guilt and shame. For example, Judy noted in an earlier childhood story that she "stole" a crayon. She wasn't supposed to have the crayon; she wasn't supposed to be drawing a ball; she wasn't supposed to be *playing.* Playing itself was bad, so playing was done in secret. And if anything is done in secret, as Roland Summit noted (1983), it has the flavor of being bad. The double bind for the natural child here is that Stage 3 learning of initiative necessarily involves the activity known as play. If you have to play in secret so your abusers don't find out you are playing, then once again being who you are—a child—and doing child things become bad.

Many multiples have had only a very limited opportunity to experience playfulness as children. Like Judy, many were isolated and severely neglected under the age of five. Because play may have been a bad thing when she was a child, playing may be frightening to an adult multiple. She doesn't know *how* to play; she feels awkward and different; playing doesn't seem to "fit." Stage 3 is the play age; the particular activity of playing involves not only initiative but something called imagination. If a child doesn't have a normal range and variety of experiences to stimulate imagination, then she is left with her own narrow, tiny box of experience and she must imagine from that. The child can only imagine from what she knows.

> JUDY: *"When I was a child I played with real toys only when a [pornographic] movie was being made of me. And what I was allowed to play with were the props for the movie."*

In addition, when the child has been given something to play with and the result of playing is that something bad happens to her, she learns to expect that something bad will follow something that feels good or fun. The toy she is given may also be taken away or used in an abusive way after the child has played with it or held it, so playing becomes something that she expects will soon hurt. When playing brings negative consequences, she learns to avoid playing.

JUDY: *"When I was a child I had to play mostly in my imagination — I played in my head. I don't remember using my body at all for play, in the way kids usually play — using their hands in mud, or skipping, or just moving freely. Even to this day I feel stifled within my own body, unable to make it move freely. When a child's experience is only in her mind, it leaves her frozen, unable to move about freely with the body. Other multiples I know also look stiff; they too are still locked up in their bodies."*

A multiple's whole body is a metaphor for her restricted childhood, one in which she could not risk trying new things or even initiate moving beyond the boundaries of her outer body. The belief this child learned was, "I have to be careful and not ask, not test, not try things out for myself, because I am going to get hurt if I do." Therefore, for an adult multiple, as for the child, any new situation, any change in the familiar, feels unsafe. In particular any new social situation may be extremely frightening.

The constant checking for safety also affects the multiple's development of conscience and moral values, which is another personality aspect beginning in the third stage, between ages three and six (Kohlberg, 1969). Living in a rigidly closed family system, the abused child tries every day to be "good," and being good comes to mean *not* being punished — being safe. Normally egocentric at this age, she thinks that if she were just good enough then bad things wouldn't happen to her. These early beliefs become part of the child's developing conscience: "I am being punished because I am not good enough, and if I were good, I would be loved and bad things wouldn't happen to me." At an age when the child is beginning to be aware of right and wrong, the reinforced parental message "You are bad" causes a guilt so strong and an anxiety so great that the feelings have to be dissociated or put away inside. (See Figure 3.2.)

Kohlberg (1969) notes that at the child's first stage of moral development, between ages four and seven, children are punishment-obedience oriented. That is, they base their moral judgments of what is right and wrong on a desire to avoid punishment, to *protect themselves.* Because punishment comes when parents are disapproving, children quickly learn that what is "good" or "bad" is what pleases or displeases the parents. The child's conscience begins to say, "I did something that is right, my parents approve, so I feel good," and, "I did something that is wrong, my parents disapprove, so I feel bad." In this third develop-

FIGURE 3.2: A crayon drawing by a child personality, age 6, showing punishment for being bad and how feelings of guilt, anxiety and anger were dissociated into three separate personalities.

mental stage the child is experimenting with trying new things and learning which of those things are all right to do, which of her feelings are OK, which feelings and behaviors are not OK, and how much of herself and her world is really her responsibility.

Once again, the healthy family with a three- to six-year-old child sets the appropriate boundaries for safety and responsibility, explains what is real and not real, and provides good mirroring by feedback, such as, "This is what is right, and this is what is wrong. What you did was not good, but we love you and you are OK." When the egocentric child feels bad about or responsible for something that has negative consequences in the family, the healthy parental mirror says, "This is something you *do* need to feel bad about," or "This is something you *don't* need to feel bad about"; "This was your fault," or "This was not your fault." The mirror is constantly reflecting reality versus nonreality, what is right versus wrong, what is true and what is untrue. In the severely abusive family, that family mirror is extremely distorted. The normal guilt any child that age would feel becomes magnified when abusive parents reinforce the child's responsibility.

The child's search for what is morally right and safe versus what is wrong and unsafe (or followed by punishment) becomes incredibly confused when the parental mirror includes double bind messages. In the child multiple's typical family, communication is usually unclear. The parents may say, for example, "This is really, really wrong" (even if it isn't), but on another day they may say, "I never said that was wrong!" And the child may be punished following either statement. Even more destructive double bind messages are communicated from parent to child in some abusive systems: "You are bad, so I punish you to make you good"; "You are good when you feel bad"; and "I feel good when you feel bad." With these kinds of messages, every moral value in the child's world turns upside down. This can be the case especially when ritual abuse has occurred. Here the developing child learns that in her parents' eyes she is "good" to participate in ritual abuse, during which the child *feels* bad about what she is doing. She earns praise and approval for doing what feels — to *her* — bad.

> JUDY: *"In my case I developed two different personalities to handle ritual abuse: one who did feel the guilt, who felt horrible about what happened in the rituals, and the other child part who participated in horrible things in order to please. She tried to be as 'good' as possible at what she was doing in the rituals, to fit the mirroring she was getting from my abusers."*

The abused child must find a way to accommodate the widely differing messages that she receives from her abusers versus her own internal, inborn moral monitor — her feelings. When the abusers' moral values are so different from what the child feels inside to be true, when she is told that what she feels inside is just not real and not right, when she can't be herself but has to be "good," then the child must split to accommodate that. So the self which is good and real becomes bad, and another "self" that accommodates the parents becomes good — only it *feels* bad. So what feels bad is good, and what feels good is bad. The child develops two sets of guilt: the guilt of displeasing the parents if she fails to do "good"; and the guilt that what she is doing feels really wrong inside.

The confusion of misinformation at this early developmental stage remains with the multiple into adulthood. A self-abusive personality who cuts herself shows the old confusion about what is good versus bad and what feels good and what feels bad: "I must punish myself so I will be good. I hurt myself to get approval, because what makes me feel bad makes you [the inside or outside parental figure] feel good. If I hurt myself you will love me because you will feel good." When someone says to a child, "I love you" and then hurts that child, the message sent is that love hurts; therefore, she believes that she needs to be hurt to get love. When this child grows up, she continues to look for someone who can abuse her or she abuses herself—physically or with substance abuse, food, or even promiscuous sex—so she can be good, so she can make the other person feel good, so she can be loved. (See more on this in Chapter 8.)

Stage 4: Ages Six to Twelve—Latency

Stage 4 occurs when a child is between six and twelve years old. This is called the child's latency age, when sexuality goes underground and the child focuses on developing competence in physical, intellectual, and social skills. The child's relationships branch outside the home into the school and the neighborhood. With successful completion of this stage, the child feels confident and competent in his basic ego skills; if s/he fails to develop these skills, the child feels inferior to his/her peers.

"Latency" is a key concept of stage 4. While most children's sexuality is downplayed during this stage, the child who is being molested is sexually active. Even if the child were molested only prior to age six, her knowledge and awareness of sexuality and her own sexual feelings would be advanced for her age. The child who is sexualized at this early age may become focused on her own and others' bodies and the sexual aspects of life at a time when she would normally be concentrating on intellectual development (school) and platonic friendships or social skills (Summit, 1983).

Adding to the distraction is the chronically abused child's continuing need to feel safe. Going to school means leaving the home and its familiarity and dealing with a new set of rules, new people, and new situations, which may feel threatening. The child watches and then acts, always alert, always reactive. She copies what she sees other children do that looks successful, so she can be like them, so she can do things right, so she can please the teacher, etc. Her behaviors are based not on striving for competence but on striving for safety and survival.

Research shows that most multiples have already begun splitting before age five (O'Regan, 1985). By the time they start school, most multiples will have several personalities. The child multiple doesn't know how to be like other children; she doesn't know who she is. She looks at other children to see how they behave. This child is always "outside" of herself, always watching, watching, watching. This is a metaphor for the split-off selves already outside of her. She cannot feel competent about herself because there is no one "self" anymore.

The child multiple learns at this age to create parts to be in the world and get by—parts who can be separate from the abuse the child has suffered. She creates parts to get through school, to play with others, etc. The child makes "created selves," each one an intellectualization of what she sees in others and creates from her own head; the created selves then perform as needed. In a sense, the child multiple "grows her own child," creating an actor to fill a role. The created personalities, because they are intellectualizations, cannot internalize the developmental competencies and feelings other children have. Each split-off personality, although created intellectually, may have feelings about what she experiences in the world and may certainly form her own identity. But because she is only a part of the whole child, she won't have the same sense of "me-ness" or of having accomplished something for herself as another (whole) child would.

Between the ages of six and twelve many child multiples begin to create what become *dominant personalities*. These are not necessarily the parts of herself who survived the abuse; rather, they are social personalities who help the child survive in the outside world. When she starts school the child begins to deal with outsiders, people outside the closed family system. Now she must be even more cautious that the family secret of abuse is not discovered. In a sense, to be kept inside a home isolated from contact with people who could discover the secrets puts less pressure for concealment on the child.

At school, the child suddenly becomes visible in a new and frightening way. She must look as "normal" as possible—immediately. Here again is the necessity to split off new personalities. She creates a child who can be outgoing, social, academic, and visible. The hurt and abused parts, who are terrified of visibility, retreat further into the child's unconscious. In addition, the personalities who must be out in the world and do so much of the child's living for her cannot always withstand the extra pressure of dealing with the abuse that happened or that may still be continuing. The new personalities are created to go to school or to be social, but may not be able to deal with the home situation. And although the "school" personalities may be quite accepted at school, the abusers may not want to see those parts back at home. The child may create a new personality who can handle being at home, so the other ones can go to school. This may be a denial part who will help keep the abused hurt parts safely in the unconscious—a personality to be at home and deny right along with the family that any abuse is happening.

Of course, not all multiples will split to this extent. Some multiples may have personalities that are more flexible and can tackle several different functions. The above scenario illustrates the extent to which some children may split in order to accommodate the various demands of their lives. By age twelve the child multiple may be quite skilled at creating personalities to fit situations. Using her dissociative skills this way makes a lot of sense; these are her very own survival skills she is sharpening, and they allow her to have a life and to grow up. They allow her to keep living.

In addition, creating new personalities to function in the world allows the multiple to have something in her life that makes living worthwhile. By leaving the home to go to school, the child gets a taste of the outside world; the personalities created to handle that world get to experience some pleasures. For example, the part who can be athletic learns to play ball and may feel some enjoyment and success in that while she is out. The social child part (or parts) who is created to go to school gets strokes from teachers and peers for being like other children—and it feels good. Success at mirroring what she "should" be becomes internalized as "this is what I *will* be." Receiving positive reinforcement for not being different and for not having problems builds more denial; being in denial in turns gives relief from problems. Is it any wonder that denial becomes such a strong part of a multiple's inner system? With both the child's family and the outside society reinforcing denial, the abused dissociative child is encouraged to split off and strengthen her denial part(s)—the parts with which she gains acceptance from others as well as some pleasure for herself.

Survival is difficult for the multiple in the outside world despite the protection afforded by dissociation. The child creates personalities to fit her world, but she cannot completely control which personality is out or when. An angry part may come out on the playground and force the adaptive social personality to be inside for a while. The dominant child personalities, like the ones in the adult multiple, will experience lost time. And because their time outside is fragmented, they cannot develop a clear ongoing picture of how to behave. They must learn to hide missed time and to cover for each other. For the child multiple, it is not only the secret of abuse that must be protected but also the fact that she—whoever she is—is not always present. *The child multiple has her own secret to guard: the secret that she is not whole,* that she doesn't even know about everything that happens to her or everything that she is doing at a given moment.

Perhaps now it becomes easier to understand why the abused child fails to disclose about the abuse once she is given the opportunity by being outside the home (see Chapter 1). The child multiple is busy creating personalities to get by in the world, busy building the denial system within that will aid her survival inside and outside her home. The child multiple will be difficult for a teacher to spot. Until a child is eight or nine years old, she may not even realize that other children have a different inner world; by that age, denial has already been so reinforced that it is entrenched within the personality system, and the wounded parts have been buried in the unconscious with layers of protective amnesia. Even if a caring teacher endeavored to question her, the child multiple by this age would probably not be able to retrieve the information about the abuse.

Finally, if ritual abuse has been part of this child's experience, disclosure is even less likely. By age six some programming may already be in place. The child may go to a school where the school personnel are cult participants; even if that is not so, the ritually abused child may be told that school personnel are part of the cult. There is no way out for the child, no one she can trust, no one she can tell. When you consider that a six-year-old may have to learn to read and write from someone she thinks may be a cult member, when she must struggle with the developmental tasks of productivity and competence under the cult's watchful eye, the need for denial and for personalities who know nothing about abuse becomes obvious.

Stage 5: Adolescence

The autonomy a child learns in stage 2 is the foundation for the learning that takes place in adolescence. Between ages 13 and 19 the teenager's task is to develop a sense of identity and an integrated image of herself as a unique person. Teens normally begin to separate from their parents and identify with peers and other adult role models in their efforts to individuate.

As we noted earlier, children who become multiples are unable to successfully complete stage 2. Instead, they often begin splitting at that age — or even before. The two-year-old dissociative child's act of autonomy is to split; this is her only avenue for control. Ten to twelve years later, the child has spent her whole life creating separate parts. How can a multiple, who has spent so much time disintegrating, complete the developmentally appropriate task of ego integration as a teen? It is an unlikely, if not impossible, task. The teenage multiple's many parts may experience themselves as unique, but not as a single person. She is many persons, many selves. At this age the multiple's dominant personalities become more behaviorally autonomous, more separate from each other; the amnestic barriers between the parts may become strengthened and rigidified.

The teenage multiple may have major issues with control, issues remaining from stage 2. Her dominant personalities may have some real conflicts over which of them is going to be in charge. While most teens experience some battles over control with parents, teachers or peers, the multiple must do battle with her own parts as well.

If an adolescent does not successfully complete stage 5, she will fail to develop identity integration; instead, identity diffusion may occur. Normally the teen years are extremely vulnerable ones because diffusion and confusion may be unavoidable temporary by-products of the tremendous physical and emotional changes taking place in the body (Duvall, 1971). For those teens who cannot weather this biological storm, personality disorders may begin to appear which can become fixated: narcissism, borderline personality, dependency, etc. For the multiple these various personality disorders may become embodied in *personalities*; there may be a narcissistic personality, a borderline personality part, a schizoid withdrawn personality, a very dependent part, a histrionic performer part, etc. Because many adult multiples have *parts* who exhibit symptoms of a personality disorder, they may be frequently misdiagnosed.

For the normal adolescent in a developmentally appropriate state of diffusion, successful completion of stage 5 is marked by ego stabilization or integration. A multiple of this age is in a different kind of diffuse state; her ego has been split into many separate and individual parts that function autonomously. She would have to integrate her personalities before she could do the normal task of ego integration. But the teen multiple may not be interested in integrating at all; instead, her dominant personalities may be more interested in developing autonomy and separateness from each other.

Sexuality is a big issue for adolescents, since this is the time of life when hormones begin to course through the body. A teenage multiple may create a sexual personality during this time—someone to carry the adolescent's sexuality. But because sexuality has almost always been connected with abuse, her many parts may have different opinions about sexuality and sexual activity. There may be several sexual personalities that have sexual desires and act on them—perhaps with a family member, or on the streets, in school, or with whomever s/he wants. He or she may become what is considered "promiscuous." A sexual personality may not communicate enough with other more inhibited parts of her inner family for the others to put limits on sexual activity. Figuring out what is appropriate and what is inappropriate—sexually, as in every other area of life—is what normal teenagers struggle with. However, without inner communication and cooperation among parts, the sexual personality—like the others—develops his or her own sense of what is OK, in relative isolation. As a result, a sexual personality may be rejected and considered "bad" by the other personalities and may be rejecting of herself as well.

> JUDY: *"My sexual part was named Gerri, and she was a teenage personality. Gerri didn't like the fact that she had orgasms and enjoyed sex, because that in itself was punishable according to the old family rules. You weren't supposed to enjoy it. But Gerri's role was very important; she was angry at men, and she always told Doris in therapy, 'I am out to use men just like they used me.'"*

While both male and female multiples may have personalities who identify with the abusers, males are more likely to identify with a male abuser simply because they are boys. A teenage multiple who is male must also have a sexual part, and it may well be modeled after an abuser. Because sexuality for the boy is so connected with abuse, the male multiple may act out sex abusively toward other teens or children. Again, the multiple does not have sufficient contact between all his parts to necessarily monitor that sexual behavior in a way that would be comfortable for all of them. Abusive sexual behaviors only bring more inner family rejection, more guilt for the sexual personality, and more shame. Denial may be even more necessary to allow this sexual part to continue to function. The male multiple, as he continues from adolescence into adulthood, may well become a perpetrator of sexual/violent crime and wind up in jail.

So for a multiple the chaos of adolescence is increased a thousand times. Adolescence solidifies and separates the more dominant personalities. If the process of splitting is not interrupted before the multiple reaches school age (first grade), the child is likely to continue to create personalities to cope with life, which may include continued abuse, and she will continue to build the amnestic barriers between parts as needed. Without early intervention, the child is fated to keep being "multiple" as best she can. The normal sequence of the growing up years, in which the child gradually develops an identity and an integrated ego, becomes just the opposite for a multiple: the more developmental stages she passes through, the more she is pushed into multiplicity.

Stages 6, 7, and 8: Adulthood

In early adulthood, between ages 20 and 30, people struggle to develop intimacy in significant relationships with partners in friendship, sex, the workplace, etc. If successful, people complete this stage with the ability to form positive close personal relationships and/or make initial career commitments; if unsuccessful, personal isolation is the outcome.

Multiples often have two (or more) personalities to deal with the two extremes of intimacy and isolation: one part to be social, and one to be alone. The twenties are often a time when personalities choose among themselves who is going to live in the world and how they shall be in the world, given that others see them as one. Decisions must be made about intimacy, marriage, children, and career, for example. The multiple who opts for marriage may have to create a personality to be a wife, one to be a mother, etc. A multiple who chooses a career may have to repress many conflicting personalities. Drugs and alcohol are often used in early adulthood to help repress memories and feelings about abuse, as well as to keep the drug-using personality in control within the inner family. The twenties may be a time when a multiple's dominant personalities strengthen even more their own ability to stay out in the world. During this time, a multiple may have one personality so dominant that she does very little switching and experiences little loss of time.

One of the problems that multiples have is making and maintaining friendships. They don't know what a friendship means, what to expect in a friendship, or what the "rules" of friendship are. Multiples usually have not learned about give and take; they only know about giving— giving a lot. They don't know about boundaries; they don't know that they have the right to say "no" to a friend. They never had any rights as children, so they don't know about having rights as adults. So multiples can find themselves being taken advantage of or victimized in friend-ships, as well as in relationships, repeating the pattern of the abusive family of origin.

> JUDY: *"I am just now, since I integrated, learning about friend-ships for myself. A normal give and take relationship or friendship is almost out of the question for an adult multiple, because she is just trying to survive—period. If I were still a multiple, I couldn't be thinking about how to be in a relationship, but only about surviving. I am just now setting up boundaries; I don't have any limits on giving, or even sometimes on taking. 'You always give all' was a family rule for me; I always had to do that as a child. I still tend to think it is wrong if I don't give all, because somehow the rule is: If I don't give all, then I won't deserve anything back. And then I might get hurt."*

Middle adulthood, ages 30 to 50, involves the tension between generativity and stagnation. This is the stage when we want life to make sense; we create or do things and find meaning in them. If we do not, we find that life seems meaningless. Sharing, both at home and at work, is important, and in a sense the commitment level of early adult-hood deepens, since this stage also involves concern for one's children and future generations.

In middle adulthood, a multiple's stable inner system may begin to break down. For anyone who has been abused as a child, it is possible to block off the memory of those events for a certain period of time, but in the late twenties or early thirties it may begin to resurface. A multiple, like others who were abused in childhood, may begin to have body memories, anxiety, and depression when she reaches her thirties. And as the memories begin to surface, the dominant personalities begin to lose their ability to stay out in the world or in control.

We don't really know why repressed material often begins to surface at this stage of life, but we do have ideas. A certain amount of psychological energy may be required to keep important memories down (even for people who are not multiples) or to keep amnestic barriers up between dissociated parts; after 30 years of life, one's energy may simply wear down. In addition, by age 30 a multiple has a myriad of outside stressors to deal with, all requiring energy: her children, if she has some, are growing up and may have problems that need attention; her marriage is probably in transition; job changes may be required either for herself or her spouse; maybe even a relocation comes up. It is as if somehow the multiple is able to block out for a period of time many or most of the environmental triggers that are occurring all around her; however, when she gets married, enters relationships, or has children, she must deal with many different aspects of someone else's life as well—and these are all things for which she has had no training or experience of her own.

Many of the situations that come up will be frightening to the multiple, and the dominant personalities may not be able to keep other personalities from emerging due to the onslaught of pressures brought about by so many stressors. When environmental triggers cause her anxiety to skyrocket, post-traumatic stress begins to expose the multiple personalities lying beneath the surface.

Chaos, in both her inner world and her outside world, is the result at this stage of life. A multiple who has chosen to be a wife and mother may face a divorce when these inner changes begin to happen. A personality may surface who does not know or like her husband, for example. The wife and/or mother personality who may have been dominant for years is now forced to spend much more time "inside" while other personalities emerge to take a turn. In fact, the husband may have married a part who is now seldom out.

> JUDY: *"So often I have heard multiples say, 'Everything was fine for years; I'd been married to my husband, nothing seemed different, we lived a certain way, and then all of a sudden I began to change and the memories began to surface. Suddenly I had multiple personalities. I couldn't bear to be with my husband. I couldn't stand to have sex anymore, I didn't want to be around him. I didn't marry him—I don't even know the guy!'"*

With the absence of the personality who got married comes the worsening of marital problems and conflicts; when the mothering personality cannot be out to mother, there are problems with the children. A female multiple may find that she has married an abusive man, which also restimulates memories and feelings of old abuses. Children may be triggers as well. A multiple will have many personalities who are younger than her own biological children, leaving the mother personality in dismay. The advent of all these problems causes the multiple to go right back into her old family system beliefs. She thinks she is not lovable, that there must be something wrong with her. If any one of the personalities feels even a little self-esteem by this stage, e.g., about being able to create a home, have a husband, have a career, etc., her mounting losses may cause even more chaos and dissociation. This, too, feeds back into the old belief system: "I don't deserve anything good; that's why this is happening."

Multiples often come in for therapy in their thirties when all this chaos is occurring. And along with the expected symptoms of panic attacks, or depression, or post-traumatic stress, they often show a deep confusion that would be reasonable for someone in their circumstances. Middle adulthood is a time when "normal" people go through transitions and struggle with the meaning of life. A multiple at midlife is experiencing a life that does not make sense. Questions lead to more questions, and the client who arrives for therapy may be asking, "Why do I lose time? I want to be doing things, but I can't seem to get them done. I don't know who does these other mysterious things around the house or at work—but it isn't me. My life is crumbling around me; I have nightmares; I can't sleep at night; I hear people talking in my head. What is happening to me? Nothing makes sense anymore."

Maturity is the last of Erikson's eight stages. The conflict at this stage, from the sixties on, is to develop integrity and a sense of satisfaction with one's life. Whereas the human being is designed to grow into maturity, a multiple redesigns her being for safety and survival. All her component parts are created to do that; all her personalities are working not to mature but to protect her, to keep safe that which was born. The multiple is like a flower that closes before it opens. The flower still develops petals like other flowers, but each petal, when it is formed, closes in or curls over itself. The flower stays in a tight bud, protecting the original birth child who is hidden deep inside—deep down, dormant, and still undeveloped.

The task of therapy is to gently lay back all the petals one by one, opening up the flower to find the center.

chapter 4

A View of the Multiple's Inner Family

T HERE IS NO WAY TO estimate the number of personalities you will be meeting and working with when a multiple enters your office. You can be certain, however, that ages will vary and roles differ within her inner family just as they do in any family system. In this chapter we explore different personality types and their roles.

Dominant versus Nondominant Personalities

Dominant Personalities

Dominant personalities are those personalities who are created to fill very specific roles in a multiple's life. For instance, a child will create a child personality whose main function is to please; she will be one who does her best to figure out what those around her want and then act accordingly, becoming the "good little girl." A "pleasing" role may manifest itself in several personalities as the multiple grows up, and by adulthood there may be one who is two, one who is four, another eight

71

years old, 11, 16, and so on. An adult pleaser personality will continue to be the "good girl" and attempt to please those around her by observing what is acceptable and what isn't and acting accordingly. This personality can be a major denial part.

Other dominant personalities take on other roles. There may be one whose specific duty is to attend college; another may be the family breadwinner. Whatever roles these dominant personalities play, they are each unique in how they view and interact with the world. For example, some personalities may speak foreign languages while others do not; some may be musical or artistic and others not. Many personalities are even unique physiologically: some may need glasses, others may not. Some may be affected strongly by drugs or medications; others may be able to tolerate a high intake.

Personalities who are opposite in one or more important features often become dominant personalities. A multiple may have a socially aware pleaser personality and another who is a rebel or a good-time party person. There may be a self-conscious churchgoer and one who is promiscuous. The polarities balance each other out, because both are needed for the whole person.

In Judy's inner family, two dominant personalities were created at age 18. Jane remained more a teenager in her style of living, less likely to take on responsibilities growing up, whereas Judith, a personality created at the same time as Jane, became super-responsible. In therapy, however, dominant personalities may round out or learn new ways of thinking and behaving. Jane, for example, retained her ability to play but matured into acting as a co-therapist, taking responsible care of younger personalities and helping Judith out of her denial. She was very mature by the time she integrated.

The more dominant personalities, or their forerunners, are likely to be created during or after the multiple's school years. During the teenage years, those personalities who have been created to be out in the world begin to develop autonomy and more stable roles. They may either remain fixated at the age at which they were created or continue to grow in age.

DORIS: *"From what I have seen in multiples, most of the major personalities usually remain fixated at the age they were created. For instance, a 17-year-old dominant personality remains 17, but as she spends more time out in the world she learns a lot and her social skills improve. She interacts with people who are the multiple's actual chronological age and may pass for a much older person; yet she retains her teenage thinking patterns."*

LYNDA: *"A multiple may have parts who think they get older, but other personalities will often later tell you they are not really older. The part in question knows, for example, 'I was created at 17 and I am now 25.' Academically or intellectually a personality may mature, but in other functions, e.g., socially, she remains the age at which she was created. Overlapping or blending that occurs at times when one personality influences another may also cause age confusion. Child multiples I work with tell me, for example, 'I am six years old, I'm in fifth grade, and I can do the school work—I get lots of help from [another personality] inside.'"*

When a multiple comes in for therapy, her intellectual skills will be good, but her developmental difficulties will still exist. Multiples, because they are often extremely intelligent people, have been able to connect with other people in society by using their intellect, creating personalities to perform social roles as needed. However, as discussed in Chapter 3, they have copied from others around them, and the dominant personalities created lack developmental experience on which to base their skills. In a way, intellectual achievements make up for the losses in other areas; a multiple lives by her "wits." A therapist can easily perceive the client's wonderful intelligence and intellectual maturity and expect a more global developmental maturity as well, when it does not exist. The combination of intellect and the desire to please may give a therapist the impression that the multiple will or should move along very quickly in therapy.

JUDY: *"I once had a therapist who expected me to be able to cope with situations that were just beyond my understanding or my skills. He became frustrated with me for not handling things more maturely, saying: 'Why can't you stop doing this behavior? I see you handling other things in mature ways—why can't your emotions be handled in a more mature way? You should know better.' I just didn't have the experience to draw from."*

Some personalities may become so dominant that they stay out and in charge for years, allowing others to come out only periodically. For example, a dominant personality may be quite competent — even brilliant — in her career, and able to carry that off for some time. Occasionally a trigger may precipitate a switch during which another personality will emerge; during these times the multiple's behavior will become what others see as bizarre or "unlike her" for a while — until the dominant personality reemerges. A dominant personality seems to have ways to maintain the energy that allows her to stay out for longer periods of time. She may allow another personality to come out for a "R & R" time for herself, and then return. However, at some point there is apt to be a breakdown.

It seems that each personality must draw from the body's total energy supply and that energy is split among the different personalities. The dominant parts have to draw some of their energy from other personalities if they can; when that energy is depleted, another personality must come out.

JUDY: *"Judith, Jane and Gerri were three very dominant personalities in my teenage years. As they became more autonomous I think they had more energy, and they assumed the roles of adult dominant personalities. Jane was able to take her place as a dominant personality because, at the chronological age she was created, her abilities were so needed. Jane was given a one-way ticket to California as a high school graduation gift and she left for California. Her role was to forget or deny all the memories of the abuses at that time. Jane did drugs and forgot. Because she had the ability to make use of the timing of her creation and live life 'to the max' using drugs, she became one of my dominant personalities.*

"Now if Judith, who was also created at age 18, had been able at that time to be more dominant, she might have denied the situation by staying with my abusers, even living with them and staying the good girl. Thank God she didn't. It was Jane who had the most energy then and who became most dominant during that time of my life. Jane married my husband, who had no idea I was a multiple; I was Jane for many years. It wasn't until another critical social situation arose that Judith came back out because she had skills that could handle that. Then Jane began to retain less and less energy, and Judith took a turn being dominant for several years. Judith now

had a job to do—so she became dominant. Jane could not function in the straight world Judith created and belonged to socially, so Jane, who was a party person, began to recede."

DORIS: *"During the period Jane was dominant, Judith couldn't handle the drugs that Jane could; the use of drugs alone helped Jane to be more dominant and Judith to recede. In fact, using drugs kept a lot of the personalities, including the children, from coming out for years."*

JUDY: *"In my own case, the few times Jane did break down and no longer had drugs available, I ended up in psychiatric wards. This always happened when Jane withdrew from drugs. Other personalities came out in the hospitals when Jane wasn't on drugs. Dominant personalities, as they became stronger, have the ability to reduce the energy of nondominant personalities. By taking the body's energy and staying out longer, they become even more dominant and the nondominant personalities become more recessed. So a therapist may not see the whole inner family for a long time, because it takes time for the layers of personalities to 'work themselves forward.' This is especially true of nondominant personalities who were created only to handle specific traumatic events."*

DORIS: *"If we speak systemically, what does that mean? Each personality has a role to play. In order for some to be more dominant, certain parts of the system give up their energy to other parts. This is not a cognitive thing; rather, as in any system, others will give up power to someone who is more dominant in order to maintain the system. If there is a breakdown and that dominant personality—for whatever reason—does not have the skills to handle a life stressor, then change begins to take place and another personality may emerge to be more dominant."*

LYNDA: *"We also know that at about the age of 30, the system does begin to break down and more switching takes place; that is when multiples often begin to come into therapy. At the midlife stage, it does seem to take more energy for one personality to maintain dominance—and of course that is the age when so many changes and transitions begin to happen, whether one is a multiple*

or not. Career problems, marital changes, children growing up — all
are stressors that could cause a loss of balance for the dominant
personality."

Nondominant Personalities

Nondominant personalities are many and varied. They are usually
created during a specific traumatic event and may be found in splits or
clusters of the same age. Other nondominant personalities may appear
in groups, those in one group having similar ages. These personalities
are again created during specific abusive events, although they may not
have a specific role assigned to them in the multiple's life except to
carry the memories and feelings associated with one or more traumatic
events that occurred. Many of the nondominant personalities will be
younger ones who actually suffered through the abuse. They were
created to get through that, rather than to be out in the world like the
dominant personalities.

It is important in therapy to validate these nondominant personalities, each of whom has had an important role in keeping the multiple
alive earlier in life. A multiple is like a jigsaw puzzle; there are big and
small pieces. If you leave out some of the pieces because they are not as
big and do not seem as important, you are going to have an incomplete
picture with holes in it. So every little piece, every personality, no
matter how small, is important.

Dealing with nondominant personalities can be challenging, since
most of them have fewer skills than the dominant parts in living in the
here and now; however, once therapy starts, these parts who once
stayed inside most of the time begin to come out and see what the
world is like. A two-year-old personality, for example, who has a tantrum
or giggle fits, can require a lot of creativity from a therapist. There will
be personalities of all ages, who have differing abilities to cope with
stressful present-life situations. And each one was created for a specific,
important reason.

The little child personalities see themselves as small. Some multiples
have all sizes of clothing in their closets to accommodate the personalities of different ages. When the child parts speak from a child's point of
view, they are being not resistant but congruent. For example, a client
may remove her shoes during therapy, and then, when she goes to put

them back on (having switched to a smaller child part), she may say, "Those aren't my shoes, they don't fit, they belong to someone else." Therapists must realize that they are actually dealing with personalities of all different sizes and shapes. Each one's visual perception is different and will match his or her age and the size s/he would have been at that age. A four-year-old personality may not be able to see over the kitchen counter at home and may get out a stool to reach for something on the counter, even though this child part in reality has an adult body and can easily reach over the counter. Reality looks different when one is small, and the child parts will reflect that.

The child parts are especially vulnerable to the expectations of the therapist. That little person looks up to the therapist; if this adult tells her how she should be or how she should act, that child may not be able to say "no." A therapist is too big. To protect themselves, those little ones may either not come out at all or come out and try to do exactly what the therapist wants them to do. This isn't progress—it's a recapitulation of the old family system.

> JUDY: *"It is important to each and every personality to be validated. The little pieces that are put back into the whole, who feel as good as they can about themselves, help make the integrated person feel more human. It's about our humanness, and about feeling valued as well—because you can be validated as a human being and still not feel valued. The gift to each personality is that sense of being valued as a part of something. Each is a part of something that is good, and without each part there couldn't be a whole. That brings some value to an integrated person and to each part; it makes a difference."*

Clusters

Clusters consist of three or more personalities, usually young children, who were created during the same traumatic event. Each part was split off in order to survive that event. In a cluster all the personalities will be the same age, but they may not be the same sex. Each one will have been created to do something different and specific to handle the trauma. For example, one may be created to hold the memory, one the pain, one the fear, and one the anger. And then one may be created to participate in the abuse, to please the abusers so the child can survive. (See Figure 4.1.)

Groups

Groups are personalities who may be of different ages but who "hang out together," so to speak, in the inside family. Groups are created not to deal with one specific abusive event, but to deal with different aspects of a certain developmental stage. They can be children or adolescents who were created for specific developmental events, which may or may not have been traumatic at the time. They may each hold a different feeling; for instance, one personality of a group may carry the anger and hold it for a particular period of time. This was true of the teenage personality named "Candle" in Judy's inner family, who carried the anger through the teenage years, allowing others in that age group to take other roles. In a single age group there may be one personality who likes drinking sodas, one who learns to drive, one who likes going out on dates, etc. Groups are more likely to be formed during adolescence than in any other developmental stage. Since at that age teens are searching for identity, they hang out together. Just as teenagers hang out with one another for comfort and support, the multiple's teen parts hang out together.

In the multiple, when one of the group is out in the body and comes to session, it is easier for another one of the same group to emerge as well. One member of a group of personalities may be the "leader"; if this one comes out, all the other ones may follow. This can be a plus when it comes to meeting all the inner family members. Members of a group may have a lot in common; although there may be some range in their ages, there is a commonality about them that holds them together.

Fillers

DORIS: *"There are non-personality parts that I call "Fillers" who come to fill the body space when no other personality is available.*

FIGURE 4.1: A crayon drawing by one of Judy's inner children depicting the story and creation of a cluster. Each torch represents a split-off personality created during one specific event of ritual abuse.

During therapy, when a personality who has been talking to the therapist leaves, occasionally it may happen that no one else comes out to take her place; the multiple may have a vacant look. When there are neither dominant nor non-dominant personalities to switch to, there can be at times a particular silence. A Filler may come to be in the body for a very brief time when no other personality is available to do that.

"I don't see this Filler as a newly created personality; it comes, and when it goes, it is gone for good. Each time a Filler comes to a session, that Filler seems to be present for the first time ever. A Filler is not a personality; it doesn't have a character or an identity, a history, etc. There may be no personality present at the moment, but there is a human being inside of the body. A Filler sits in the chair when no other personality can be out. The Filler looks nondescript, vacant in the eyes. In a sense, when a Filler comes, all the personalities inside are dissociated from the body at once. It's a completely dissociated state. It is important for the therapist to treat that Filler just as she would treat any personality who comes to a session. I see a Filler as someone who comes to hold things together until some personality can come back. And this is an important role: to be in the body until someone else, a personality, is ready to be there."

JUDY: *"It makes me sad to realize that a human being may have been so abused, so traumatized, that during her work she may present to the therapist an unfilled being. At that moment she is totally separated from her body, so dissociated that she is in a state of nonbeing."*

Remember that, just because all the personalities are for the moment inside, this doesn't mean the multiple is not *there*; rather, she simply does not have the perception of being there. When the Filler is in the body, something very important is taking place inside. As the therapist, do not demand that another personality return. This is not the time to ask to speak to so-and-so. If you do that, you have interrupted the therapy that is going on and the multiple's inner processing. There is a reason a Filler comes; there is a reason all the personalities went inside; it is important for you to acknowledge that. Let it happen, and know that the multiple is not trying to create a problem for you.

Male and Female Personalities

A multiple's inner family may include both male and female personalities. Some of the reasons for this are listed below.

1. During an abusive event, the child may have identified with the abuser. When the child is forced to participate in an event that is so abusive that she fears loss of her own life if she resists, then that child may identify with the abuser in order to be able to participate in the event. When life and death are on the line, a child may see this as the only way to survive. When the child is a girl and the abuser is male, she may create a male part to complete the identification. Sometimes the child may believe that she actually takes on the identity of the abuser and becomes him or her. In therapy the multiple may have problems separating herself from the powerful abuser. Between the ages of two and five, a child can become very confused about what is real and what is not real, particularly when the abuser deliberately adds to this confusion.

2. Extreme discomfort in a sexual situation with a same-sex abuser may lead to creation of an opposite-sex personality. When a child is required to have a sexual interaction with an abuser who is the same sex as she is, the child may feel a sense of revulsion; it doesn't feel right. It may even feel less right than being abused by a person of the opposite sex. So what the child creates is a personality of the opposite sex to participate with the same-sex abuser in a more "normal" kind of relationship. Even at an early age, a child knows inside what fits for her and what doesn't. If sexual behavior with someone of the same sex doesn't fit, the child makes it fit as best she knows how. The abuser and the situation won't change, so the child adjusts herself to fit: she becomes the opposite sex. Changing herself to fit the situation is what a multiple has had to do all her life.

3. A male may be seen as stronger and better able to protect. There is often a sense that being male is more powerful than being female. So if in an abusive situation a girl child feels the need for an extremely powerful protector or the need to be very strong, she may create a part who is male.

4. The child may have been forced by the abuser to "be" of the opposite sex. In ritualistic abuse, for example, the abusers may require a child victim to be both male and female; they may actually encourage splitting so a child can perform in both roles.

5. The child may have perceived some parts or functions as more male than female. For example, feeling "prissy" about bugs

may be seen as female or being smart may be seen as male, so these personalities can be created in what the child deems the appropriate gender. Feelings that are not acceptable or which cause too much anxiety for the child to own as part of being a boy or a girl can be dissociated into a personality of the opposite sex.

These are some of the reasons for having both male and female personalities. There could be many more. When the male personalities in a female client come to therapy (or vice versa), it can be a time of confusion and questioning on the part of the client and the therapist. it is not helpful to say, "It's not possible to be a male because you are a woman." These personalities need extra respect and belief in their importance from the therapist.

Negative Introjects

According to *Webster's* to "introject" is to "incorporate or assimilate into oneself subconsciously or unconsciously (attitudes or ideas of others esp. parental figures, or in infantile fancy actual parts or all of another's body)." Introjects, which affect us all at a very early age, originate initially with our primary caretakers. Introjects may be positive or negative; here, however, we are concerned only with the negatives. A remark from an exasperated parent, such as "You *never* do anything right," especially if said frequently, can have long-term effects on a child. Other remarks, such as, "You're just like your father" (who is alcoholic and irresponsible), or "You'll never amount to anything," illustrate the types of negative introjected messages most of us struggle with into and even during our adult lives. For a multiple, the introjections are even harsher and may become embodied in actual personalities who continue to give the multiple negative injunctions. While many personalities carry negative introjected messages that they may verbalize or act out, other personalities may represent an actual original abuser.

What we call negative introject personalities are those personalities who represent major powerful people in the multiple's life, usually one or more of the people involved in extreme abuse. The introjects invade that inner family and continue the abuse that the multiple heard and experienced as a child from the external environment. That external abuser is now internalized. The abuse from a negative introject personality can take the form of an abusive voice that other personalities can hear, or, when the introject personality is controlling the body, s/he may use abusive or self-destructive behaviors.

We draw a distinction between negative introject personalities and the usual abusive or punisher personalities. Some writers lump these two types together into the category of "persecutor personalities" (see Putnam, 1989, and Ross, 1989). Bloch (1991) refers to a type of "malevolent alter" that is a "toxic-introject" of an abusive early attachment figure (pp. 30, 55). These sources believe that all persecutor and toxic-introject personalities can be reframed and transformed into positives over time and that they can eventually be integrated into the whole. In Frank Putnam's excellent book, *Diagnosis and Treatment of Multiple Personality Disorder,* he states: "In personality systems that contain persecutor alters, the therapist must engage and work with these personalities. They will not go away spontaneously, and they cannot be exorcised" (1989, p. 205). This is an important observation. We have continually referred to the importance of accepting all personalities, including those that are negative or destructive. To "remove" or attempt to remove any of these *essential parts* would be to deny the client the right to reclaim part of herself and negate the importance of the wholeness necessary for integration.

While we agree that these persecutor personalities can be transformed in the majority of cases, we believe that in some multiples there are differences between negative introject personalities and other abusive or persecutor personalities in the inner family who continue the family of origin system. Rather than being bona fide dissociated parts of the client's original personality, some negative introjects may be interlopers, "uninvited guests" in the multiple's inner family. In some cases, negative introjects do *not* belong in the inner family, may never be transformable, and may depart with the help of the therapist and the multiple's inner family. Judy was one such client. Judy's inner system contained several persecutor personalities. However, three of them were adult negative introjects. One (female) was able to transform, join the family, and be integrated; the other two (males) were not. All three were adult personalities whose names and behaviors clearly duplicated those of the original abusers. This adultness differs from the description others give of more common persecutor personalities.

Putnam (1989) states: "Beahrs (1982) makes the observation that many of these 'demons' are angry children. My experience supports his observation that persecutors tend overwhelmingly to be child or adolescent personalities" (p. 207). Ross (1989) also states: "Another type of persecutor is the internal demon, the alter identified as the incestuous father, and other paranormal alters. . . . Usually one is dealing with a school playground bully who really wants to be contained and loved" (p. 257).

We have found that intractable negative introjects are *not* child or adolescent personalities, but adults. They speak with the abuser's voice, use the same language and tone of voice, and are similar in age to the abuser. They are personalities reported as older and more powerful than the child parts. We do not believe these introjects are demons or evil spirits, and we do *not* equate them with some specific alters created to do "evil" during ritualistic abuse. Rather, our theory is that these negative introject personalities represent specific adult abusers who were "swallowed down whole," becoming deadly forces inside the system, where their purposes were not to *protect* the inner family but to perpetuate the original abuse. Therefore, they have no true "place" within the inner family system.

Although they were given months (in one case years) of opportunity to transform, to be loved, and to belong, two of Judy's negative introject personalities refused. They were asked to leave by the inner family. These negative introjects left, they never returned as themselves or as any other type of persecutor, and their particular forms of abuse ceased following their departures. We do not know why in some cases the type of intervention we used works; we do know that it does. (See Chapter 8 for interventions.)

It was only after researching every aspect of these negative introjects with the other personalities, and after giving these introject personalities every chance to be loved and reframed, that the whole inner family reached an agreement that they were to leave. We did not see this process as an "exorcism," but rather as the removal of foreign objects whose presence created a deadly irritant within the body of the system, preventing healing.

Because it is crucial to know the difference between an introject and other abusive/punishing inner family members, particularly before any departure is encouraged, we will discuss these differences in detail. A personality who does or says abusive things and who *does* belong in the multiple's inside family is punishing in order to protect the system (albeit in a misguided way). The overall purpose is to protect the inner child. This personality may not be aware that she is being protective, and this awareness can only come about as she and the therapist work together in accepting and reframing her behavior. Most punishing personalities will at some point come to see themselves in a positive light and the others in the inner family can learn to accept those parts in a positive light as well. The abusive or punishing behaviors change as these personalities learn more positive ways to accomplish their purposes.

Negative introjects, however, may be *unwilling* to be reframed if their only function is to duplicate the original abusers. These do not exist within the inner system to protect; they are there to control and keep the family secrets, just like the original abusers, even if it means destroying the multiple. That is why they may not belong as permanent members of the multiple's inner family.

To determine whether an abusive personality is an introject, it is very important to spend adequate time with reframing, to discover whether that personality is eventually willing to see herself differently. This is a process that involves many sessions, over a period of at *least* months and possibly longer. What that means is that a therapist must take the time to get to know every personality, including the ones she sees as abusive. The therapist may draw conclusions for herself, but she must also check out her hunches with the other personalities; other personalities may have a clearer picture of what this abusive personality is like and what his or her underlying intent is. Give that personality every opportunity to join the family, to change the behavior from something destructive to something positive. If that personality refuses to accept reframing, then, putting that information together with the information from the other personalities, you can determine that this personality is a negative introject.

When you and the client discover what looks like a negative introject personality, the first thing to do is to try to reframe that personality, to allow that part to transform into a positive family member. Find out when it was created, what feelings it may or may not have, and what its underlying goals and functions are. Judy had a negative part who appeared to be a negative introject but who transformed herself in time into a positive part. Her name was Rosalyn, and she spoke and sounded like one of Judy's abusers; she was the introjected mother figure. She was extremely abusive and colluded with Leon, the negative introjected father figure. Rosalyn accepted reframing: she learned to see herself in a positive light; others were able to see her in a positive light; and she remained with the inside family. Rosalyn was a necessary, integral part of the whole; she had taken on the role of the mother figure who had carried Judy as a baby in the womb, and who had given Judy life. And because this particular abuser had been quite cruel, Rosalyn sounded abusive from the start. Leon, the father figure introject, was able to connect with Rosalyn because she took on the role of his wife. Rosalyn was not a lovely person to work with initially.

Don't get caught up in how awful these abusive personalities are. What you are hearing is what your client heard as a child; this negative personality is introducing you to the multiple's world as a child. Use this information to enlarge your picture; it will be good information to give back to the client, to help her separate from and have more objectivity about the very abusive people she grew up with.

Here is an example of using reframing with a negative introject, or any negative personality.

> DORIS: *"Rosalyn had the female abuser's voice. A session with this personality was an hour and a half of the most intensive verbal abuse I have ever experienced in my life, and it was exhausting. At the end I said, 'Thank you for showing me what it must have been like for Judy growing up with that abuser.'"*

With Rosalyn reframing eventually worked, and this personality stopped abusing. With Leon, the introjected father figure, it never worked. In this case, the whole inner family worked with the therapist to ask him to leave (see Chapter 8).

Here are some other clues to help you distinguish a negative introject who doesn't belong from an abusive personality who does belong in the system.

1. Abusive inner family members who do belong in the system will frequently talk about punishing a particular personality to keep that one in line with the other family members, and they may express anger at the one who "needs to be punished" for the things she does. An abusive personality might say ugly

things about the multiple, such as, "She's no good, I want to get rid of her, I don't like what she does." Although this abusive one wants to hurt the multiple, she always has a reason for her anger. In contrast, *a negative introject does not express anger*; its abusive behaviors are done purposefully and without feeling. However, an introject may collude with another angry/abusive personality to accomplish its destructive goals. A negative introject wants nothing other than to control, just like the original abusers. It will not ever do good; it will consistently undermine therapy and undermine the existence of other personalities; it will undermine cooperation.

2. A negative introject that chooses not to be reframed will not have more than one aspect; it will not have a good side and a bad side as many of the multiple's parts will. If an introject cannot be reframed as having a positive side, it may be because there *isn't* any light side. There may be nothing positive about it; moreover, the introject may not *want* to have a positive side.

3. There are nonverbal cues that signal a negative introject personality. While many of a multiple's inner family members sound alike, there is a different tonal quality, a different tone of voice, to a negative introject. There is no softness to a negative introject; as therapist you can't sense or elicit a soft side, as you can with another abusive inner family member. The body movement, the tone of voice, the facial expressions, and the look in the eyes are all very different from the usual abusive family member. Such an introject has a very single-minded, goal-oriented destructiveness that is not based on anger or rage. This negative introject is intellectual and without feeling; it has a cold-blooded quality. It seeks to hurt and control.

An inner family member can be suicidal or try to kill another personality but she will have a reason and is usually angry or depressed. An abusive family member may also want to punish or get rid of another personality if she believes that one has done something "wrong." But a negative introject doesn't use reasons of right and wrong; its only concern, its only mission, is to control.

4. Another clue that a negative introject personality may not belong in the inner system is that when it loses control, it typical-

ly seeks to *destroy the system*. Realizing that a multiple's inner system is set up like the family of origin system, you can expect that it will include one or more abusive parts who watch to make sure somebody doesn't do something to change the system. When an abusive member sees that another personality is behaving in a way that will change the system, e.g., telling the secrets or expressing feelings, the abusive member thinks she ought to punish that part. Breaking or changing old rules means upsetting the whole system; from past experience, changes mean something awful is going to happen—it means death. So when that abusive personality tries to punish the rule-breaker, she is not seeking to destroy the system, but to maintain the system. *A negative introject, on the other hand, uses abuse not to maintain the system but to control the system and if necessary, destroy it; it has no concern for the system.*

5. Art is another avenue for discovering a negative introject who cannot be reframed.

JUDY: *"I drew a picture showing a family circle of some of the inside family members, and there was an elaborate line connecting that inner family to Gloria, my spiritual part. In that drawing there was a picture of Leon, a negative introject. Gloria, my spiritual part, and the other inner family members had given Leon many chances to join the family, and when he refused, one of the child personalities covered over his picture in that drawing with black crayon. So in the drawing there is a black box in the corner, which is separate from the other members shown; it represents Leon as a negative introject, unable or unwilling to join the family. My spiritual part, Gloria, drew a heart over the box, symbolizing that only through love or light could he change. But Leon never did; he refused." (See Figure 4.2.)*

You must give the negative introject every opportunity to join the inner family and to use that negative energy in a positive way. Use art, sand tray, or any type of projective work that you would normally use with adult or child clients; all are helpful in gathering clues about each personality, including any introjects. When you work with a multiple, think of yourself as doing family work. Use the same techniques that you would in doing family therapy and see what comes of that. *Don't be in a hurry.*

FIGURE 4.2: A crayon drawing of some members of the inner family circle.

DORIS: *"In Judy's case, it became clear that the confusion about feeling bad versus being bad, together with the constant physical and verbal violence during her childhood, caused her to introject the punishers into the inner family system as a child. In therapy, the child personalities said that Leon, a negative introject, 'wants to kill us all.' This introject was seen as a powerful, destructive force; I was told, 'The Killer stalks everyone, he's behind everything bad, and he's ready to kill anything that (Judy) does because she is unworthy.' During one session after Leon was introduced, Judy made a clay sculpture showing depression. Leon stuck a knife in the piece and set it on the back porch of the office. We were getting too close to Leon for his comfort; he didn't like the way the therapy was going, and he was beginning to worry about losing his power in the system."*

When you begin to expose a personality as a negative introject, and other inner family members begin to realize that s/he doesn't belong in the inner family, the introject will often accelerate its threatening talk or destructive behaviors. The introject may make death threats, exactly as the original abusers used to do.

Many other personalities, including abusive ones who belong in the family, will react similarly to being exposed; they may be afraid of being rejected or "gotten rid of." Be very, very careful about labeling any negative introject personality as intractable. And if you are not sure, take your time. *It will be impossible for any personality, abusive or otherwise, to leave the inner family system if it is not a negative introject personality.* If you encourage departure prematurely, that personality may withdraw and go into hiding, and you may believe you have succeeded. However, what the multiple has done is just repress that part. If you make a mistake and try to remove any personality who is not really an introject, you won't be able to do it. The rejected personality will go more deeply "underground" and you will have much more work to do afterwards to make up for the rejection that personality experienced during the process. You can't work towards wholeness if you try to take away a part that belongs.

It is important for multiples themselves to know that each personality, whether abusive, angry, hurtful, or not, remains safe inside the inner system. Personalities need not worry that "maybe I am the introject and will be gotten rid of." All the parts are important. Each "negative" part will be given as much time as needed to see herself differently and to understand how she can belong in a positive way.

An example from family therapy with other types of clients may illustrate this. Let's say you (the therapist) have a family come in for treatment and you find that one of the family members is acting out—perhaps this person is a teenager and he's using drugs or beating up on a sibling. What you don't do as a therapist is say, "This person is acting out so let's get rid of him, and then your family will be OK." You wouldn't do that with other families, and you don't want to do that with a client who is a multiple. Again, in a multiple you will discover teenage parts, little children, and adults—all are part of the family. All of them are very important and all of them need to be affirmed, valued, listened to, and involved in the process of working towards wholeness. In contrast, a negative introject existing in a multiple's inner family might be characterized as a mannequin or robot that walks and talks, and which has been carried around inside by the rest of the inner family for so long that everyone has come to believe it is real. It can be removed without loss to the inner system — but not necessarily without a fight.

Positive Introjects

The multiple will usually introject those aspects of the therapist that resemble mothering or fathering. Multiples need a model or image of a good parent. It is not helpful for a therapist to say to a multiple, "You can be your own parent." We all have an introjected parent image in the beginning. If the multiple's only parent image is an abusive one or a non-protective one, then she has no source of inner nurturance.

The therapist will not be introjected as a personality, but her words and beliefs will be introjected as internalized messages. Be attentive to the verbal and nonverbal messages you give to the client as an authority/parent figure. If your messages as a therapist are, "I don't trust you to do (your work) right, I know what is good timing for you, I know which personality ought to come out right now, I know this is the time for integration," etc. the multiple introjects the belief that she is not competent, capable or responsible as a human being. No matter how loving it is on your part as a therapist, these kind of messages reinforce the old system belief: I (the parent/authority) know what is best for you.

A more subtle negative message from the therapist might be: "I want you to express your feelings; I want you to be able to express your anger — and I want you to do it this way. Express your anger, but not at this time, and not at me, and not in this place." This is too much to ask of a child. Remember, when it comes to issues like this, the multiple is functioning back in early developmental stages. You are doing trust work and teaching; you are the child's mirror. Rather than being a negative mirror that reflects distorted self-images, you must reflect clearly and honestly.

> JUDY: *"As a multiple in therapy you have the opportunity to know the feeling of acceptance, of warmth, of caring, from your therapist — but you only know it from her behavior. You may have a connection to your own spiritual part who has nurtured you and this may have been the nurturing that has kept you alive; but as a multiple you may know very little about nurturing behavior from another*

human being. The positive reflection your therapist mirrors back to you may be the first. It is within that intimate setting of therapy that a multiple experiences what it is like to have a parent who gives nurturing to a child. I think that if a therapist is not willing to give that to a client, then she will not have the same growth."

What we are talking about is valuing our clients so that they can value themselves; multiples may have never felt valued. And if they feel *devalued* in therapy, they cannot grow. Safety for multiples is important, so they can take the risks they need to take to change. Part of the safety you provide is in your valuing, your trusting, your belief in her own process. You create a mirror. If you stand before a mirror and put the light on it in a certain way, then the light goes in and is reflected back, lighting up the one looking at the mirror. So the multiple (child) begins to make her own mirror for herself because of yours. And the self-image she makes will be a mirror image of whatever picture you give her.

The Spiritual Personality

Blume (1990) states,

Psychiatrist Elizabeth Kübler-Ross, renowned for her work on death and dying, describes the heightened spiritual strength of the otherwise damaged, ill, or deprived child. I have seen this strength over and over in the existence of an "inner guide" in many incest survivors. The inner guide is not some other-world spirit or "past life" guide, but an aspect of the incest survivor herself. This internal caretaker ensures that no matter how complicated or painful the incest survivor's outer life becomes, she protects herself enough to "keep on keepin' on." In many instances she is uncannily wise.... The inner guide meters out the defenses ... guiding the incest survivor by blocking and releasing memories and feelings. (p. 80)

An adult multiple will have a spiritual personality who may act as a protector of the inner family and as a guide for both client and therapist during treatment. Some therapists (Allison, 1974; Putnam, 1989) refer to a special helping or guiding personality as the Inner Self Helper (ISH); however, it is possible that a spiritual personality may be different from some ISH personalities. The spiritual personality may be seen as a positive introject, taken in from whatever positive or nurturing sources were available to the multiple as a child. The child may connect with someone outside herself and then connect that powerful nurturing to something within herself, creating a spiritual personality. For other clients, the spiritual personality may personify a part of the self that is present from birth, a part whose power is connected to a higher source. We don't really know whether this spiritual part is innate or introjected. However, many cultures around the world believe that humans are more than thought, behavior and emotion, that we are endowed with a spiritual dimension from birth as well. Our work and experiences with multiples have led us to believe they, like all human beings, are born with a spiritual aspect.

What does it mean to the client to have a spiritual personality? This personality is a resource to draw from, a resource available when no other resources exist. The spiritual part is something within that gives the multiple an anchor even in the midst of utter chaos — something on which she can focus, something to cling to.

JUDY: *"My spiritual part was named after the one person in my life who during the short time she was with me personified nurturing, caring, and unconditional love. For me, this spiritual connection or resource was available to me when death was imminent. I took this little bit of love from this one person and connected it to my world inside in order to make life bearable. I used this part to create a safe world that is and was beyond anything that I know now, beyond what we know and understand as human beings to be our natural, physical resources.*

"During times when I thought I was dead, I experienced a physical warmth that was similar to what one would feel as a child being held close by someone else. It was a warmth that filled my whole body, my whole being; it gave me nurturance from beyond myself, yet within myself. This place of warmth was void of anything other than love; there was an absolute absence of evil there. It was a place where I could exist without punishment, fear, judgment, pain or violence. Sometimes this place had such a strong light that I couldn't

look directly at it; instead, the light surrounded me, held me, and kept me alive. And there was a peaceful place within the light where there was a meadow with a river. The personalities called this place 'The Shining Place beyond the stars, where eagles fly.' This sounds really mystical, but this was my experience. I don't equate it with a Christian experience of God at all, because that seems too limiting. On occasions when I came very close to death and needed to be in that environment, it kept me alive. I think my spiritual part has always been the connection to that special place inside; she is the personification of my spirituality. I truly believe she is my own angel."

DORIS: *"When Judy's spiritual part appeared in session, there was a definite change in Judy's whole being. She would sit up very straight and her eyes would change — they became very big and direct in gaze. I sensed that sitting before me was an extremely powerful, very wise, personage. The spiritual part came at crucial points of therapy and gave instructions not only to Judy but also to me. For instance, during one difficult time period, when I had many concerns about Judy, the spiritual part came and told me, 'Judy must walk her own path; you cannot walk it for her.' That was pretty straightforward talk! Judy's spiritual part became essentially a cotherapist. She was a great source of information, telling me when certain parts of therapy were finished and when it was time to go on to the next stages. I found her very helpful, and I paid attention to her advice. There were times when I wished she had come more frequently, but she let me, the therapist, walk my path also."*

JUDY: *"My spiritual part was also available during the integration process to take the child personalities to the Shining Place inside. This made the integration safe. She provided the inner children with a feeling of peace, an experience they had never known before but which could finally be theirs — it was the coming home.*

"I have felt at times that I was pushed from the inside to continue my therapy and my journey to be whole, even when it seemed beyond my control. Sometimes I still want to give up on the work, to be at peace; but there is something more I am to do and I must keep going on. Part of it is that I now speak for all the inner children who were abused; I am their voice. I think that responsibility was given to me as a gift. My spiritual connection is still available to me. I have a

very hard time talking about it, because spirituality is the one part of my life I don't want anyone to trash. My spirituality is strong, but I don't often go into detail about it; it is something I cherish so much I don't want it open to abuse from others.

"I think that in therapy, when someone's spiritual personality is introduced to the therapist, the therapist's reactions—positive or negative—will determine whether she's able to have an alliance with that personality or not. It would be helpful for the therapist to be open to the possibility of the multiple allowing that part of herself to connect with the therapist. The multiple's spiritual part may not match the therapist's religious beliefs, but the therapist should be respectful of the client's reality. To open up communication, it is important for a therapist to believe in the multiple's reality, in her world; otherwise you can't build that bridge between therapist and client, and the multiple won't be able to cross over to a safe, accepting world beyond herself.

"Other multiples I know have told me that they have personalities within themselves who are their spiritual parts. A spiritual part is seen differently by each multiple, but it is always connected to something beyond herself that is bigger than she is, a power that nurtures and guides her toward something good. All of the people I know talk about the spiritual part as having something to do with light, with peace, and with guidance. I think that, without these spiritual parts, none of us who have survived horrible abuses would have lived."

The Core Personality and the Essence

DORIS: *"When we talk about the Core personality, we are referring to the original child—the child who was born into the world and from whom all the other parts were split off or created. In some cases, such as that of Truddi Chase (*When Rabbit Howls, *1987), the personality system may refuse to allow a certain highly protected part to emerge; I would consider that one to be the Core person.*

"The child who is abused and becomes a multiple splits off parts of herself to survive. However, if the abuse becomes so great that the original child, after splitting many times, can no longer tolerate it, she in effect 'shuts down.' Then the amnestic barriers become thick-

*er and more rigid, enveloping this Core child in a protective manner;
the split-off parts continue to exist as separate personalities, protecting the original child for whom they were created. This Core person
will not emerge in therapy until all the other personalities can trust
that she will be safe, for they have spent the child's lifetime making
sure of that.*

*"In Judy's case some personalities said they believed the original
'Judy' was dead or asleep. The Core person is usually hidden under
layers and layers of personalities, dominant and nondominant, but
she is not dead. The personalities who come into therapy early on
probably will not include this Core person. But there is one personality who will give you a preview of what the Core will be like, who has
a special connection with that Core child. This is the Essence personality."*

When we talk about the Core and the Essence, we're referring to
something different from the "host" personality. Kluft (1984, p. 23)
defines the host as: "the one who has executive control of the body the
greatest percentage of time during a given time." "Frequently this is a
personality that presents for treatment and the one who becomes identified as the 'patient' prior to the diagnosis of MPD" (Putnam, 1989,
p. 107). We believe that there is another personality who may present
herself to the therapist; we call this personality the "Essence."

DORIS: *"Essence is the name I give the one adult personality who
reflects what the original child would have been like as an adult. The
Core is hidden inside, but the Essence is like a shadow or a silhou-
ette of the Core. The Essence personality is usually not a dominant
one and may only appear occasionally at first. The other personalities will be very protective of the Essence as well as of the Core
person."*

How do you identify the Essence? Here are some clues. The Essence
may have little or no knowledge of the abuse, the memories, or the
early life history; she will only live in the present. However, she will
appear very confused about what is happening in the present. She will
often hear the voices of the other personalities, but won't know what
that means. The Essence personality will be the actual age of the

client; for example, a multiple who is 34 may have personalities of varying ages, but the Essence personality will be 34. The Essence may be called by the multiple's birth name — but not always.

> DORIS: *"Making contact with the Essence personality is like making contact with a wild animal. A wild animal that lives in the forest is very fearful, especially if it has been shot at by hunters. To get this creature to come out, you must wait patiently at the forest clearing with food. The animal ventures out a little bit, and then a bit further; eventually, if you are patient, she will come out far enough to eat the food you brought before rushing back into the forest. In time, she will come out for longer periods, staying out as you watch her eat, and finally letting you get closer.*
>
> *"This is the way I see the Essence getting to know you, the therapist. Very slowly, as the other personalities build trust, the Essence begins to emerge. As you continue therapy, she will appear more frequently. While you are first getting to know the Essence, she will probably not yet be connected to the Core person. She is the reflection of that Core child, but the Essence doesn't know that. The Essence will be curious; she will have a lot of questions. She may say things like, 'I don't really know who I am, or what I'm for.' She will have very little feeling, except confusion. The Essence personality has no specific role or function, in contrast to the other personalities; she will not go to school, clean house, be the mother or the wife — she just 'is.' Any time a trigger occurs, the Essence will disappear inside again, where she is safe. The Essence may not be in control of her coming and going; other personalities may be in charge of her. And she may not have memories of childhood until she unites with the Core person."*

You will be looking for the Essence personality from the beginning of therapy, and it is rather like detective work. It may take over a year to discover this key personality — but don't be in a hurry. There are no hard and fast rules for identifying the Essence. However, since multiples live in a confusion of paradoxes, they may present another one for you, the therapist. We have also found that it is possible for the Essence to be one of the more dominant personalities. In this case she may have some memories, feelings, and awareness of other personalities. This is particularly possible if your client has had previous therapy and the Essence has had more time to grow and be out in the world.

For the rest of this section, we will refer to the Essence as a non-dominant personality. However, the process that the Essence undergoes in therapy is the same whether this personality is nondominant or dominant.

As the other personalities do their work in therapy, they and the therapist pass new information along to the Essence. Initially, the Essence gains information through the intellect. For example, she begins to make sense of the voices, to know that many personalities exist, and that the abusive events they talk about really happened. She gets acquainted with the other personalities. As therapy progresses, the Essence personality will receive the memories that the other personalities have been carrying, as well as the feelings. As she begins to receive memories, she "fills out"; she begins to grow and to become more dominant, spending more and more time "out" in the outside world. Eventually, this Essence personality will be the one who joins with the Core person. Connections made within the personality system work from the top down to the Core, and back up again, adding memories and strength as they occur.

Unlike the Essence, the Core person is often a child, the child who thinks she went to sleep or died. When the Core person returns, she will see that she has changed, that her body is different, that she is older. It is important not to assume you have met the Core person after you have met several child personalities. Even an infant personality may only be a split-off part of the Core that was made in babyhood. You may find some clues as to how old the Core person is by mapping out all the personalities by age and historical events. Sometimes this helps to show when the original child had had too much abuse to bear and shut down, and when the parts begin to create parts on their own.

The difference between the emergence of the Core into the outside world and the emergence of other child personalities may be small — but it is discrete. Other personalities, including children, continue to see themselves at their reported ages of three, five, seven, 15, 26 or whatever, even if the client is actually 34. But when the Core person emerges, her perception will be, "My God. *I* have changed." Other child parts may notice, "These shoes are too big for me," or "How did I get this big?" The Core person not only remembers herself as a child but also perceives herself now to be physically an adult. There may be variations in how the Core emerges, but the important thing is not to confuse the Core child with other child personalities.

JUDY: *"My experience was of waking up in a world I didn't remember. I thought I was still a child. I remember looking in the mirror and seeing not the child I thought I was but this person who had aged, was older. I was shocked that I had aged. I didn't recognize myself, yet I knew it was me. There was a knowledge that it was me; only the Core person can have that experience. The other personalities didn't have that experience of connecting with the self like the Core did."*

For some multiples, the reemergence of the Core person may coincide with joining to the Essence.

JUDY: *"I remember that I was in a room sitting on a white couch—and I had no idea how I got there. I didn't know what to do; I felt traumatized just by being in a place I didn't know. I was feeling hot and cold at the same time, and dizzy. I looked around the room, trying to figure out where I was and who was sitting there looking across at me. There was nothing in the room I could recognize, but I had a sense that it was all familiar. I was peeking out of myself for the first time. I felt invisible because nobody knew I was there. Once I got through the mechanics of figuring out I was OK, I began to take notice of myself. I felt a shock wave go through my body when I noticed my hands; they were old. How do you describe how it feels to wake up after being asleep for 30 years? I thought I was five years old, and I was in the body of a 37-year-old woman. I thought, 'My God, where have I been?' I was horrified and afraid. To recognize yourself after being gone 30 years is a shock the other personalities don't go through."*

DORIS: *"I felt some surprise and confusion when Judy's Core person first merged with the Essence. I thought I had met all the inner family members already, yet this seemed to be someone new. This personality talked like an adult yet knew nothing about being an adult. This was my first indication that the Core person had finally joined with the Essence. I had not known that this 'new' person existed, because the Essence personality I'd been working* with was so similar. *The Judy who appeared this day, however, was different; this Judy knew the child, this Judy was the child. Before this experience, the child Core had been a separate part not connected to the adult.*

"The Judy (the Essence) I had come to know and who had appeared in therapy frequently was a young woman who was growing, evolving, interacting with people, becoming more sure of herself. As I looked at this person before me who claimed to be a new creation, I realized that the child Core had joined with the adult Essence and the loss of 30 years had become clear to her. All the work we had done with each personality had been but a prelude to this first meeting; I knew that for the first time in over 30 years, Judy was really here."

chapter 5

Techniques of Treatment

T HE VALUE OF OPENING up communication channels among the multiple's personalities and between the therapist and all personalities cannot be underestimated. The following are some of the techniques we have found to be particularly helpful in this area of therapy, as well as in retrieving and expressing memories and feelings.

Art

Multiples often seem to be very visual people—and with reason. They have had to be extremely watchful in whatever environment they have lived in, in order to know how to look, how to act, how to feel, and how to protect themselves. Also, multiples hold many of the memories of their past abusive experiences in images, so it fits for them to express those memories in visual form.

Art is a great way for personalities to communicate with the therapist when they are too young or too frightened to speak. Particularly at the beginning of therapy, some personalities may be too frightened to verbalize even small details about themselves or other personalities. Having paper and pencils or crayons available is a great help. If a certain part is having a hard time talking, ask her if she would like to draw or write; many, many times this mode of communicating feels safer.

Art is also a way for many inner family members to "come together" to describe an abusive event. When one personality draws a picture about abuse, it may trigger a switch, and another personality may appear in the session to continue drawing on the same picture or to tell the rest of the story. A second personality may also appear to deny or distract from the story just told in a picture, by drawing a very different picture or coloring over the original. This allows the therapist and the client to view the multiple's inner process, bridging several personalities.

> DORIS: *"This switching process in a session can seem very chaotic, even disruptive to a therapist, but I believe it is important for the client to be able to communicate her system in the best way she can. For the therapist, this process is like meeting all of the cast of characters in a play; you must get to know each of them, learn what their roles are, and validate each one in order to understand the 'play.' Art gives you, the therapist, a great opportunity to meet the personalities and to discover each personality's role. When a client switches personalities after making a drawing, you can ask the next personality, 'Do you know anything about this picture? Can you tell me or draw me more about this?'"*

Art can be used as a means of expressing feelings—feelings that the multiple may be unable to express in any other way. Art allows the client some distance between herself and the feelings. The personality who creates the art may be expressing feelings for several other personalities as well. Art is a way of communicating about something that may seem foreign to personalities who do not experience those feelings, and as such is a teaching tool from the multiple to her many parts. The creative process and the finished product show some personalities inside what others are feeling. Those personalities inside who are watching may voice such realizations as, "I didn't know she felt that way—I don't have that feeling," or, "No wonder so-and-so feels that way." Other personalities who come during the session may also want to tell you what they see in the art form or add to it to express feelings of their own.

JUDY: *"For me, expressing any feeling was difficult, partly because I didn't know exactly what my feelings were. I would do some art work, and there on the paper was an expression of a feeling I didn't even know I had. Although I distanced myself or dissociated from those feelings, I was able to see in concrete terms that I did in fact have feelings of sadness, anger, etc. Art was a way for me to begin to make contact with my feelings. Art also helped me to see the chaos I was going through on the inside, particularly in the beginning of therapy when there were more amnestic barriers between personalities. When I looked at a piece of paper filled with symbols and lines, obviously drawn in different styles and hands, and saw how chaotic it looked, I began to understand and believe. Because the art was so concrete, it confirmed for the personalities in my inner family that in fact they were parts of a whole, and I began to acknowledge, 'Yes, I am a multiple.'"*

The therapist can use this expression of feeling through art as an opportunity to reframe the client's negativity about certain feelings like anger, fear, and sadness, or even her negativity about having feelings at all. Art also is a way to ventilate feelings and soften them to the point that the multiple can cope with her sometimes extremely intense emotions.

As a therapist, interpreting a picture or art form may be very tempting. However, it is not up to you to interpret for your client what her art is expressing or even necessarily to share your interpretation with other personalities. You may see something in that drawing that means something to you because you've talked with several other personalities, some of whom may have told you a story that might fit the picture you're looking at. The personality who is making the drawing may not be ready to hear the whole story that someone else inside knows — and she may say she's not ready. She may simply communicate something *she* knows, letting others inside listen in. The client's timing is important, and if she feels the support of her therapist and safety in the therapeutic environment, she will progress as she needs to, receiving information as it becomes appropriate for her.

JUDY: *"When I look back at the early drawings I made in therapy, I found that my inner family used symbols such as a chair, a closet, a light bulb, etc. to express abusive situations. The personalities who drew those pictures were much too frightened to tell the whole story at first, or to even verbalize about the secrets. These symbols didn't always have a story attached to them; someone just came and drew a single picture. In the beginning they could not have understood or dealt with the whole story. It was important to the inner family, especially the child parts, that they weren't pushed into knowing the whole story of each drawing. It took a long time to uncover the meaning of certain symbols, but over a period of years the stories could be pieced together, like a jigsaw puzzle." (See* Figure 5.1.)

As a therapist, it is wise not to assume that you have the whole memory when you begin to see a story drawn in art forms. The story may not be told in its totality for a number of years.

Art is also something the client can do at home without the therapist. If, for example, you are on the telephone to a client who is having some very hurtful and intense feelings, and she doesn't seem to have a place to "put them" or a way to dissipate them, you can say, "Would you like to paint or draw those feelings? Just draw how you are feeling." This often helps. When certain personalities are awake at night and frightened, putting their feelings down on paper may help to diffuse them. When the client brings those drawings into the next therapy session, other personalities get to know those nighttime personalities as well. This is one way to help the multiple to become less dependent on the therapist and to learn a way to handle feelings other than dissociating them.

When the multiple feels especially self-destructive or finds she cannot rid herself of an obsessive, self-destructive thought, wish, or picture in her head, drawing the wish or self-destructive behavior can lower the intensity of the feeling and give her some relief. This can be helpful in between therapy sessions as well. Putting the feelings on paper releases them in a way that is not destructive; she puts the anger or the need to harm herself on paper instead of on herself. (See Figure 5.2.)

Clay is a wonderful medium for multiples. Using clay involves touch and physical contact; the multiple can really get involved physically in the art. Child parts should be given permission to be messy and not be scolded; this encourages them in freedom of activity, something they had no chance to experience in childhood. Clay allows control and

FIGURE 5.1: A typical drawing Judy's personalities made in the beginning stage of therapy.

manipulation by the artist; she can push it around, hit it, squish it, chop it up, etc. She can make a figure of a person and vent her feelings on it in the safety of the therapy room and with the support of the therapist. After the client has expressed these feelings however, she may be afraid of what she has just done; some personalities may be especially triggered. It is important for the therapist to reframe the client's work with

FIGURE 5.2: An example of how Judy's personalities drew their feelings of rage.

the clay as good and as a safe way to express the feeling. When working with clay, you don't need to tell your client what to make; you need only say, "Here is the clay — go ahead and play with it and see what you'd like to make." Let the client interpret it for herself. Then you can ask, "What would you like to do with that?" and encourage her to do just what she wants to. (See Figure 5.3.)

Most multiples are extremely creative, and for many art is a special gift, as well as a means of self-expression. Satisfaction and self-esteem are reflected back to her when the multiple sees a finished work that she has created and realizes it may be viewed as beautiful and artistic and even admired by others.

Journaling

Journaling, like art, is a visual experience. A personality who is out can see differences in handwriting or begin to recognize the different ways

FIGURE 5.3: A clay lion sculpture made by Judy well after three years of therapy, describing her feelings of anger toward the abusers.

that various personalities typically express themselves. The journal becomes a means that the personalities can use to identify themselves and the differences between themselves and other inner family members.

Multiples may not be able to visualize their other parts; but if they use journaling or art, they can use those media to "see" other parts of themselves that they might not be able to meet in another way. Journaling helps the multiple come out of denial about her diagnosis. A personality in denial can see for herself that she didn't write a certain journal entry. The concreteness of writing and of the information in it confirms that another personality was out. She'll notice, "That's not my handwriting," or "I don't talk that way." The journal offers evidence from the inside and as such is more meaningful and believable for the client.

Journaling is another way of communicating among different personalities and of gaining access to information held by various parts. It is also a safe way to network between the inner family and the therapist. Journaling can be a good way for the multiple to express something to the therapist that she is afraid to verbalize. Many multiples have a lot of fear about "saying" and "talking"; writing down the information or the experiences may feel much safer. Even after the multiple writes something down, it may take some time before she has the courage to allow the therapist to read it. Be sensitive about putting pressure on your client to share information before she is ready. Just writing it down for herself helps get the experiences "outside." Writing thoughts and feelings down helps desensitize traumatic material; experiences that have been written down may be easier to verbalize later on.

If the client is ready, ask her to read a journal entry aloud, to let you read it aloud, or to let you read it silently as she reads along with you. Be careful of interpreting information; give the client the opportunity to tell you more about what she has written. Personalities who are present in session and are reading the entries may have information to add then or at a later date. Repetition of the material, whether by journaling, art, or verbalization, is important; it gives the client some distance and a chance to desensitize to the information. Repetition allows the intensity of the feelings about revealed information to lessen.

Different personalities can get acquainted through journaling. Encourage the personalities who come to therapy to write something about themselves, to write their thoughts, their dreams, or something they would like other personalities to know about them. The client may want to write in her notebook something important that came up in session so that other personalities who weren't present can read it later.

It may also be helpful for a therapist to write something in the client's journal or in a separate notebook that the client can take home. As therapist, you may want to use writing yourself as a way to help other personalities learn about something important that came up in session; other inner family members who are out at home can use that as a way of obtaining information and passing it around. You may also want to write to some personalities just so they can get to know you.

If a client keeps a journal over a period of a year or more, she may begin to see a pattern in it; she may use it to identify which personalities are out at certain times of year, or what personalities emerge and what feelings follow certain current experiences and triggering events. The following is an excerpt from one of Judy's early journals, written by a dominant personality named Jane. This segment illustrates how journaling can help the inner family communicate among themselves and how it can be used to express feelings about past trauma and current life experiences. It also shows the process of therapy.

Jane's Journal

"*Friday August 2*   The beginning of a search, created by the questions of Who Am I? Why do I exist? The search has begun. Now I realize I am existing within a structure considered to be not my own, but a shared existence with others within the same human form. Possibly. Well, I doubt it seriously, but it's explained by my therapists as 'Multiple Personalities.'

"*Saturday August 3*   Sleep was impossible last night. So many questions. Even the process of falling asleep seems to have significant questions. Do I sleep or do I leave? I feel confused, not being able to sort out things clearly today.

"*Thursday August 8*   I started to cry uncontrollably and nothing can stop it. It's like a dam giving way. Why am I crying so hard? I'm becoming aware that I was reliving childhood experiences of which I had scarcely any conscious knowledge, until today. I had remembered only isolated fragments, but now the entire sequence is being revealed that was surely stored within my head. This reliving is very painful. And I can see that in burying it, my life has been altered.

"*Saturday August 10*   I have continuing feelings about the possibility of my childhood being so horrible. Was it my experience?

"*Monday August 12*   The idea that I may not be who I am fascinates me. How can I be, but not really exist? It's like a Chinese puzzle; take one piece out at a time. There seem to be so many pieces in my puzzle.

"*Tuesday August 13*   I've done it!!! I've made contact with Practical Judy. I've got to admit it, she sure is practical. My life is like a series of isolated events; nothing is tied together. It's like noise. I'm beginning to accept myself along with Practical Judy as a unit of one. Not together — separate — but [parts] to make a whole.

"*Monday August 19*   I lost three days. Dazed and confused. It's my responsibility to find out what and where I have been. No words are flowing to communicate. Feelings are to be experienced, but it's hard to communicate. Sometimes I feel painfully alone, searching for the answers to integration. Anxiously alone and nowhere. Lost in pain. I feel the pain of living. To live in pain is to live in a broken world. Everything is smashed into nonsense. It's painful to see the truth.

"*Thursday August 22*   I wish I could say I will survive the pains of childhood, but will I have to see the darkness to know from where we came?

'Dear Jane,

I did not promise you an easy journey—for that which seems most simple is often most difficult. I can promise you a large reward at journey's end and the steady summoning of your own strength as you begin to apply this childhood knowledge to your own existence. It will only make you stronger. Together we will undertake this journey, your hand in mine, my hand in yours. Prepare to face your enemy; and as you do so, breathe deeply of the feelings from your heart and know that you are loved.

Gloria'

"*Tuesday August 27*   Gloria says that everyone in our inner family belongs to everyone else. She knows the connection and is showing me. My role seems more defined as I become the one who wants to know how we exist.

"*Monday September 16*   It has become apparent that the problem is with myself. I believe I've been cheated out of my childhood, and denied even the remotest possibility of a childhood at all. It hurts. It is part of the unchangeable past. As I add this all up, I am a person who has recognized painfully that I was blocking out everything in my life about my childhood. I felt I hadn't even existed as a person. As long as I can cry about my lost childhood, I am in touch with its reality. This reality has brought about a grip on life."

As with artwork, information from journaling comes from the inside to the outside. This process parallels what the therapist tries to accomplish over and over with the client: to get what is inside and unknown (unconscious) to the outside. Not all clients are willing to do artwork, and some will not want to use journaling. Find the medium that works for your client. Especially during the initial stages of therapy, journaling may be the only way personalities can talk together; many clients do not begin therapy with a good internal system of communication or co-consciousness.

Support Groups

The Multiple in a Group with Nonmultiples

DORIS: *"When I began working with Judy I felt it would be good for her to have a network of friends or a support group. I was leading a support group of women who were dealing with everyday problems that we all encounter: family problems, relationship issues and so on; these women accepted Judy into their group knowing that she was a multiple. The benefit to being in a 'regular' group of people is that it allows the multiple to see that many of the problems she is having in relationships or with her children, as well as many of her feelings of anxiety or depression, are normal—that other people who are not multiples also experience these problems and feelings.*

"I like to keep reassuring multiples that they are normal people, that MPD is something they created to cope with extremely traumatic abuse and not something they were born with. Some of their ways of coping are similar to others'; many of their fears about their families or their relationships are like other people's fears. Issues about being intimate, making friends, raising children, and feeling accepted are ones that many of us have to deal with in life."

JUDY: *"As a multiple I had had few friendships, because I just wasn't able to trust people enough. I knew I was losing time and that things inside were very chaotic. Being in this group was a way for me to learn how to connect with people and to be accepted as a multiple. It gave me the feeling that I was not an oddity and helped me believe that MPD was a coping system. It also helped the others in group to see MPD as a way of coping with traumatic abuse, and because of that, helped me believe the abuse was not my fault. As I watched other women in group use their own coping skills, I began to feel more 'normal.' Slowly I began to trust someone outside of myself to be supportive. It was a positive experience to learn to trust someone other than my therapist, and helped me to live more in the outside world rather than so much within myself."*

If you choose to place your client in a support group of this kind, all members must be well informed as to the nature of MPD and the differences within one person they are sure to encounter. Not every group will be able to tolerate the switches or changes of behavior that occur. The health of the group and the health of your client must be constantly monitored if all are to benefit.

Support Groups of Multiples

We believe that support groups for only multiples should be structured yet noncontrolling. Activities and conversation must be directed by a therapist to assure that the group functions to provide support and does not become an arena for therapy work. We believe that abreactive work is not appropriate for a group of multiples. A support group of multiples should be designed to allow socializing, making friends, being understood as a multiple by other multiples, lessening isolation, etc. Multiples who do personal work in such a group will only trigger the others, creating chaos and leaving behind feelings of vulnerability, exposure, and mistrust.

Each participant in a support group of multiples must have a bona fide diagnosis of MPD. In addition, each member must have a therapist and be involved in ongoing treatment outside the support group. The support group cannot provide the multiple's therapy. Issues that may surface in the group must be taken to the multiple's individual therapist, where they can be worked out safely and confidentially. The group facilitator (therapist) must also have signed releases that enable her to contact the individual group members' therapists if any problems occur in group.

A support group of this type provides an opportunity for multiples to come together and be with others who understand what it is like to live in their world. It provides a setting for them to do things together that is nonthreatening and fun. As they experience one another, they may have their first chance to *not* feel different. They are with others who also never had a chance to learn many developmental skills; they are with people who will be more aware of their losses than any others could be. The often unspoken understanding is, "We know what it was like for you, and what it's like now." A support group for multiples gives the members an opportunity to support each other as they live their lives *as multiples*. Sharing how they are making it or not making it is important, as is validation and confirmation of each other.

It is not possible to have a group like this without having some triggering occur between people. It is important that the therapist leading the group stay alert to the conversations between group members and steer them away from delving into specific memories or details of abusive events that someone has experienced.

In a support group outside a hospital setting, members will tend to share telephone numbers or addresses and may meet outside the group. There are positives and negatives to this. Multiples can be helpful and supportive to each other outside of the group; or, depending on which personalities connect with each other, they may meet to do some negative things, such as using drugs or alcohol. The therapist must weigh the risks and decide whether the positives outweigh the negatives.

In deciding whether to refer a client to a support group of multiples, the therapist must consider the client's current level of stability. Factors to consider are: the amount of previous therapy; the amount of cooperation already achieved within the client's inner family; the amount of chaos the client is experiencing. Some multiples may not do well in a group, including those whose internal systems are quite chaotic, where cooperative efforts to maintain safety of the whole are lacking, and those who have abusive personalities emerging who might want to connect with another multiple to engage in activities that are harmful or abusive. Multiples who were ritualistically abused may not be appropriate for groups, especially if they have personalities who are actively in contact with a cult.

Hypnosis

We do use hypnosis on some occasions (see Chapter 8 on introjects); however, we have found it unnecessary to use formal hypnosis in order to work with a multiple. Ross (1989) says:

> When people ask me if it is necessary to use hypnosis to treat MPD, I usually say "No," because I don't want them to think they can't do anything with these patients without years of experience in hypnosis. I also point out that the aim of therapy is to bring the patient out of trance, not to put her in it. (p. 273)

The multiples various personalities are already in natural trance states; when the client switches, she merely changes from one alternate trance state to another.

Hypnosis is usually employed when the *therapist* wishes to speak to a particular personality. This may or may not seem important to the client. Rather than formal induction techniques, which may feel like control, the therapist is more likely to be able to enlist the cooperation of her client by asking the multiple quite simply to go inside and ask so-and-so if he is willing to come out and talk. This is an easy way to make contact or to let a personality inside know that you are aware of his existence and that you are willing to talk with him. And if a certain personality can't come out at that moment, that is OK. Some therapists get into problems with the thought, "I need to talk to that one — right now." There are other ways to get information to and from an inside personality. If a certain one cannot or will not come out, you can use other personalities to communicate with that part.

Always assume that many personalities inside are listening in on your sessions with the client. Even if you don't get a specific response, trust that the information is going in and that it will be passed around the system in one way or another at the appropriate time. The multiple's own timing is important and will be used to the advantage of the inside family.

Using hypnosis in controlling ways can trigger a pleaser personality to placate the therapist. A therapist is a major figure of authority and power in the multiple's life, and the client will have personalities who don't trust or who cope by attempting to please. She may try to be or do what the therapist wants her to, as she has done in the past to survive.

If you ask to speak to a specific personality, be careful not to give the impression that the personality who is already out and sitting in your office is not as important as the other one, that you don't want to talk to her, or that she shouldn't be there. Such messages imply that the client is not "doing it right." Let the multiple have as much control as she can, as much as she needs. If there is a personality you want to talk to but can't, or if there is a piece of information you wish to get from a specific personality inside, you'll often find that the multiple will find a way to retrieve the appropriate information for you. She'll process it in her own way and work it from the inside to the outside and back to you.

JUDY: *"My first experience with formal hypnosis in therapy was in a hospital setting. When during hypnosis a child part emerged or an angry personality came out, it really scared the therapist; he immediately tried to get me out of that state or personality and into another. That experience left me with the fear that those personalities were not good or OK — that it was not all right to be angry or to tell secrets, as the child personalities had done.*

"I think that my therapy with Doris and Lynda took less time than it would have if they had used hypnosis. I was allowed my own timing; my therapists did not try to control me. Also, it is very frightening for people who have been ritually abused to be hypnotized, because often the abuse involved hypnosis or a type of brainwashing to help the abusers control the child. To be hypnotized can recapitulate the old abuse, so a therapist must be sensitive to each client's issues."

If used judiciously and caringly hypnosis can be an invaluable tool; however, a therapist should not use hypnosis unless s/he is trained in its use. The error is in using hypnosis to control the agenda or schedule of the therapy, to control what issues are worked on when, etc. Such practices only reiterate the multiple's old family of origin rule, which is that there is always someone else who knows what is best, and that is the person with the most power.

Gestalt Therapy

Virginia Satir's work was based primarily on Gestalt therapy. Her "parts parties" allowed people to bring their many inner parts into the here-and-now and to work on old issues and feelings that continued to affect their present lives in negative ways. Gestalt therapy stays in the present; it permits the therapist to work with the client right where she is in the moment. Multiples do their work naturally in the present, since the old memories and the feelings are all captured in the moment and remain accessible to therapy in their original real-life state.

For this reason Gestalt therapy offers excellent concepts to use with the multiple. It allows the therapist to be with whatever personality comes into session, acknowledging and listening to her even as she switches. As therapist, you can give permission for whatever each personality needs to say, noting the relevance of that information and reframing it when necessary. This is quite different from using your

own agenda to get into an issue *you* think is important or asking some
personality who is not there to "be in the present." Fill in each personality you meet about what is current with the other parts; orient each one
who comes out to the present — make her aware of what room she is in,
the body she now occupies, what other personalities have said, etc.

Abreaction of past history is the telling and experiencing of that
history in the present. Each personality needs permission and acceptance to bring the past abuse to the here-and-now. Many personalities
are trapped in the past; the past is their "now." But when they abreact,
that old experience comes into the present — and this time, when they
experience the trauma, it is different. It is different because the therapist is there with the client to give her respect, comfort, safety, and
validation, which were lacking in the old experience. Replaying the
experience this way in the present gives that experience another dimension; it becomes a shared experience.

In Gestalt terms, as the multiple completes one picture or finishes
old business, that picture recedes to the background. Each personality
must complete her own Gestalt — each must tell her own story and
integrate it into the total picture. That is why it is important not to
deny or overlook any individual personality: there is a reason why each
personality was created and there must be closure to each experience
before the client can have "finished business." A multiple cannot complete her total picture until she can put all her pictures from the past,
whether large or small, together and connect them one with another.

When each personality can "finish the Gestalt" for which she was
made, when she can fulfill the role for which she was created, express
the feelings she was created to hold, and when this accomplishment
reverberates throughout the system, then that personality's purpose is
complete. For example, a child personality or a cluster of personalities
may have been created to hold the memories and feelings of a specific
abusive event. This young personality may be fixated at that early point
in time. When she is able to emerge, tell her story, experience her
feelings, and complete the experience in therapy, that may be all she
needs to do; that personality may then be ready to integrate.

DORIS: *"If you look at the dynamics of a multiple, there is constant movement from the background to the foreground with each
personality. Different triggers in the present may bring them out.*

Until their "foreground" work is finished, these personalities will recede and reemerge in the foreground over and over. Until they have their Gestalt, they cannot integrate with the whole and become an integrated part of the background.

"Each personality's individual Gestalt cannot be completed until that one can connect with the other parts of the multiple. As long as they are separate, they will keep coming to the foreground. In addition, there cannot be a Gestalt until there is a connector available; therapy may bring out partial pictures, but there can be no whole without a connector. The dissociated experience must become a system experience. So you may see a memory/feeling fragment repeated over and over in therapy until it can be shared by the system and until there is another personality available to integrate with the individual part who is holding one piece. We have found that the Essence personality is very often the bridge or connector between these individual parts when the time comes for integration (see Chapter 9)."

Don't feel discouraged with the amount of repetition that occurs in working with a multiple. There is no way to speed the process. However, time and energy are never wasted; every time a particular story is told or a feeling is expressed about one incident, more and more of the other personalities in the system become aware of that one experience. Each time something is told, more permission is given to others to tell their own stories. Retelling allows gradual desensitization to the remembrance and to the trauma of telling.

Finally, pay attention to the Gestalt of each session with your client. The multiple will need closure at the end of each session — as much closure as possible for the individual experiences that occurred within the session. This process happens again and again: there will be more closure over a period of months, and then years — until you reach the final Gestalt of finished integration.

Play Therapy

Play therapy is a means of expressing feelings, telling and reexperiencing memories, and regaining missed developmental stages in an atmosphere of safety. Play allows the child personalities in particular to get what is inside outside. Sand tray, puppets, dolls, storybooks, building materials, a dollhouse, paints, clay, and games are all useful materials. Make as many materials available as you can, and let the client use her imagination.

Using the sand tray or dollhouse, the child personalities can construct the pictures they carry around inside. They can show you, the therapist, what life was like growing up and what the various people in their lives said and did. Adult personalities can also use the play materials to show you things they remember or information they receive from other personalities. While one personality is playing, others inside are watching and listening; while the child is showing you, she is showing other parts as well.

While it is important to refrain from interpretation, it is helpful to comment and ask questions while the client is reenacting a story. Open-ended questions are helpful, such as: "What did the mommy do then?" "Tell me about this person here," and "Then what happened?" You will get feedback from observer personalities to clarify parts of the story or provide interpretations, such as, "Oh, now I know why so-and-so is always angry or afraid of that," or "I hadn't realized that was such a hard time in my life."

It is also extremely helpful for a multiple just to play. Many multiples missed out on the developmental skills that children acquire through play and the simple joyfulness of the experience of play. Some may have never had a doll of their own. Playing in the presence of a caring adult gives the child personalities a therapeutic experience.

> DORIS: *"I played with Judy's child parts a lot. We dug holes in the sand, played with stuffed animals and dolls; we bought doll clothes. We played on swings at the park, bought ice cream cones, and read storybooks. No one had ever simply read Judy a story. Just providing these experiences has a tremendous impact."*

Some of the books, toys, or decorations you have in the office can be accidental triggers for some child personalities, and as such they can be scary. You may offer to put away something that scares one personality, being aware that another personality may want to use that same toy at a later date to show you something scary that happened.

Play therapy can often be worked into the therapy time as part of a session or all of some sessions. For some clients it may be more comfortable to have the play time at the beginning of the session. The child personalities can come out first, and the older personalities can come to session later on and be available to drive the client home and continue with adult responsibilities of life.

Dreamwork

Dreamwork allows both therapist and client insight into the multiple's inner processing and her progress in therapy through dream symbols that are both universal and unique to the dreamer. As well as communicating symbolically, dreams may be a way that some personalities use to show others concrete information about specific past traumas. A word of caution: get some training in using dreamwork in therapy before you begin to incorporate this useful tool. We recommend the following sources: *The Portable Jung* (1971), edited by Joseph Campbell; and *Dreams and Healing: A Succinct and Lively Interpretation of Dreams* (1978), by John Sanford.

Judy has always had a rich and powerful dream life, one that has consistently tracked her progress and relayed information in symbolic form. Here are some excerpts from three of her dreams, covering a period of one and a half years in her therapy.

> Dream One: First Scene
> JUDY: *"I hear a noise in the house; I know the killer is out, stalking me; I feel very frightened. I ask my husband if the doors are locked. I don't feel safe, I know the stalker will kill me."*
> DORIS: *"The 'killer' in the dream represented an introject of an abuser, one who was involved in extreme abuse that included many death threats and near-death experiences for Judy. She was at this point in therapy revealing more of the family of origin secrets."*
> Second Scene
> JUDY: *"I am in an old house with a garage; it is very messy. Mother and I are cleaning and find something in the rubble as we are sorting things out. Some things are going in boxes, others into the trash. One object I find is old and unrecognizable to me. Mother holds it up and says it's not trash but a valuable antique piece of silver used*

for Thanksgiving dinner. She looks closer and it says 'dedicated to Judy Kessler.'"

DORIS: *"In Judy's dreams old houses have symbolized her 'old self' and the sorting out in the dream shows what was occurring in her life at the moment: going through 'old stuff' in therapy, sorting out which was trash and which was of value. The mother figure in this dream is significant; she represents for Judy the carrier of old messages in which Judy was told that she was not capable of knowing what was good or bad. The last part about the antiquity and value of the silver, and the 'dedication' continues the confusion, since celebrations of holidays during Judy's childhood were ominous events."*

Third Scene

JUDY: *"A man comes in; my husband is there instead of my mother. The man has a letter saying my mother is in danger. Then we realize he is the killer. The next car that comes by holds the killer, who has a huge gun."*

DORIS: *"The confusion continues. A new messenger arrives. He is both the messenger and the killer, and the former messenger is now in danger. The presence of Judy's husband in her dreams indicates passive support."*

Fourth Scene

JUDY: *"I run to a small, old dollhouse full of spiders and webs; I squeeze in and hide. The killer starts shooting and killing everything in sight: people, children, it doesn't matter. He's going to find me and kill me."*

DORIS: *"Hiding in the old way, in a space that is for children (dissociation), does not bring protection now or stop the killer."*

Fifth Scene

JUDY: *"The killer and I are face to face. Knives are used. I slice him and he still chases after me. I jump into a car but I can't go fast enough. He finds me and we fight to his death. Ugly, bloody fighting. I'm exhausted. I don't know if I can finish killing him."*

DORIS: *"The dream comes to its conclusion with the message that the old ways of believing and the old ways of dissociating from past traumas are under siege and there is a primal battle going on as the old system fights to survive the changes a new system is bringing."*

Dream Two: First Scene

JUDY: *"I am in a construction area and go into a room. It is very old and dark. Almost like a barn with old theater props in it. I found they weren't real but made of hard wax."*

DORIS: *"Being 'under construction' was also a recurrent theme in Judy's dreams. The theatrical props again touch on the 'unreality' of past traumas. The new Judy under construction is full of old stuff."*

Second Scene

JUDY: *"I looked in a corner and saw a baby in distress. I crawled near the baby and tried to pick it up. The baby struggled and screamed, 'I'm not good enough to be loved.' I held the baby close and tried to comfort it."*

DORIS: *"This part is self-explanatory. The struggle around love is a continuing paradox: the desire to love and be loved and the belief that she is unlovable."*

Third Scene

JUDY: *"I walked out of the barn and realized the construction had been completed and the barn was now a huge modern university. Many people there knew me. I walked into a lounge where a woman was giving a piano concert."*

DORIS: *"The university represents new learning and the many people a new visibility (as well as acquaintance between many parts of herself). There is a sense of being at ease in her surroundings."*

Fourth Scene

JUDY: *"Next I was running away. I was afraid of something. I felt as if a man was going to hurt me."*

DORIS: *"The sense of being at ease doesn't last long. The system once more reacts to change and sends old messages designed to maintain homeostasis."*

Fifth Scene

JUDY: *"I got stuck back in a dark room. I'm crying and no one knows I'm there."*

DORIS: *"Challenging the system is overwhelming. Even though change is occurring, fear causes the dreamer to return to an old survival pattern: hiding to feel safe, and at the same time feeling abandoned."*

Dream Three

DORIS: *"This last dream is one Judy had just prior to integration. I'll tell it in its entirety, just as it was told to me. I believe after you read it you'll agree that the dream is self-explanatory."*

Scene One

JUDY: *"I was going up the stairs with broken jagged glass cutting my feet, and crying 'it hurts so bad.'"*

Scene Two

JUDY: *"I was on a ship seeing the world for the first time. I saw old and ancient cities; Malaysia, Greece, and old unsettled islands."*

Scene Three

JUDY: *"At the port, I miss getting off the ship. My husband had come aboard and taken my suitcase off the ship, then he left again. I was still on board."*

Scene Four

JUDY: *"I found a roommate who was the daughter of Ghandi, but she didn't know that. She had a child and I showed her how to take care of it."*

Scene Five

JUDY: *"I knew a large storm was coming, a hurricane. I showed people aboard ship what to do to survive. After a few days, when no storm appeared, no one on board would listen to me; they sent all the children aboard the ship to play on the beach at an old ancient port in Malaysia."*

Scene Six

JUDY: *"As I prepared for the hurricane I looked out at the children on the beach. Each was mutilated, retarded, or somehow damaged, and yet they were able to play and enjoy themselves. I felt so sad for them, my heart ached. 'It hurts so bad,' I kept saying."*

Scene Seven

JUDY: *"The ship began taking on water; the storm had arrived. The children were in great danger on the beach. I called to them to get on the ship. It was so hard for them. They had to crawl up the stairs, then up a great wall into the ship."*

Scene Eight

JUDY: *"As the storm got closer, growing in intensity, a small child—the last to come aboard—stood crying. She was crying hard because she hurt so bad in her body she couldn't make her arms and legs move enough to climb up to the ship. I risk my own safety, reach down for her, and bring her closely to me, using all my strength. I say to her, "You must survive, you are the last one. Find the strength inside and you will be able to do all you can do to survive. Find the strength within yourself, for it's there for you to survive. Reach in and survive."*

DORIS: *"I am aware that you, the reader, may see that there could be many different levels of interpretation other than the ones I have discussed. However, the main interpreter of any dream must be the dreamer herself. The therapist can point out possible clues and pass along information, but it is up to the dreamer to see what fits for her. As in other aspects of therapy, don't press for interpretation even when the message may seem quite clear to you. If your client seems 'resistant,' remind yourself that the dream belongs to the dreamer. She will receive the message when the time is right for her. She will have other dreams."*

As we bring this chapter on therapeutic techniques to a close, we are aware that the uniqueness of each multiple will determine which techniques will be the most useful in her particular case. As a therapist, do not predetermine which will work; rather, explore with her the possibilities available. She will choose those that fit for her.

chapter 6

The Beginning Stage
of Treatment

A MULTIPLE MAY SHOW few signs of multiple personality disorder when she first appears for treatment. In some cases you may spend months (or longer) with another diagnosis, such as anxiety or depression, before a trauma or other life stressor triggers overt dissociative symptoms. However, if you are patient, curious, nonthreatening, and trustworthy as a therapist, a multiple will eventually give you some clues of MPD (see Chapter 2).

When you suspect MPD, check out the symptoms you are seeing directly with the client. At the time of diagnosis, it helps to give the client some basic information about multiple personality disorder and how and why it develops, as well as reassurance that she is not crazy to be the way she is. A good way to begin is by talking about dissociation, which is something we all do. Most clients will feel relieved that someone actually sees what is going on, knows what MPD is, and is not afraid to talk about it.

For the remainder of this chapter we are going to assume that you have already diagnosed your client as a multiple. She may be someone who was referred to you with this diagnosis, a new client you diagnosed yourself, or a client you have been seeing for some time for other problems. If you suspect your client may be a multiple but have not reached a sure diagnosis, the following suggestions for the beginning sessions will still be quite applicable. Treatment will be primarily the same, since the work related to multiple personality is just beginning.

The First Sessions

First sessions are times of observing the multiple's behavior and creating a safe environment in which she can feel free to speak about her history, her problems, and her feelings. A therapist must be sensitive to the fact that many multiples have been in treatment for years for various diagnoses other than multiple personalities, and many have had negative experiences as a result. Although previous therapy may have been unsuccessful, the multiple may still know that there is something wrong; she wants to feel better, but she may lack confidence that her work with you will be helpful. Her fears during those first sessions will include:

1. Fear of talking to you. This may be difficult at any time for a multiple, but especially with a new therapist, particularly if the client's past experiences were negative and included encounters with doctors and therapists who were too intrusive.
2. Fear of being disbelieved. A multiple's stories may sound quite bizarre; she may have past experience with professionals who may have implied that she was making them up or simply lying. This type of response triggers the multiple's old feelings from her family of origin, where her abusers told her: "You didn't see that, you didn't hear it; you didn't experience that—you're lying; you are making all this up; we never did that." The mental health system may have unwittingly recapitulated the early abuse.

When a multiple first comes into your office, she will most likely be checking you out to see how much you, the therapist, know and how much she can disclose. Before she can disclose, *she must first trust her therapist.* Initial therapist comments such as, "Tell me about yourself," or "Tell me about your history" may be perceived as too threatening for the client, who may be asking herself, "What will be expected of me? And what do I have to give up to this therapist to get his/her help?" Be aware of the client's fear of therapy and of being invaded. Too many expectations on the part of the therapist may result in the multiple's assuming a helpless role. A therapist, simply by her role is in a position of power and must use that power wisely. Based on her growing-up years, a multiple may have every reason to fear powerful people.

Here are some suggestions for establishing nondemanding, non-threatening contact that will lead to a good bond between client and therapist.

1. Don't rush into doing therapy; take your time getting to know the client and letting her get to know you. Move slowly and gently; let her observe you and your office. It is more important in the beginning stages of therapy to be a safe person than to show a complete knowledge of multiple personality.

2. An important rule to use throughout therapy is to *follow the client's lead.* Be nondemanding and nondirective and take your cues from the client in your office. (An exception would be a crisis situation where the therapist must take charge.) De-mands contribute to chaos and can create fear because de-mands, to a multiple, may signal immediate danger. Even ques-tions may be seen as demands.

3. As a therapist you must be congruent. During the first session and all the sessions that follow, the multiple will continue to check you out — and she is a master at picking up nonverbal cues. She will recognize any insincerity, manipulation, or at-tempts at control on your part. You cannot fake congruency with a multiple for she has developed an intuitive sense and a trained eye that will catch any inconsistencies between verbal and nonverbal communication. This ability is a learned surviv-al skill.

   As therapist then, bring to the therapeutic setting not only your cognitive skills and all that you have read and learned about multiples, but your own personhood, your genuine self — without pretense or arrogance. The first sessions set the stage for following sessions and if there is any display of gran-diosity on your part, or if you have a hidden agenda, you will be recapitulating the client's family system by bringing issues of power and control into the therapeutic setting.

Although you may have the desire to work with a multiple, and although you may find a multiple very interesting and exciting, this work may not fit for you. Keep in mind that it will be long-term therapy and very demanding at times. If you are a behaviorally oriented therapist or only comfortable being direc- tive, it would be wise to refer the multiple elsewhere; you can- not pretend to be what you are not. If a multiple is to work through the many layers of fear beneath which the original child is hiding, safety and permission for each personality to emerge at her own pace are of major importance. If you have an agenda or time schedule of your own for the therapeutic process, this will be interpreted as a "demand" by the multiple, who will then do her best to comply. And you will have re- created the old system your client knows so well, the one that has told her all her life to do as she is told in order to live.

4. Be sincere and accepting. Acceptance is a key word. Nurtur- ance, while extremely important, might feel overwhelming to a multiple at first, since in the past what appeared to be nurtur- ing may have been twisted into abuse. If you are too nurturing at the beginning, the client may say to herself, "So — what do you want now? Now that you have given me this, what do I have to give you in return?" As a child, if this person ever re- ceived anything, she was expected to give something back; and that something almost always hurt. If you are by nature a very nurturing person, that doesn't mean you have to change your- self; simply allow the client the time to get to know you, to realize that you are a genuine person and that there are no strings attached to your nurturing.

If in the first session you have made a good contact, you are on your way. But don't build up expectations about how other personalities may feel about you! You may have to have an "initial session" experience with many personalities who may not have been to your office that first visit. Treat each emerging personality with respect and move slowly, continuing to create a safe place and a trusting relationship with each inner family member.

Before the client leaves your office, you will also need to establish the frequency of sessions and the contacts apart from therapy. The structure you set up will depend upon your own schedule, whether the multiple is currently in crisis or not, and whether the client is just beginning to be aware of her multiple personalities or whether she has already done some work as a multiple.

Who's the Expert?

It is important for the multiple to know that her therapist will be honest about what she does or doesn't know during the process of therapy. Although there are many similarities, each multiple is truly unique; the design of her inner family system will corroborate that uniqueness. A good way to establish a sense of equality, as well as your acceptance of her, is to incorporate the multiple immediately into the therapy process by using terms that will do just that.

> DORIS: *"I like to establish in the first session that I see her as the expert on what it is like for her to be a multiple. She can then educate me as to what she has discovered about herself and share as much of that information with me as she can at that time. She may even question me as to whether or not I believe she is a multiple, and ask me to explain why. With the information she's given me, I'm in a better position to do that. In addition, she may have switched once or twice while she was talking to me, which I can point out to her. As her therapist, I make it clear to her that I will initially be getting acquainted with her and with all the other personalities, that she and I will be exploring together what that inner family system is like, and that I will pass on to her any information from other personalities that she hasn't had access to. Together we will build a network with the other inner family members and begin to create a communication system.*
>
> *"Don't overwhelm her with too much information during the first sessions. There may be a number of onlookers inside who are making sure the personality in your office knows what they think of you, and she has to process that while she's talking to you as well. Always remember that when you are talking to the personality who is 'out' there will very likely be others listening in."*

Intellectualization as a Problem
of Early Treatment

During the first session(s) with a multiple, you may encounter one of the more dominant personalities, particularly one who has learned to intellectualize or socialize. An intellectual personality may have read books on MPD, talked to many professionals, and be quite articulate. As time passes, this may appear to you to be the one member of the multiple's inner family who will enable you to access the inner family system. Not necessarily so. For some multiples, an intellectual or historian-type personality may indeed have access to the inner system, and she may be able to empathize with the experiences of other personalities or have feelings of her own. However, in many cases this personality may have been specifically designed for the job of seeking out information; rather than a denial part, she may be a searcher part — one who wants the facts, wants to learn all she can. She may not experience feelings. This personality may be one who has learned to work with a therapist in a way that encourages the therapist to believe she is making progress, when what is happening may be quite the opposite.

Because she "stays in her head," this part may prevent major changes from occurring within the system if she continues to stay in control during sessions. The personalities who are historians and fact finders may want to stay out in the world, avoiding the painful work of experiencing feelings and retrieving the memories. They may have discovered that if *they* talk, they can hold back other personalities who would talk about abuse or feelings, and so protect the secrets and system. This is understandable; why would any human being want to reexperience the pain and terror he or she endured as a child? The intellectual, nonfeeling personalities may search for another way to do therapy that will not be painful; as such, they are endeavoring to protect the inner family system as best they can.

If you as therapist collude with this kind of cognitive dominant part early on by following every intellectual lead the client offers, you may find yourself becoming attached to this very intelligent, capable personality who seems to make your job as a therapist so much easier! However, she will be watching to see whether you are willing to go beyond that with her, to encourage expression of feelings in spite of her protectiveness. If you find you have colluded with her and gotten caught in this intellectualizing format of therapy, it is not necessary to reverse yourself and see that part as negative or manipulative; you need only to realize that this personality is a protective part, who maintains the system and alleviates as much discomfort as she can in addition to gathering and accessing valuable information. As you recognize this, you can encourage this helpful personality to use her skills and knowledge to teach others within the inner family.

Establishing a Structure for Treatment

Length and Frequency of Sessions

When deciding length of sessions and how often to see a multiple for therapy, it is helpful to take the following issues into consideration. First, is MPD a new diagnosis or has the client already been diagnosed with MPD? If a dominant personality is just learning about being a multiple or if the client was just diagnosed, you may want to move rather slowly, giving that personality time to accept the diagnosis and to get as much information about it as she wants. If this is the case, you can start off your work with one session a week, lasting a full hour. Later on, you may want to increase the time to an hour and a half or two hours once a week. If your client has known she is a multiple and has been working already for a while, e.g., with another therapist, longer and/or more frequent sessions may be appropriate from the start.

An hour may not be long enough for a multiple, who may have several personalities appear in session for short periods. The therapist is the one who must keep track of what is happening in session and make sure that there is time enough at the end of the session to tie up loose ends. Allow enough time for the multiple to reorient herself so that she can leave the office. A longer session gives the personality who originally came to the session time to return at the end if needed. For example, after several switches, an older personality who can drive the car may need to return before the client leaves for home. Saving the last 15 minutes of the session for "regrouping" also allows the therapist time to transmit any information to this last personality that she may have learned from other parts. This process may give the multiple a better sense of continuity.

If at the beginning of treatment you create a structure for the sessions, the multiple can begin to rely on that structure. Knowing the format helps give the client a sense of safety and control and promotes trust as well. For example, if the client knows she will have enough time at the end of the session to reorient herself, she won't need to panic with a thought such as "What if I'm not the one here at the end of the session—what's going to happen to me? Who will drive (us) home?" Sometimes a therapist can help with this, if a bond of trust has been created with a particular personality. The therapist might say, "I would really appreciate it if you would come back if you can at the end of session, so you can drive home."

While this can help the client feel as if she has some control, be careful how you coach the return of particular personalities. What you *don't* want to do is cause your client to feel as if she has failed if a certain personality does not return at the end of the session. State the idea in terms that it *will* be possible for someone to come at the end of session who will see them (all) safely home, which is an affirmation of her own ability to do that. Over time, the client can use that ability more and more if needed. It is important to encourage the multiple to take as much charge of her life as possible, without giving her the message that it is her responsibility not to dissociate or that she had failed if a personality cannot be out when wanted.

The second factor to consider when establishing an initial schedule for therapy is whether the client is currently in crisis. Are there external or environmental factors that are causing a lot of stress at this time? If so, you may need more frequent sessions for a while. The first year of work in particular may contain crises at holiday times. For many multiples, birthdays, Christmas, Easter, Halloween, etc., were occasions for abusive events. Days that most of us see as very special were days of horror for many clients; you can anticipate these as times the client may need extra support or networking.

Finally, is the inner family system currently in chaos; is a lot of switching of personalities occurring? When many personalities are available to talk to the therapist, they may appreciate a longer session. As the work continues, more switching will occur, and therefore more chaos will be experienced inside by the multiple's inner system—this is part of the therapy process. At this time, it helps to increase the number of sessions, e.g., from one to two sessions per week, or to schedule telephone calls in addition to therapy time. While some therapists may be able to see a client as often as every day in a hospital setting, other therapists in agency or private practice settings may not be able to do that—nor is it necessary. If you establish a certain schedule early in treatment and adhere to it, that schedule becomes comfortable for the multiple. While two or even three hours of contact may seem long when you first try it, you will need the extra time when the client's work becomes extremely difficult and internal chaos is extreme.

Contact Outside the Office Setting

Contact outside the office may be necessary or helpful. If telephone calls are needed, schedule those for specific times during the week. If the therapist is consistent with office and telephone contacts, the schedule itself may lessen the need or extreme urgency for extra contact that the client may feel during times of stress. If she knows she will be meeting with you on a certain day, for so many hours, or that she can call you on the phone, for example, on Wednesday at 7 p.m., and talk to you for a certain length of time—if she knows she can count on it—she will be less likely to panic.

As the therapist, it helps if you know, or at least come to learn, what your own boundaries are, so that you can be truly present for your client during scheduled contacts. If you find yourself taking telephone calls but resenting those calls as intrusions into your own time, then telephone contacts will not be very therapeutic and countertransference issues will develop. It is important that you, the therapist, know when and how much time you have outside the office for calls. After you have determined your own limitations, take the time during a session with the client to preschedule specific times that either you or the client will telephone to make contact for continued support. There will be times of crisis in which she may need more time, but if possible limit the calls to 10 to 15 minutes. If possible, the client herself should be in on the decision about how often she needs to call and how long the calls are to last. Do not get into doing therapy over the telephone. Do your best to say, "This is something we can talk about in our next session."

Some fine therapists have found that they must refer a multiple to someone else when they find themselves drained by the intensity and duration of the work. If you are a therapist who resents any telephone calls after office hours or any extra crisis scheduling for sessions, you may not be a candidate for working with a multiple. Changing therapists halfway into the course of therapy may be devastating for the multiple, and the therapist may find herself struggling with some issues of her own. Both therapist and client must accept that this is going to be long-term therapy. In order to do the work required of her, a multiple needs to know that her therapist is willing to go the distance with her.

If the client is abreacting at home and intense feelings or memories are surfacing at a rapid rate, you might want to schedule an extra therapy session at the office sooner than the one already set up. Many therapists fear that a client will take advantage of extra time or contact offers; however, if you have established a specific structure, *and you are clear about your own boundaries*, the client becomes comfortable with that and usually will not take advantage of it. If several phone calls turn into hourlong contacts, you and the client must deal with that issue during a therapy session. Be aware not only of your own boundaries, but of your client's boundaries as well. Remember, telephone calls at the client's home may seem invasive to her also—so check it out.

Consistency in scheduling will be helpful not only for the multiple but also for you as the therapist. You will not be using up energy making and receiving extra phone calls or scheduling extra sessions in the middle of an already busy week. We learned that with multiples, if you can give them a structure, they can live with that. If, on the other hand, you tell your client you will call and then don't, this may have negative consequences. You cannot break a promise to your client—any more than you can to a child, a spouse, or a business partner—without having some negative reaction. A multiple needs that consistency from you in order to trust you. For any adult who was severely abused as a child, lack of structure and consistency creates chaos and fear.

Creating a structure for therapy is actually setting up therapist/client boundaries. It is a healthy process that helps clarify messages and expectations; it sets up trust. If you, as the therapist, need or wish to make any changes in the structure that is formulated, be sure to discuss that change with the client during session. Even a helpful change can create chaos. For example, if you begin to add telephone calls during the week without prior discussion, you will throw the structure off balance for the client. Inconsistent behavior creates the same kind of confusion in a multiple that she experienced as a child.

*Setting Boundaries for Safety in
Times of Crisis*

Often, a directive approach on the therapist's part may hinder rather than speed the therapy process. However, there is a time to be directive, and that is when the client is in crisis and in such chaos that she loses perspective or a sense of reality. During these times she needs to be told in very clear terms what she can do to lessen the chaos. There may be something she can do at home; if the crisis is more serious, she may need an extra session at the office or she may need to be hospitalized in order to be safe and to feel protected.

When a person who has habitually dissociated from feelings begins to reconnect with intense emotions, those feelings may overwhelm her. Overwhelming feelings can arise from an environmental trigger or from work done in therapy. When feelings take over, the ability to think logically recedes; the client begins to act instinctively. Because she has been terribly traumatized as a child, some of the behaviors she uses now will be old ones, and they may appear irrational—especially with her feelings out of control. During this time, it is important that the therapist act as a stabilizer, enabling the multiple to reconnect with her own ability to mentally process and organize information, without preventing the expression of the intense feelings. This allows the client to regain control and once again feel more comfortable.

Some of the crises that can require immediate attention include threats of suicide; other behaviors that endanger the client, such as sexual encounters or contacting ritual abusers; being contacted by family of origin or former abusers; and self-destructive behaviors such as cutting or mutilating. It is very helpful at times for a therapist to have support from other professionals in the community mental health system. Get to know the multiple's family doctor; network with physicians and psychiatrists at the local hospital. Some crises may require intervention from a hospital crisis team; others may not. If a client is extremely suicidal and the risk is great—particularly when there is no outside support except for the therapist—hospitalization is an absolute must.

When you know your client well, and when you become acquainted with the personality or personalities who use self-destructive behaviors, you will learn just how far they will go. You may find that there is a certain amount of self-mutilation that you cannot prevent, especially in the beginning stages of treatment before a lot of inner cooperation has been achieved. You may also find that some forms of self-mutilation do not necessitate hospitalization, even though such a remedy would seem helpful from both your perspective and the client's. In some hospital systems, superficial cutting may be perceived as "attention-getting behavior," particularly if this client has used "superficial" self-mutilation previously and was attended at the hospital.

The therapist may then find herself between a rock and a hard place; she may not be able to get hospitalization for her client if the hospital crisis team does not consider the risk serious enough. In such a case, a strong bond of trust between therapist and client becomes critical. The therapist must be in contact with the personality who inflicts the harm and be directive about limiting the behavior for the protection of all personalities. It is also extremely helpful for both therapist and client to be aware of who in the multiple's personal outside network of friends or family can be of support in an emergency. Perhaps a husband, a grown child, or a friend can stay with the client.

As the therapist for a multiple, you must also remember that your client is first and foremost a survivor. You have to trust that your client, as a survivor, will pass through difficult times and move on. For more information on causes of self-destructive behaviors and treatment with hurtful or violent personalities, see Chapter 8.

Setting Up a Nurturing Triad: Using Co-therapy

Changing the client's self-punishing, closed system to a self-nurturing one will be one of the goals of therapy with a multiple. A good way to begin is to bring in a co-therapist. Virginia Satir believed in the power of the nurturing triad, the representation of the early Father-Mother-Child triad. A nurturing co-therapy triad can provide for a multiple an environment that is supportive, accepting, and affirming. Figures 6.1 and 6.2 schematically show the family of origin triad and the therapeutic/nurturing triad.

With two therapists in a session, the multiple has the opportunity to see positive confrontations between therapists and positive resolutions to conflict. When the multiple has a personal issue with one therapist,

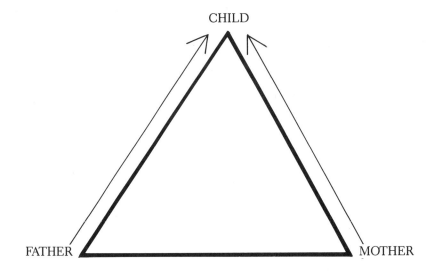

- · Role-reversal: Child in care-taker role

- · Child given blaming messages

- · Child scapegoated

- · One-way communication

FIGURE 6.1: Abusive family triad.

the co-therapist can support the client in addressing the therapist on that issue. The therapeutic triad models for the client a different system than the one the abused child experienced (see Figure 6.3).

DORIS: *"My own personal experience in working with multiples has taught me not only the great advantages of having that extra pair of eyes and ears a co-therapist brings, but also the importance of the co-therapist's healthy interaction as it relates to the triad. A co-therapist must be chosen wisely. Trust and respect between the primary therapist and the co-therapist are as important as trust and respect between client and therapist. Because of the intensity of the work, each therapist needs to enjoy the support of the other, and each must honor the integrity of the other.*

"Confidence in the co-therapist's ability to be an effective thera-

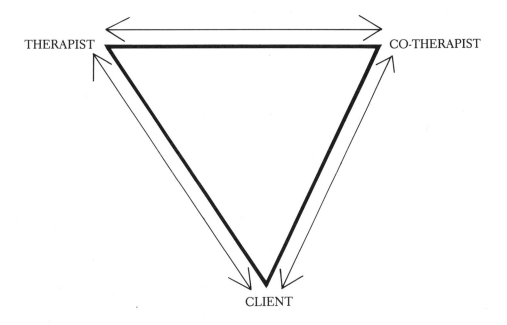

THERAPIST   CO-THERAPIST

CLIENT

· Nurturing of client
· Open communication
· Therapists model healthy relationship

FIGURE 6.2: Nurturing therapeutic triad.

pist and to handle emergencies as they arise is essential on occasions when the primary therapist decides there is a need for extra therapy sessions or for additional contact with the client through telephone calls. Not only does the primary therapist receive support, but the client, having bonded with the co-therapist, doesn't suffer the anxiety of change. The therapy continues in an uninterrupted manner.

"A co-therapist is also beneficial in other ways. I have found that as a primary therapist, I am able to work at a deeper level when I 'join' the multiple's inner family if I know there is someone on the 'outside'; my co-therapist watches to see that I don't get caught up in the very system I have joined to change. As we work together, always with the uniqueness of the individual client in mind, a healing environment is created for her."

LYNDA: *"When the co-therapist joins the sessions, the resulting triad will feel much more open than the previous dyadic system, and*

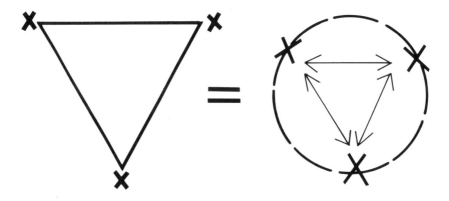

FIGURE 6.3: Nurturing triad allows client to experience an open system.

the multiple will feel even more vulnerable for a time. As a new co-therapist, be prepared to be a silent partner for several sessions, even for months.

"Those first months will be trust-building sessions between you (as co-therapist) and the client, in which the multiple will be checking you out. She and the other inner family members who remain inside will be observing your reactions and your body language, and getting used to having one more person see them and hear the secrets—both of which are great risks for the multiple.

"Take your time in moving to therapeutic interventions; use the initial period to get to know the client and to observe the client-therapist interactions taking place in front of you. Your powers of objective observation will be called upon later in the therapy process, for one of your major roles as co-therapist will be to support the client in her attempts to make her needs known in therapy, and to clarify the interactional process between client and therapist when transference and countertransference issues appear (see Chapter 8).

"My own experience as a co-therapist was very positive. I found the first months as a silent member of the triad gave me time to adjust to Judy and Doris' way of being together and working in therapy, and time to find my own place in that process in a way that would be helpful to both of them.

"Being in a triad requires learning to 'dance' with the other two members. I learned to be flexible, for co-therapy demanded a con-

stant shifting and adjustment of my role in the triad. During the extended process of therapy I was at times the observer, and at other times a support for Judy or the mediator between Judy and Doris. At times I was the active therapist in session, at other times a support for Doris, and at times I was the one supported. My presence in the therapy allowed Doris and Judy more flexibility also, and gave Judy a chance to observe the interchanging of roles and the exchange of support that occur in a nurturing triad."

The results of using a co-therapist to create a nurturing therapist/ client triad are extremely positive. The multiple can experience having her feelings without punishment from the parental figures in the triad. The nurturing therapeutic triad becomes a complete reframing of the family of origin. In this healthy new family, the multiple is not punished or abandoned for having and expressing feelings, needs, and wants. All the old rules are broken.

Methods and Techniques

Using Satir's Concept of Parts

The initial phase of therapy with a multiple consists largely of acquainting the therapist and the client with her many personalities. This is no small task in itself and requires time, perhaps more than a year for some clients.

Satir's concept of "parts," as well as her method of connecting with, accepting, and affirming each one (Satir, 1978), is extremely helpful when working with a multiple. The therapist works with personalities rather than parts, yet the concept remains the same.

As children growing up, none of us knew at first which parts of ourselves were acceptable to our families, but we soon learned. In many families, anger was a bad part and loving was a good part. Since we were told we were too young and inexperienced to make judgments about ourselves from our own resources, we learned to accept the judgment of others. We began to disown and to project onto others those parts that kept us from winning the approval of other family members on whom we depended.

Satir believed that there is energy in every part of ourselves. To project or disown whatever part we see as bad means the energy of that part becomes destructive and the part converts itself into a negative. To see the positive in a negative part. is the first step to owning it and connecting with it. This releases that energy so it can be used in a positive way.

How does this concept apply to a multiple? Multiples have not only been totally confused about what is good and what is bad, but they certainly don't want to connect with any of their "bad" parts. Unlike most of us, whose parts "float around," as Satir would say, the multiple's parts are clearly defined, to the point that the parts actually assume different roles, taking on identities as different people. (In this book, we use the terms "parts" and "personalities" interchangeably.)

With each dissociation, the child splits off or creates a separate personality to assume a role in the inner family. Some walk in the outside world, and some hide inside; some only come out at night. Each part or personality carries her own set of experiences, memories, emotions, and ways of coping with those emotions. In a multiple, one part may also split into more parts when an extremely traumatic event occurs; in this case each split may take on specific tasks (see Chapter 4).

Mapping the Inner Family

Family mapping is very helpful in working with a multiple. With other types of clients, family-of-origin mapping is a great way to create a visual pattern of what most of us manage to recreate in our own current families. However, with a client who is a multiple, the map is of the "Inner Family." Since the family-of-origin map for a multiple may be difficult to obtain, or may contain information that is frightening for the client to give initially, it is often best to work from the inner family map. Mapping the inner family will give many clues about the family of origin.

Begin by creating the map as different personalities or parts appear in therapy sessions. As you start, write down a descriptive adjective for each personality. Soon a picture will emerge of the ages at which particular traumas occurred in the client's life, which will indicate the timing and duration of the traumatic events that caused each split to occur.

As the different personalities appear, the map continues to grow, and you will get a clearer picture of the inside family of the multiple. Each

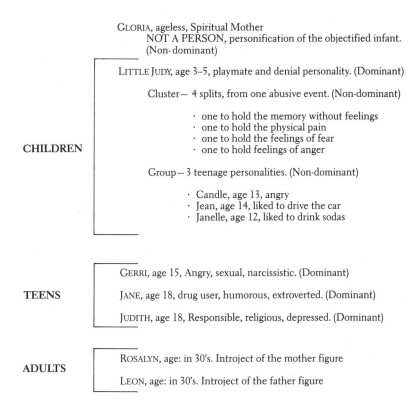

GLORIA, ageless, Spiritual Mother
NOT A PERSON, personification of the objectified infant. (Non-dominant)

CHILDREN

LITTLE JUDY, age 3–5, playmate and denial personality. (Dominant)

Cluster— 4 splits, from one abusive event. (Non-dominant)

· one to hold the memory without feelings
· one to hold the physical pain
· one to hold the feelings of fear
· one to hold feelings of anger

Group— 3 teenage personalities. (Non-dominant)

· Candle, age 13, angry
· Jean, age 14, liked to drive the car
· Janelle, age 12, liked to drink sodas

TEENS

GERRI, age 15, Angry, sexual, narcissistic. (Dominant)

JANE, age 18, drug user, humorous, extroverted. (Dominant)

JUDITH, age 18, Responsible, religious, depressed. (Dominant)

ADULTS

ROSALYN, age: in 30's. Introject of the mother figure

LEON, age: in 30's. Introject of the father figure

FIGURE 6.4: Map of Judy's inner family of personalities.

member will have a certain age, a time at which they were "born" or created, and a role they play in the inner family.

As you gradually construct the inner family map, it should be shared with the client, so she can begin to understand the parts and personalities. In fact, the client may begin the map herself, adding more members to it as she begins to open up communication between her many parts.

Figure 6.4 shows personalities taken from Judy's inner family and illustrates Satir's concept of family mapping as used with a multiple. The map shown here is in introductory form and is meant to illustrate a possible format for family mapping; it does not necessarily show the order in which the personalities depicted appeared in therapy sessions, nor does it show all of Judy's personalities.

In Judy's case, the first split occurred as an infant when she had already begun to view herself as an object. She even gave herself the name "Not A Person." The loss of self begins very early. The second split occurred between ages three and five, when a playmate was created to relieve severe isolation. She was named "Little Judy," a friend and namesake. From then on Judy was able to create other parts/personalities as specific traumatic events occurred. The following are some of the important personalities of Judy's young adulthood.

Gerri was created at the age of 15. Angry and a fighter, she hated men. She was narcissistic, which is normal for a teenager. Other personalities could not accept her behavior, saw her as bad, and rejected her. Gerri rejected them in turn, yet also saw herself as bad. She required a lot of individual therapy. Jane was created at age 18. She was outgoing, bright, full of humor, and used drugs; she knew how to play the Mental Health Game. Jane was protective of the younger child parts and closely connected to Gloria, the spiritual life force. She could express both anger and love.

Judith was also created at age 18. She was super-responsible and very religious, often depressed and suicidal. Judith denied the existence of other inner members, denied the childhood abuse, and maintained contact with the family of origin. Judith was not well liked by the others. She was too "square" for Jane and Gerri, and her connection with the abusers terrified the children inside.

Rosalyn was an introjected mother-figure, and she was abusive. However, because Rosalyn also symbolized giving baby Judy life, she could be reframed as a positive part and was able to remain in the inner family. See Chapter 4 for more information on negative introject personalities.

Leon was an introjected father-figure, called "the killer" by other inner family members. He continued to express the poisonous family of origin messages and threatened death if the secrets were told. He refused all attempts at reframing or transformation, and therefore could not be integrated with the rest of the inner family. (See Chapters 4 and 8 on negative introjects.)

Gloria was the Spiritual Mother or guardian angel of all the personalities. She was ageless and powerful.

On this map you will notice there is no personality named "Judy" after the age of five. This is a metaphor for a multiple's life. Where is she, the child named "Judy"? As the abuse in childhood worsened, the child who was so adept at creating others "went to sleep," and her parts were able to create other inner family members themselves. The Core person, the self that all the other personalities are created to protect remains well hidden in adulthood. For some multiples, the inner members will say she is asleep; others may say that she is dead. To find her, one must often connect with what we call the *Essence* of the Core person, the personality who represents her in the outside world. Identifying and building a rapport with the Essence personality will be one of the therapist's important tasks in the beginning stages of therapy. (For more about the Essence, see Chapter 4.)

Using Satir's Concept of Reframing With Personalities

Applying Satir's concepts about parts enables the therapist to recognize and validate the importance of each of the personalities as they present themselves. For every negative aspect of a particular part there is a positive aspect. Your task is to help the client own *all* her parts, even those that are most painful and seemingly destructive.

This means the negative parts have to be *reframed*, helping each part accept not only itself, but also the others. For a multiple, reframing is most essential, since negative personalities are in a position to bring pain and even danger to other inner family members as they reenact the abusive family of origin system. For example, the angry parts will act out in ways that are painful or frightening to other parts, so some personalities will want to control or reject those angry parts. This is a cause for constant conflict in the multiple's inner family. The following is an example of reframing personalities to each other.

> DORIS: *"As an example, when working with Judy's inner family I reframed Judith's behavior for Jane in a way that Jane could accept, noting that both she and Judith were trying to protect the family inside. I told Jane that Judith's denial was an attempt to alleviate the inner family pain and chaos. I helped super-responsible Judith to see that Jane's drug use and good times were also an effort to take away pain. Although Judith's way was different from Jane's, their goals were the same."*

A family systems therapist views all these parts—the angry parts, scared parts, denial parts, etc.—as important, because they make up an internal family and interact like a family. It is apparent that the inner family was created over time for a specific reason: *survival of the original child.* Keep in mind that the multiple is the result of the most horrifying, destructive, and demeaning abuses, and you will appreciate this exquisite design for survival, created by the mind of a human child.

Building Communication
at the Beginning

Opening Communication With the Therapist

Beginning communication means beginning a relationship with the multiple's personalities. The personalities' future relationships with each other are often built on the relationships with the therapist. An example using Judy's inner family of personalities follows.

> DORIS: *"In order to access Judy's inner family I had to connect solidly with one of the dominant personalities. Although I had met Judith first, her personification of denial made the kind of connection we needed impossible. I was glad when Jane came to session. She not only acknowledged the other family members, but she had no illusions about the abuses. Whereas Judith questioned my professional skills, Jane viewed me as a challenge.*
>
> *"It was easy to get acquainted with Jane; she was outgoing and lively. I had to connect with her in a way that would also make it possible for her to connect with Judith, for Jane was the personality most likely to help me lead Judith out of her denial. Jane, Judith and I formed another therapeutic triad."*

Your personality as a therapist will help determine which of the multiple's parts you are able to make this kind of relationship with. Watch out for collusion. (A discussion of transference and countertransference occurs in Chapter 8.)

Another way to build communication and trust is for the therapist to keep no secrets about her client. Satir believed that to create and maintain an open system, there could be no secrets. From the beginning, allow your files to be open and available to your client. Any information you, as therapist, receive from one inner family member you can pass along to other personalities. Such information may be as basic as which personality came to the office last session, who was in the office just a moment ago, and what was said.

As simple as this sounds, a major family rule is being broken when you do this—the rule of absolute secrecy. You can expect chaos to follow even from this simple beginning. For example, when one personality tells secrets, anxiety follows; the multiple knows from her family of origin that something awful will happen. This anxiety frequently occurs at night, a time when many of the old abuses happened. This is part of the misery of being a multiple. There will probably be a personality who stays up at night, watching and waiting for the "something awful." Revealing a secret triggers reliving of the past abuse during the night—and the personality who told the secret may not be the one who gets up at night. Thus, one revelation unleashes anxiety and chaos in many other personalities, who are endeavoring to cope.

In the family of origin, breaking the rule of silence meant severe punishment and the threat of death; however, breaking this rule is essential in changing a closed system to an open one that communicates freely and can allow change. As the therapist, be sensitive to the fears of each personality. If there is an introjected abusive personality, he or she will be terrorizing the others over what they have disclosed. Expect chaos to follow, in the form of manic behavior, insomnia, anxiety, body memories, depression, and suicidal ideation and behaviors. This process is discussed in depth in Chapter 7, which covers the multiple's cycle of feelings and behaviors.

As trust in the therapist grows, the multiple's inner family members begin to express the ugly secrets and the painful feelings they have hidden for so long. The therapist's loyalty and commitment to the multiple will become a major factor in the client's life. Expect to be tested, for you *will* be, and by a personality who is an expert in the field. One of the most powerful testers may be an inner family member who has borderline traits, and she will put to the test the new system you are creating in therapy. Chapter 8 will discuss this in more detail.

A therapist using a systems model in working with a multiple will recognize that the client desires change, yet is caught in a powerful struggle between this desire and the need to survive. A closed inner family system has made survival possible up to this point, and the family fears that any change means the end of the system, the end of the inner family, and therefore death for herself. The multiple expends a tremendous amount of energy to maintain the inner family homeostasis. Releasing that energy and allowing it to be used to achieve change depends upon the relationship with a therapist who is sensitive to the depth of the client's fears.

The therapist's goal is not to set up rules for the client's inner family, but to find out what those family rules are, how they are communicated, and what purpose they are serving. Rather than setting herself up as the expert, the therapist enlists the aid of each personality as she appears, so that each may appreciate how their separate roles achieved a common goal—survival—and thereby work toward a new goal, acceptance of one another.

Using Touch in Therapy

Touch is another important way for a therapist to begin to build communication with the personalities. Satir emphasized the importance of touch in therapy. Because of repeated abuses to the body, multiples expect touch to be painful and avoid it. Multiples may also numb themselves to keep from feeling. To avoid feelings of pain and shame, multiples have disowned their bodies, becoming completely separated from them. Helping them reclaim their bodies is another goal of therapy. This will be discussed in greater detail in Chapter 9.

Responses to touch vary from one personality to another. Some will accept a hug, while for others the touch of fingers is all they can risk. Yet it is important to help them take that risk, since it brings them into contact with the world outside themselves. Painful touch was a cruel form of communication in the multiple's life. Gentle touch teaches a healthy form of communication and helps her reclaim her body. Some parts may find, for the very first time, that touch does not have to hurt.

Until some indication is given as to what touch is acceptable, maintain a hands-off attitude; be very careful not to invade your client's personal space. This does not mean that touch is to be avoided. Including touch as part of therapy teaches multiples about personal space and establishing boundaries. By being sensitive to each personality's personal space, the therapist gives them control of that space; in this way they learn how to establish boundaries for themselves.

Learning about loving, nondemanding touch is important for the healing of the child and adult parts alike. Do not push touching; let it happen in a natural fashion. Fingers may touch while handing a child part a crayon; as time passes, a handshake or a hand on the shoulder might be acceptable. Ask permission to hug.

How the therapist feels about touch can be important as well. If you are a therapist who feels awkward about touching, be congruent, and go slowly when you begin to use touching in session. It's important to know and accept your own personal boundaries; if you try to be easy with touch when you are not, the multiple will be aware of your discomfort and will probably believe something is wrong with *her* because her therapist is having those feelings.

The therapist's ability to be comfortably creative and to move around can be helpful in creating contact. Don't just stay in your chair when you work with a multiple; be flexible and sensitive to the needs and age of each personality who comes to session.

> DORIS: *"I sat on the floor with Judy's inside children when they came out, and played with them during many of the sessions, particularly in the beginning. Judy now indicates that these and other gentle overtures toward contact helped her overcome many fears of touch, and that now when she thinks of a hug it is with warmth and not apprehension."*

Other forms of contact between client and therapist are important. A multiple may be as sensitive to eye contact as she is to touch. Be careful not to stare or try to make continued eye contact during the session if it bothers your client. Even very brief eye contact may be considered staring. Some multiples have been forced into child pornography at some time in their lives and feel exposed, embarrassed and shamed when looked at. (See Figure 6.5.) Videotaping sessions may not be helpful for the same reason. Even taking notes is suspect, since it sends a nonverbal message. Making a verbal contract with the inside family that the notes you are taking are open and available to them at any time is a good way to reframe the experience of being observed and to open up a system that has relied on secrecy for survival.

The Therapist as a Family Member

The acceptance of the therapist by the multiple's inner family is of major importance. A therapist gains access to the multiple's closed inner family system by establishing trust. Yet, at the same time, s/he

FIGURE 6.5: Drawing showing Judy's experiences of pornography. Note the large intrusive faces, staring eyes, and camera.

remains a powerful authority figure in the client's view. How you as therapist use this authority is an important factor in enabling the system to open up and the inner family to heal. A critical task is to assure each of the multiple's personalities that you are a strong, capable therapist, rather than a powerless child, and that you are quite able to receive and process any information that they may need to share. At the same time, trust the client's process and allow the information to come from the inside out.

> DORIS: *"The therapist invests a great deal of energy in joining with the collective goal of the multiple's family system: ensuring that the original child survives. I believe that the reason Judy has been able to do the work she has is not only because of her own strong will to live, but because I, as the primary therapist, was accepted by her inside family. This allowed us to work together throughout the course of therapy, exchanging information and receiving guidance from one another. Without this mutual cooperation, I do not believe a multiple would have a chance to become whole."*

The desire to be seen as a person, rather than as an object, is paramount for a multiple. When she experiences safety and acceptance within the therapeutic setting, all kinds of feelings are released. As the trust level grows, however, so does the transference, and the therapist can be overwhelmed. The therapist becomes role model, parent, and both the hated and loved family the multiple never had.

As with any family, not all inner family members view the therapist as the great savior; some will see her as a real threat to the safety of the family—and indeed she is, at least to safety as they know it. Over time the therapist will find herself living through a wide range of experiences with many individual parts: children, adolescents, young adults—all with their own ways of being, their own defenses and demands. Dependency needs, denial, and rage will rule many sessions.

The demands on the therapist are great. If the *therapist* (as well as the client) has suffered abuse or was overly controlled as a child, and has not completed her own work in this area, she can find herself caught up once more in the role of victim and react in that role with her client. The client will then have to take care of the therapist. It is important that the therapist who works with a multiple deal with her own issues. (See Chapter 8 on transference and countertransference.)

For example, suppose a bond has been established between a therapist and a client who is a multiple. Trust is growing, to the degree that memories are returning and secrets being revealed. A major family rule—"Don't tell or you will die"—is being broken, and change enters the inner system. It is at this point that the multiple depends upon her therapist to be powerful and help her survive this frightening experience. Although trust is growing, the client is in chaos at this time, as different family members fight any change in a system that has kept them safe all these years. Many want to stay with the old rules, one of which is, "Don't trust anyone outside the family."

However, despite these injunctions, the therapist has accessed the system and has become an introjected member toward whom every other inner family member has ambivalent feelings. (See Chapter 4 for more information on the introjected therapist.) This puts the multiple in a double bind, one that is all too familiar. Past experiences have taught the multiple to trust no one, yet she very much needs to trust the therapist if the system is ever to change.

The client may offer the therapist a double bind. Because survival in her old family of origin demanded that she be ever watchful of others, the multiple is hypervigilant, able to read all the nuances of nonverbal communication. If the therapist is tired, the client may interpret this as "I am the reason my therapist is tired." The following conversation is an example of what might occur.

CLIENT: "You look tired today. Everyone I know gets tired of being with me after a while and they just go away. I make it so hard for everybody."

THERAPIST: "No, I just had a particularly long day yesterday and that's why I'm tired."

CLIENT: "Do you want me to leave so you can get some rest? You take care of so many people; you need to take care of yourself. I can come back another time." (Client is checking out the therapist's strength and commitment to her, and expressing her own fear that if anything goes wrong it is her fault.)

THERAPIST: "No, no. I'm fine. It's not your responsibility to take care of me. Let's go ahead with the session now." (Therapist attempts to reassure the client, but in doing so also attempts to *take control of the session*, instead of staying with what is going on with the multiple. She might have said, "You are very concerned that your therapy is a burden to me." Instead the therapist ignores her own feelings about needing to be in control and the importance of the client's issues of control as well.)

CLIENT: "Are you sure I'm not the reason you're so tired? I know how hard I am to work with . . . " (The multiple, with her acute perceptiveness, again tests the therapist. Her fear increases as she watches for signs of impatience or rejection on the part of her therapist. She attempts to take care of the therapist in the same way a child attempts to take care of a parent—out of fear of having no one to take care of her if something should happen to the parent. Feelings of helplessness are mixed with anger at the parent's/therapist's weakness—and probably also at the parent/therapist's efforts to control her.)

THERAPIST: "No, you are not the reason I'm tired. Now let's get on with it. I see you brought in a dream?" (The therapist is beginning to feel a bit testy and frustrated.)

CLIENT: "I don't want to talk about the dream. I want to talk about what we did last time. Something really bothered me."

THERAPIST: "What was that?"

CLIENT: "You don't remember?" (You don't care.)

At this point, the multiple and her therapist are headed for chaos—chaos in which the therapist can become a participating "victimized" family member, who is left with feelings of anger, helplessness, and battered self-esteem as she gets locked into a power struggle with her client.

If the therapist dissociates herself from this "abusive family member" (her client) by intellectualizing or blaming, she helps maintain the abusive family system of the multiple. Optimally, the therapist can maintain enough distance from her client to be objective yet caring, and remain a powerful, positive, and stable new member of the family.

If the multiple perceives at any time that you, the therapist, are trying to dominate her or lead her in ways that she discerns are against her own best interests, she will again feel objectified and respond accordingly. She will present an adaptive self who will please the therapist, she will attempt to gain control herself, or she will disengage from the therapeutic process. If this happens, you must get in touch with your own control issues and review very carefully what is happening.

Building Communication Between
Inner Family Members

When talking to any member of the inner family, child or adult, assume that there are other family members listening in. Taking this into account gives the therapist a great opportunity to acquaint other personalities as to the reason some parts behave the way they do. Even those parts who dislike each other intensely will begin to have a better understanding of one another. As they listen to the rage, the terror, the pain, and the memories expressed by others, the personalities' knowledge of themselves and of the system increases. With greater knowledge comes the possibility of greater acceptance of one another.

Another way for the personalities to communicate is through journaling or writing notes (see Chapter 5). In the journals each can express what is happening in her life and the feelings or thoughts she may be having about herself or other family members. Journaling is also a good way for one member to make herself known to a part who wants to remain in denial and ignore the existence of others.

In Judy's inner family, for example, Judith had a difficult time denying Jane's existence when Jane began to move Judith's things around in the house and left journal entries signed "Jane." Written communications may be signed, but even if they are not, there may be recognizable differences in handwriting, composition, and use of language. As a way of communicating, writing is generally nonthreatening.

Dreams are another form of communication. Dreamwork gives insight into process and progress in therapy. It can also be a means of transferring concrete information or memories from one personality to another (see Chapter 5).

In summary, successful work with a multiple will depend only partly upon the "head knowledge" of the therapist and her ability to skillfully implement this in therapy. Success will depend more importantly on the integrity of the therapist and her commitment to another human being for what may well be a long and frequently arduous journey.

chapter 7

The Middle Stage
of Treatment

IMAGINE A STREAM IN which, over the years, debris has collected, creating a dam that obstructs the flow of water. Over time the dam becomes thicker and higher, creating behind it a holding pond. Then one day the dam breaks; heavy rains change the stream into a powerful force that sweeps the dam away and the current, now out of control, floods the surrounding areas.

Now imagine that this dam is a human defense mechanism built by a multiple to hold *one* of hundreds of memories, and when the dam breaks down, the entire physical, emotional and psychological system of the multiple is flooded. The intensity of the feelings and the loss of control are terrifying and overwhelming. Vivid inner pictures may arise, and the multiple experiences the memories as if they were happening at that very moment. Her body again suffers the excruciating pain that occurred, and her mind fills with terror. She becomes once again the child who was dragged from her room in the middle of the night, abused and humiliated by the very people upon whom her life depended. The psychological term for this reexperiencing is "abreaction"; for the multiple, the word is agony.

153

At the midpoint of therapy, the multiple's work involves retrieval of memories and feelings, abreaction, and possibly the beginnings of integration. The bond or connection between the multiple and her therapist is solid; communication and trust have evolved among the inner family members to the degree that the multiple's life stories can now begin to be told in more detail. The stories, originally told in fragments and with little feeling, can now be told more completely. Emotions begin to be connected with the memories. Even so, an entire memory may not be retrieved all at one time; only a little part may come back, and that will be enough to process for the moment. One memory may be told and retold again and again, with more details or feelings added to it each time from different personalities. The majority of information from memories will be integrated into the Essence as well as the whole system during this midpoint of therapy, prior to the integration of personalities.

During this part of the work, the client experiences even more internal chaos, which can seem confusing. She may say to herself, "I've been in therapy for three years; why does it feel so much harder now?" The reasons will become clear as we discuss the intense work of this stage of treatment.

Loss of Control and Chaos

Because trust has grown within the therapeutic setting, more personalities will begin to emerge to meet you during this stage. The dominant personalities, some of whom may have been able to stay "out" the majority of the time in the past, are less likely to be able to continue to maintain control of the system when other parts want a turn to see or speak or to be outside. Chaos increases when the delicate balance is broken, and it is at this point that a multiple, or her nuclear inner family members, may accuse you of creating more problems than you cure in therapy.

A very functional multiple may become less functional as she begins to have feelings and memories that are extremely disturbing. Many memories may appear as pictures in the mind, horrifying in content. More nightmares, more insomnia, more lost time occurs, as other family members come out to tell their stories, taking time away from dominant personalities who have been able to live a somewhat "normal" life in the world and throwing the whole system into a state of confusion and fear. The experience of remembering is *loss of control* in the extreme.

Retrieving the Memories and Feelings

By this time, the inner family has hopefully constructed a networking system inside that allows communication among at least some of the family members. While this will be helpful, chaos will still occur. The memories and feelings repressed for so long and held by individual family members, many of them small children, are now experienced as if for the first time. Because the experience has the intensity of the original event, the entire memory is not always abreacted at one time.

It is wise for the therapist to remain aware that there may be more of a memory forthcoming, even though one particular piece of work seems complete. A memory may be retrieved without feelings, but it is not firmly anchored in the present until feelings and memory are connected. The memory may in fact be forgotten again until feelings are aroused that bring it back.

When a multiple has the feelings without the memory that caused them, she will usually not know why she is experiencing such intense feelings of fear, anxiety, grief, or sadness. Particularly at night, feelings will come up and the multiple may report in session, "I don't know where the feelings came from, but suddenly I was so frightened." What often happens is that an outside trigger, which the multiple may not be able to identify, produces a feeling. The feeling then seems to her "out of sequence" with her life events. The trigger and the resulting feeling may be affecting an inner personality whom the personality who is out does not know. The different personalities inside are aware of many things that are going on outside—things of which the dominant personality, or the one who is out at that time, may not be aware.

When knowledge of the abuses and/or emotional feelings begin to return, physical feelings associated with the event also return. The body writhes in memory; welts, rashes, lumps, wheezing, burning sensations, body aches, and extreme pain in the genital, anal, or other areas may occur. The client may make guttural sounds, which may be her way of expressing terror so extreme that for the moment she feels as if she has gone mad. She may weep; she may cry out for her mother.

Body memories may precede either the feeling or the memory—there is no one rule. The client may have a body memory and not know what it is about at all. As a therapist, you will encounter a wide variety of differences among multiples in when, how, and why body memories appear. But no matter how they come, body memories are always intense. For example, if the client was raped in the past, she will actually reexperience the rape, feel on her body the actual weight of the rapist, perhaps even see and hear the rapist, even if she is alone in her bed at the present time. While the client may be at a point where she knows intellectually that this reexperiencing is not actually happening, in another part of herself she is still experiencing that event. Validate the body memories as they appear. Sometimes body memories or symptoms may abate once the client validates the emergence of a memory or actually verbalizes the memory. Even so, they may continue for days and/or recur.

The personality who originally experienced the actual trauma holds the feelings that occurred at that time and carries them through the years. Sometimes there are even several personalities created during one trauma who will each hold a particular feeling or aspect of the memory. For such a cluster of personalities, memory retrieval may take a bit more time. Let's say, for example, that during a particular abusive situation of childhood the child (or personality) split into four different parts: one to hold pain, one to hold the memory, one to hold the anger, and one to carry the fear. In this cluster, the personality or part who doesn't have the feelings must integrate the memory with the feelings, so that one single child personality then has all the pain, the fear, and the anger, as well as the memory. It is abreacted like any other memory. Once that little child personality (formerly the cluster) is whole, then she must be integrated into the larger whole (see Chapter 9). This process may happen again and again, until each once-fragmented personality is solid and able to join with the Essence.

In some cases, one personality relives the memory and the feelings, but other parts don't. The client may say in therapy, "I was lying in bed and it felt as though someone was on me. I was scared to death, I could see my father . . . but when I opened my eyes, he wasn't there." Even in this type of experience—where one personality may relive the whole event, feeling the pain, seeing who is there, obtaining the knowledge—

this remembering may remain disconnected from the whole and from the other personalities. When one part abreacts and other parts do not participate, more processing may be necessary.

Memories and feelings may appear again and again not only because they have not been shared within the whole system, but also because they cannot yet be connected to the self. During the first years of therapy, the multiple may not be integrated enough to be able to say the memory and feelings are "mine"; the memory only becomes an awareness that some of the personalities have. The multiple has no "me" yet, and the memory may fall away again unless there is a personality to connect it to. We have found the Essence to be this connector.

As treatment progresses, the Essence personality spends more time out in the world, and by midpoint the therapist will know which personality the Essence is. As the memories return, the Essence may begin to receive the memories from other personalities, along with the feelings. This is a difficult time for the Essence, who has up to this point been almost an innocent bystander concerning the multiple's life history of abuse. She may wonder, "Why is there more chaos? Why am I having more nightmares? Someone else used to take these for me." As she does receive the memories and the feelings, the Essence grows, and her connection with the Core, the original child, increases. The different personalities may have told their stories before in drawings, writings, and in session, but what happens eventually is that, as they tell their stories once again, the stories begin to become the Essence personality's own memories. And this is hard for her.

Before the Essence is ready to receive the memories, the same memories may be processed more than once. However, it is possible that reliving the memories over and over helps lessen to some degree the intensity of the feelings and experiences, and allows the awareness of the memory to trickle a little at a time into the whole inner family system's awareness, until the Essence is finally able to accept the memory as hers. The first experiences of the memories are so terrifying and so intense that the client is overwhelmed by them. Repetition allows her gradually to gain enough control over the memory to make it her own. Remembering and forgetting or denying, followed by re-remembering, enable her to put the memory outside of herself and keeping it at a safe distance after she has held it inside for so long.

As the memories and feelings come up, the multiple is forced to look at material that is extremely devastating and hurtful. Her first instinct when facing these memories is to go into denial, saying, for example, "No, this can't be true; my family loved me." Or she may believe only a part of the memory. Following denial, the multiple may dissociate the memory again; this is normal. When the Essence first becomes aware of memories and feelings, she still has no solid experience of them, because they "belonged" to someone else, to another personality; *that* personality experienced it. It is difficult to accept a memory as your own when you were not the one who lived it. This is another of the complexities of working with a multiple. What looks like denial or resistance is also—paradoxically—a truth. The Essence says, "I never experienced that; it's not mine, I wasn't there." More complete acceptance will come with time and reprocessing as needed.

> JUDY: *"During this part of my therapy I was still connected to my abusers to some degree. What I was remembering didn't fit them because by this time in my life they were not overtly abusive to me. So all the information that was coming up seemed like a lie. I thought I was crazy and that what I was remembering couldn't be believed. I didn't understand why my therapist wanted me to believe these memories. I thought, 'Why would she want me to believe something that is so unlikely?' When I looked at the people I knew it just didn't seem possible. So I was not only fighting myself, but I was fighting my therapist as well."*

The Therapist's Role During Abreaction

What the multiple needs from the therapist while she is abreacting is:

1. Belief that what she tells you is true;
2. Provision of safety and support;
3. Reframing of the traumatic event and touch;
4. Validation of her feelings.

For a multiple, the importance of being believed cannot be overstated. She has been disbelieved all her life, and threatened with blame if she ever told of the abuse. A therapist who does not believe and advocate the abused child parts will simply recapitulate the old trauma. (See Chapter 8 on revictimization.)

All the personalities will need reassurance that the office is a safe place, and that you, the therapist, are a safe person to tell the stories to. Child parts, like any child who's been abused, may need to hear that they won't be punished for telling, that you (the therapist) and the inner family won't let those bad things happen to them anymore. While one or two personalities are abreacting, you will also be working with the inner family members, encouraging them to participate by watching and listening. The inner family will need support and time to learn to encourage rather than punish abreaction (see section on the cycle).

While the multiple is remembering and abreacting, the therapist reframes the traumatic event that is being processed and gives it a different meaning. The therapist must take each of those old family-of-origin rules and beliefs (see Chapter 1) and expose them as lies, as cruel and demeaning. The multiple will need to hear over and over that the abuse was not her fault, but the fault of the abusers; that she did not deserve or require or invite the abuses she received; that she had little or no choice and was required to be obedient to survive. The facts of her entrapment, her helplessness, and her efforts to protect herself must be validated each time.

The comforting and understanding that the therapist provides make this reliving different from the original experience, and in this process the original experience is reframed. While being touched during or immediately after abreaction may be too painful for the client, appropriate touch later, especially when asked for, may also be comforting.

Validation of her feelings, along with reframing the abuse as not her fault, makes abreaction a restorative experience. The multiple needs to hear that she had and has a right to feel terrified, anguished, betrayed, and rageful, that whatever her feelings are, they are normal and important.

The Role of Denial in Reclaiming Memories

Once abreacted, the memory and the feelings may then become a part of the multiple's remembered memories, or they may not. They may be so overwhelming and unbelievable to her that she may need to re-repress them until she feels strong enough to retrieve them again and own them. This is when the personalities most able to take care of this chaotic situation will appear, and *what they will use is denial.*

At these times the trust between therapist and client is of the utmost significance. A trusting, supportive relationship allows the multiple to gradually break through the denial and continue the remembering, even when the process is so painful. Hopefully, the therapist has already established with the client that information from one personality will not be withheld from other inner family members. Although there are to be no secrets (a factor that acts as a powerful change agent in a closed system), the multiple, by moving into denial, is making a statement: the information and feelings newly emerging are too terrifying to retain at the moment. However, for integration to take place, the client must at some point retain that awful memory.

The protector/denial personality may not remember the work just done in session, but may notice some lost time and some physical symptoms (body memories). When denial comes into play, the therapist can explain to the inner family the loss of time and the body memories that are occurring. Here, the therapist's sensitivity, intuition, and knowledge of her client are important in deciding how much information to relay at one time. You may not need to insist on telling the denial personality the whole story or memory, but you can affirm to her that her exhaustion, which is sure to follow the abreaction, comes from the work that she did about the revelation of a cruel and devastating event, and explain that the body memories that exist are a physical reflection of what occurred during that event.

She may continue to deny the truth of the therapist's statement, preferring to believe she has the flu or some other illness rather than a body memory, or that her current anxiety and fears come from an outside stressor, rather than from an emerging memory. It is prudent for the therapist to hear the client's unspoken message—that right now she is unable to retain the memory—and send her home knowing the information will gradually work its way up into the client's consciousness. Trust the multiple's own timing as to when that will occur.

If you attempt to keep one personality present during a session working on a memory that has emerged, you may trigger the client's switching if that part is not yet ready to handle the full memory. The therapist must be sensitive in allowing the multiple to take charge at that time and follow her lead. Remember that there are probably other personalities connected with a memory who may be too frightened to come out right away, and they may be watching you until they have enough trust to come out and begin to talk about what happened to them.

At other times switching may occur to bring out all the aspects of a particular memory. One personality may come in very upset about a dream or partial memory or about a feeling or trigger; that person may talk about it a little, and then the client may switch. The next personality who comes may have more information about the same experience. This second personality is there to tell about what s/he knows, and when there is a third switch, the next one may know still more about that event, etc.

As you can see, switching in session may have a very specific reason and be beneficial to the therapy process. It is not helpful, therefore, for the therapist to try to keep one part talking when another wishes to come out. In fact, if you do, a personality may come and tell you that you are pushing too hard or that it is not time to do that work. Most of us, when we find something too difficult to talk about, distract or say, "I'm not ready to talk about that just yet." What a multiple does is switch when the work is too hard, or switch in order to help process that issue and to tell you about the memory through the different personalities.

When switching means "that's enough for now," the multiple's denial part becomes very important. Denial is an effort to keep the inner system from coming apart; it is a safety valve, a protection, making it possible for the multiple to live. Expect denial and disbelief to become a part of remembering. A multiple in therapy both wants to remember and wants not to remember. When the feelings begin to emerge and the body reacts, she may want to know why it is happening, but not the whole awfulness of it. The message is: "What I really want to do is get rid of these feelings, and if I could get rid of them without ever having a memory, I would really like that—and if you (the therapist) can do that for me, I would be very happy."

It is important to learn to work with the denial, since it is such a necessary part of treatment. A multiple cannot constantly stay in that chaotic process of remembering the memories and still function in the world. Over the process of therapy denial gradually fades more and more, but you cannot hope to take it away immediately, or even in a few months. With each memory, you will have to go through this process of remembering and denial.

When you work with a multiple you are working with a system set up to protect that person from horrors that she believes would literally destroy her if remembered and told. Don't look at denial as resistance to change, but as protection and as a way of saying "move slowly, move slowly." It is a necessary way of pacing the therapeutic process for the multiple.

Denial must be both honored and confronted. Find someone in the inner family system to help you with the confrontation. For example, a helper personality may come to explain denial: "That's the person who always wants to be in charge of everyone, and she doesn't like to know about those (past abusive) events." The therapist can then say, "There's a reason for that," and explain (reframe) why the other part is in denial. Of course, the denial personality may be listening in, as may others, which you must remember whenever you are doing this kind of reframing.

If the multiple's denial personality is a dominant one, it may greatly affect the amount of internal chaos or crisis that occurs. For example, when Judy's personality named Judith, who was quite dominant, began to experience a breakdown of denial, there was a greater likelihood of her becoming suicidal. If she maintained her denial, the whole system in the inner family ran more smoothly.

The process may also work in the reverse. When there has been a dominant part for many years who needs to stay in denial, and the system breaks down, the act of holding fiercely onto the denial may also cause the internal system to go into chaos. Especially when changes occurring in the inside system coincide with changes in the outside environment, self-destructive behaviors or suicidal ideation may become ways of holding onto denial.

In either of the above cases, hospitalization may be necessary to weather the chaos safely. Everything at that moment seems to be going out of the client's control—and losing control is the greatest fear of everyone in the inner family. For a multiple, who has had so many past experiences in which she was in fact totally powerless and vulnerable to the most horrible abuses, losing control strikes stark terror into her soul.

How can the therapist help the multiple with the denial? As has already been mentioned, the therapist must go with the multiple where she goes, and accept that she has very good reasons for both her feelings and the denial. Second, the therapist must not be afraid of the intensity of the feelings that will be emerging. For example, one of the client's feelings that can seem frightening for the therapist to witness is anger. If the therapist is uncomfortable when the client expresses an intense feeling, the therapist must explore her own issues if she is to continue being helpful to the client (see Chapter 8).

Third, the therapist must refrain from insisting or even implying that the multiple should control her feelings, or that somehow a feeling is inappropriate, should be lessened, etc. The multiple already has within her a personality who can come and remove that feeling for her. If the therapist encourages the multiple to "control" a feeling, the multiple may have to switch to do it, or keep certain parts from surfacing. If she is subtly asked not to feel, the client will do her best to comply, which may make it difficult for her to learn about and experience her feelings. The hardest thing for both the multiple and a caring therapist is to acknowledge that the client has to experience the pain—all of it. It's important for the therapist to be honest and say, "Yes, this is going to happen." There is no easy way to do the work. But the therapist can affirm that she will be there for the client, as much as is possible.

> JUDY: *"What I remember as a young child is that there were no feelings associated with the abusive event. There had to be a way to contain the feelings, to isolate them within myself. I found a way to put a barrier between myself and abusive events. When as a child you have never connected your feelings at all to an event, you grow up with the inability ever to understand 'feelings.'*
>
> *"Sometimes it took four or five personalities or splits to handle even one abusive event. The feelings were too overwhelming for any one of those splits, and they had to pass along to the next created personality in turn the ability to carry on with that feeling. So not only were the feelings disconnected from me, but they were also fractured. There was not a whole feeling even within one personality in some cases, because the feeling was split up among several, particularly if the trauma was extreme.*
>
> *"In my case, I was kept isolated from my own ability to think straight. The abusers kept me that way; the process caused an inability in me to stay grounded. I had to break my feelings away from myself to survive the physical pain or the emotional craziness of the situation, otherwise I could not have survived. If I could not have*

dissociated and had been forced to have the feelings at the time of the abuse, it would have been too overwhelming to me as a child of three or four. Even as a teenager, dealing with ritual abuse was too much. My body could not have contained that much feeling or pain and continued to associate with the emotional chaos, the body feelings, and the intellectual chaos. I would have died.

"So when in therapy a multiple starts connecting with those feelings and experiencing them, the fear may very well be of death. The ultimate reason for becoming a multiple and staying a multiple is to stay away from death, to survive. For example, if I have a feeling of anger—if I suddenly get in touch with the extreme rage any child would have from such terrible abuse, where is that rage going to take me? Will it burn me up? I cannot put this rage outside of myself and express it because if I do the anger might kill me or I might kill someone else. Or, the person I am angry with may kill me, just as the abusers threatened when I was a child.

"As an abused child, my whole life has been taken out of my control. So the one thing I might have in my control is the ability not to feel, through dissociation. And as out-of-control as dissociation may seem, it is the one resource for control over the feelings. Even the smallest feeling of sadness, anger, or fear that I began to experience was a feeling I had never had before, so it seemed that I was out of control.

"The feeling seems bigger than I am, because I am connecting with it for the first time from a child state. The feelings are new, and rather like the abusers: enormously big, much bigger than I am. So I again feel vulnerable to abuse or danger. To connect with something so enormous and powerful is being thrown into a situation out of my control—so out of control that it feels like recapitulation of the original abuse. The feeling is bigger than I can contain, so the feeling can get me. I cannot contain and hold anything that big, therefore it's out of my control, and that means danger, and my life is again at risk."

DORIS: "The child parts of a multiple are little people. Feelings are literally bigger than they are, and it seems impossible to get feelings that big inside their tiny bodies. To ask them to take in those feelings and feel them or express them has to be absolutely terrifying. Every time a multiple does something that frightening, that risky, that courageous, they need to be validated."

JUDY: *"It was the validation of those feelings and the hard work I did that kept my courage strong enough to go on and try risking again and again until integration was completed. And it still takes validation and more courage to continue to grow and become even more human, better able to cope with new understandings. This is why it is so important for the therapist to let the multiple decide how far she is willing to go, how much she can do at one time, and to honor the distraction and denial. The multiple must take care of herself so much. If you, as a therapist, cannot recognize and validate the multiple's way of being, her timing in therapy and in her healing, if you have to control the therapy process, you had better not work with a multiple."*

DORIS: *"As a therapist, you can revictimize and reabuse a multiple if you begin taking control and demanding something that the multiple feels puts her life in danger at every step. You, too, are bigger than the multiple and are in a position to take advantage of her. There is a certain bond created even with an abuser that is very strong, and you can easily revictimize."*

Judy's Perspective on Reconnecting with Feelings

JUDY: *"As a multiple, I awoke every day while in therapy and said to myself, 'This is a different life, this is a real world, and I will try my very best to survive.'*

"Teaching me about feelings, something I didn't know about and was never taught about, made a difference. It is still a continuous job of learning. I've had to learn when I feel sad. I've had to learn that when I feel sad it's because of something. I've learned to get in touch with why I feel sad. I've had to learn what tears of depression are or what loneliness or feeling scared is. I've learned that tears are normal.

"My therapists told me over and over that all these feelings are normal. Talking about each feeling I had and even identifying for me what the feeling was helped me to understand the emotional and physical feeling of crying, or sadness, or fear, etc. It helped me to connect the physical feeling with the emotional feeling. As a person,

I never knew these things before. I had to learn that certain feelings are normal and go along with certain situations. For example, it is normal for me to feel afraid at night, and it's OK to turn on a light for protection and sleep with the lights on. I began to connect with feelings I never had before, find a way to deal with them, and find safety as I went through them.

"My therapists also taught me that it was all right to feel any feeling and OK to talk about it. There has never been a rule in therapy that I can't talk about how I feel; instead, it was repeated over and over that it was OK. Over time I have introjected many positive things to replace the horrible memories and old messages. It took years of work, years of talking, and in therapy I am still redefining feelings, identifying them, and learning that they are OK. What I've heard so many times before, I still need to hear. However, I think I'm now learning how to do it more for myself.

"It must seem like such a little thing, something human beings would know—that it's OK to have feelings, it's OK to cry. But those of us who are abused so badly are like babies who need to be taught, and allowed to be babies who cry naturally, who feel anger naturally. Tears, anger, and fear were not accepted by those who abused, because they could not continue to objectify a child who had feelings. The child had to remain an object only, and not a person who had feelings. So, having feelings dehumanizes you; it takes away the objectification. When you become a human being you have feelings. When as a therapist you work with a multiple, you help the client become human again.

"All these years as a multiple, my job was to hide and not be noticed—not be, so I would be less tortured. To become human and have feelings is to become visible, and it is extremely frightening. Being visible means you are more vulnerable; if I am visible, I will be used and abused. So when feelings start happening, they immediately bring up danger. Somehow, someone will find out that I am visible and I exist, and therefore my life is in danger. Along with that, someone is going to get me for allowing myself to feel and be vulnerable. As long as I stay an object, I am safe; when I become a human, I am not safe.

"This is so paradoxical, because what the therapist is asking the multiple to do in therapy is so difficult: in order to be human, we have to start being visible and have feelings, which creates a feeling

of such danger for our lives. As a therapist, you are dealing with a person; and in that person, there is a being who has never been.

"This is the reason for the little steps and the slow work that takes years. To try to speed up the process is taking this person who never existed and throwing her out into the world saying, 'OK, make it! Danger doesn't exist anymore — just believe it.' It's rather like insisting that a baby be born before the nine-month period is up. A multiple is being reborn over and over every time she gets a feeling, and every time she becomes visible enough to exist and know she really is.

"For years as a child, the only thing I saw was the inside of my room or the inside of a photography studio. I had never been to a store; I had never been outside; I had never worn pretty shoes, or had my hair fixed nicely every day, or had a decent meal. I didn't know what it was like to be warm all the time or have a jacket, or bathe regularly or to have breakfast, lunch, and dinner. I had never played with another chid or played with toys at all; those things were props used in movies, things I got to see and hold during the filming, but they were not for real, and they weren't things I could really have or know about.

"Therapy for a multiple is reteaching a human being to live again, to awaken her to self and to feelings. So much safety has to be made at every step between therapist and client in order to overcome the knowledge that the visibility and the danger are always there. You must teach the multiple how to live, because she has never truly lived before."

Reentry Following Memory
Work in Session

It is extremely helpful to the client (and to the therapist) if there is a supportive environment the client can return to after difficult sessions. However, that may often not be the case. Many multiples live alone or are single parents and must return to their caretaking or work duties feeling exhausted, physically ill, and depressed. There may be a personality who can take over at this time and give the support needed for reentry — one who does not hold feelings and can therefore carry on.

However, if there is no inner support personality, the multiple may feel devastated, in pain, abandoned, and exhausted, just as she was so many times in her life after severe abuse. Self-nurturing skills are not a part of the multiple's repertoire and are not easily learned, since punishment almost always followed any happy thought or action on her part if she attempted them in the past. Remember, the old family rule and experience was that something bad must follow something good.

Here are some possibilities you as therapist may use, depending on the home and office situations that exist. As the work becomes increasingly difficult, allot some extra time and a location after the therapy session for the client to have some quiet time or even to take a nap. Perhaps there is a friend who can be called upon to take over a few household duties for the client for an afternoon or evening. Or, therapy sessions might be scheduled during times the client's children are in school so she can have some alone time at home afterward.

Each client's environment, being unique, must be tailored whenever possible to meet that individual's needs. Be creative. Remembering how creative multiples themselves are, therapist and client can believe there are resources to draw from. Remember as well that multiples, who are above all survivors, have the ability to keep going under the most difficult circumstances. This in no way negates the difficulty of reentry. It is merely a suggestion to prepare for hard times by pursuing every possibility available, while maintaining respect for the integrity and safety of the client.

> JUDY: *"After working hard in therapy and experiencing the horrendous memories and feelings, I was exhausted emotionally and physically. After reliving a memory I usually felt devastated, depressed, ugly, and distasteful. Sometimes I was even suicidal, wanting to stop the pain and the memories. It was important that a transition period be given after therapy before I reentered 'normal' life outside. If a transition period was not provided, it was like moving from one time zone to another without any chance to regroup. After leaving therapy, I often felt so broken apart by my intense feelings that I was not ready to join the rest of the world. I had to learn that it was normal to have the residual feelings inside and how to cope with them.*
>
> *"Sitting quietly during the last few minutes of a session helped me*

'come back' to the office setting. Often this was a good time to ask to be held and comforted. It was imperative not to rush this adjustment period. Another personality sometimes came at the end of my therapy session to take care of me. This was not seen as negative, since it gave me some space for healing from the work. I would have to own the work I had just done soon enough.

"Upon reentering the world outside, I needed time to rest. I tried to make plans to take care of myself after therapy by resting, napping, or sitting quietly by the ocean or in a comforting place. Since I am a wife and mother this was not always possible, but as soon as the opportunity was available I tried to find some private time. When memories begin to emerge, it may be a good time for a client to learn how to ask for help and support of a friend. A therapist can encourage a client to ask the friend to watch the kids for a short while or to cook a meal while she rests.

"Once time was taken to regroup and rest, I began to explore the newly acquired memories and feelings, seeing how they would fit within myself. This was a good time to journal or paint about them, and it also helped make them more concrete. Since the therapy a multiple does is so demanding, it is absolutely necessary that a reentry program be discussed. One cannot expect a multiple to continually go through these exhausting experiences without some kind of respite. Help your client set up a support system for herself so she can learn how to nurture and care for herself after difficult work. The time of reentry will also help her prepare for the next therapy session."

The Multiple's Coping Cycle

We have found that every multiple has her own coping cycle—as do many other clients who are dissociative, or who have been abused. Every person has defensive methods and coping skills that they learn to use over and over again to get them through the hard times in life. While most defensive skills are common, each of us shapes and hones our skills with time and use until the way we think and feel and behave in times of stress becomes a pattern that is uniquely our own. The multiple, too, will have a unique way that she uses her dissociative skills to help her cope with stress. When she enters therapy, she will already have some patterns. However, therapy itself is stressful. In the middle stages of therapy the multiple is risking reliving extremely traumatic memories and feelings, over and over. She may add to or intensify her original coping behaviors to contend with the challenges of treatment. A cycle or pattern may become very clear as the client delves into middle-stage work.

Discovering a client's cycle helps the therapist know what to expect next as the multiple progresses through her therapy. The cycle also becomes a therapeutic tool, as the client learns to recognize her own coping patterns and how to intervene to shorten the process or soften the intensity of the cycle.

Figure 7.1 is a simple diagram of Judy's cycle, presented here as an example. We will discuss it in detail in this chapter.

Phase 1: A Trigger Occurs

A triggering event usually sets off the multiple's cycle. Triggers may be generated by either the environment or the client herself. Environmental triggers may be such things as a scene in a movie theater or television program; store decorations, e.g., for Halloween; spotting an unknown person in the grocery store wearing a certain type or color of clothing; a telephone call from the former abusers, etc. Triggers from the multiple herself may include a dream, a drawing made in therapy, or a partial memory that one personality recalls. Whatever it is, a trigger causes a memory to begin to surface and starts the multiple on her cycle of coping.

Because of the memory that is triggered, the client goes into internal chaos, which is in turn reflected in her outer behavior. Voices may increase; a lot of switching between personalities may occur, and confusion escalates. Conflict rages inside as some of their personalities go into denial or avoidance of the surfacing memory and others struggle to learn the truth that memory can reveal. The multiple wants to know, but when the memory starts to come up she says to herself, "Oh, no." The paradox is that the multiple works hard in therapy to get back the information and the feelings, but at the same time she dreads them.

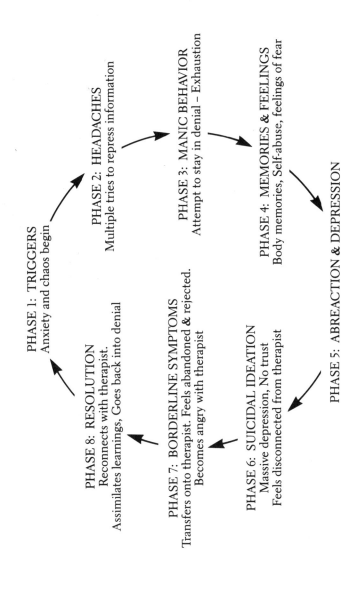

PHASE 1: TRIGGERS
Anxiety and chaos begin

PHASE 2: HEADACHES
Multiple tries to repress information

PHASE 3: MANIC BEHAVIOR
Attempt to stay in denial – Exhaustion

PHASE 4: MEMORIES & FEELINGS
Body memories, Self-abuse, feelings of fear

PHASE 5: ABREACTION & DEPRESSION
Overwhelming feelings, Extreme anxiety
withdrawal, and Paranoia

PHASE 6: SUICIDAL IDEATION
Massive depression, No trust
Feels disconnected from therapist

PHASE 7: BORDERLINE SYMPTOMS
Transfers onto therapist. Feels abandoned & rejected.
Becomes angry with therapist

PHASE 8: RESOLUTION
Reconnects with therapist.
Assimilates learnings, Goes back into denial

FIGURE 7.1: The multiple's coping cycle.

171

Phase 2: Headaches

When a memory is triggered, the inner equilibrium is disturbed; one or more personalities will resonate to the trigger, and a memory or feeling begins to leak into the system instead of being contained within that personality as usual. By the middle stages of therapy, when permission for sharing and some cooperation has been established, someone in the inner family may be ready to give important memory information to the others in the system. Or, the personality holding the memory or feeling may try to push her way to the foreground and come out in the body to express it.

Because of the chaos this inevitably causes, others in the inner family will be trying to keep that personality or memory down. The multiple begins to repress the information. The inner conflict builds into tremendous pressure, which the multiple perceives as pressure from the inside of the head. The resulting headaches may not be relieved by aspirin; they may not abate until the memory or surfacing personality can find at least a partial outlet.

During this phase the multiple may also begin feeling scared, dizzy, or vaguely anxious. She may be angry at the therapist for encouraging the kind of work that results in this acutely painful state of imbalance. Depending on which personalities are dealing with the chaos, they may blame the therapist and try harder to revert to denial.

Phase 3: Manic Behavior

If when the trigger occurs and the headaches begin the multiple attempts to stay in denial, a manic phase may follow. Manic behavior is often an effort to avoid the remembering, to avoid the pain and the feelings that come with it. In addition, a multiple may use manic behavior not only to distract but also to punish or "cleanse" herself.

When major memories begin to come up, the first feelings to surface may be vague ones of being "wrong" or "bad." Tension increases, just as it did in the abusive cycle of the multiple's family of origin. These first awarenesses of the memories and feelings match the child victim's old awareness that abuse was about to happen. Making abuse happen, i.e., punishing herself, is the surest way to shorten the suspense of this old familiar cycle.

A personality will go into action on the basis of old beliefs she may not even be aware of or able to verbalize. She may say to herself, "I *feel* bad, so I must *be* bad;" "This really didn't happen and I'm lying—so I must punish myself for telling lies," or "What happened to me means I'm bad, so I must be punished for it." Punishment (self-abuse) must happen if she tells a secret, if she lies, or if she has "bad" feelings, such as fear, pain, or anger. Going along with the belief system the child grew up with, punishment will be seen as necessary to cleansing away the bad feelings or the sensation of being bad.

> JUDY: *"Many times, I punished myself with manic behavior in metaphoric ways. I literally cleaned my house until I was hurting; I cleaned until I felt punished, and then I could feel better. After punishing myself I felt a sense of relief."*

However, all this manic behavior in the form of frenzied housecleaning or yardwork, or even overtly self-destructive acts, doesn't quite do the trick—it doesn't keep the memories from continuing to surface. Physically exhausted after all this hyperactivity, the multiple is no longer able to keep pushing the returning memories down. As phase 4 begins, the memories keep coming.

Phase 4: Memories and Feelings Surface

The body is often the first to remember old trauma. Welts, lumps, bruises, rashes, and pain often appear in different parts of the body. By now the personality who has been exerting pressure from within may be able to come out and tell something of her story. While she is out talking, some of the others inside hear the information, and it starts circulating around the system.

The system again goes into action. Abusive personalities may begin to parrot past abusers, telling the disclosing personality, "You're lying, that's not true." Fear swells among the personalities when the memories surface in earnest, because secrets are coming out. If a secret comes out, extreme punishment or death will surely follow, according to the old family system rules. The personality who reveals a memory may hear from abusive ones, "Now you're going to get it; you're going to have to be punished."

So the ones being threatened feel terrified, and others are angry. The abusive personalities who threaten the others may actually feel terrified as well, using their role as punishers to try to regain the safety and equilibrium in the system that is lost when memories surface. The multiple's system is trying everything it knows to rebalance itself, but the chaos and feelings intensify. The memory or dissociated feelings that are coming up succeed in penetrating the multiple's amnestic barriers, which causes the next phase of the cycle to begin.

Phase 5: Abreaction and Depression

At this point in her cycle, the multiple can't hold back the feelings and memories any more, and she begins reliving the trauma as if she were thrown right back into her old family of origin. She experiences feelings of shame, unworthiness, embarrassment, dirtiness and guilt. Not wanting to be seen by anyone, she begins to withdraw. During the abreaction stage, the client may feel too visible and too vulnerable; she can become frightened and suspicious of everyone, including at times the therapist. Agoraphobic behavior may appear here, as well as paranoia in some cases.

When the multiple is experiencing such a high pitch of fear, shame, guilt, and unloveliness, and when the memory of trauma is clanging wildly around the personality system in pictures, feelings, and body sensations, she may start to shut down with depression. As withdrawal and depression begin to take over the inner system, the client may begin to feel disconnected from the therapist who is helping her through all this. With the feeling of disconnectedness comes the seeds of distrust.

Phase 6: Suicidal Ideation

This is the stage where the multiple's feelings begin to connect with her thoughts; and the thoughts, when they come out of such intense feelings of guilt and shame, can be extremely self-condemning. "I am not good enough to live, I'm the cause of the problem (of the old trauma)." And finally, "There is no place and no way to feel better." Beset by emotions that have been so long dissociated, the multiple finds them unbearably frightening and overwhelming. Feelings of help-lessness and hopelessness set in, and suicide begins to look like the only way to stop the pain.

> JUDY: *"Those feelings are so intense when a memory is first at-tached to feelings; it seemed as if I was going to die, as if I should die. The 'should' came from feelings of guilt and shame, from believing it was still my fault as I did when I was a child. Sometimes I felt so physically sick from the emotional pain that I thought it would have been better to stop the pain right then instead of going through it all over again to become healthy. Part of my own wishing I could die was thinking it was my fault for still having these awful feelings. If only the pain had stopped way back when I was a child, I wouldn't have had to become a multiple, I wouldn't have had to live through more abuse, and I wouldn't have to do this work right now. As a child I believed the pain and abuse were my fault; it was my fault I turned into a multiple, and it was my fault I still had to deal with it now. Suicide in the present seemed only like something I should have done years ago."*

The intensity experienced in this phase of the cycle will vary de-pending on whether the multiple's work is still in the beginning stages or whether she has progressed to the middle stages of therapy. A small amount of memory may result in some abreaction, but the intensity will be much greater during the middle stages when the client is retriev-ing memories and feelings in larger or deeper pieces. Knowing about your client's cycle will give you an idea of what to anticipate with memory work. You will know there may be headaches coming up; there will be denial, then manic behavior, body memories, remembering, abreaction, and pain that leads to depression, withdrawal, and suicidal ideation.

Massive depression brings the multiple thoughts such as, "I can't deal with this, and nobody can help me. I can't even help myself." "Nobody wants to be around me; I'll just hide. I should be dead." The client becomes mired in the depression, unable to move out of it. In her withdrawn state, she perceives the therapist to be far away from her, or lost to her. "Surely she won't like me either." Trust in the therapist dissipates, rapidly at times. With the belief at this phase that "I am stuck here with these feelings, and there is no one who can help me—

not even my therapist," the multiple may shift into a borderline state, particularly if she has personalities with borderline traits.

Phase 7: Borderline Symptoms

The client is feeling awful and perceives herself as bad for having the awful feelings. She may at this point project her negative feelings about herself onto the therapist, assuming that the therapist views her as she herself does.

She wants to be rescued — usually by the therapist — but doesn't know how to be rescued. If the therapist tries to rescue her from these horrible feelings about herself, it will not feel right — because she cannot be rescued. And that recapitulates her childhood experience. "There was nobody who could save me, there is no one here for me now;" I brought this on myself, it is all my fault." The therapist probably hates me too, because I am dirty, shameful, etc. Terrible things happen to me, so it must mean I am bad." This last belief is true not just for multiples, but for anyone who has been physically or sexually abused as a child. Because the abuse happened to them when they were egocentric children, they cannot separate the abuse from themselves. They become what happened to them: "The bad stuff is me."

Many borderline feelings and behaviors may surface during this phase of the multiple's cycle, and a discernible pattern within this stage itself will often emerge. Below is an example of a "mini-cycle" that can occur just within this borderline phase.

a. The client experiences feelings of insecurity, inadequacy, abandonment, and fear. Suicidal thoughts follow. The client has no coping skills yet for dealing with her anger at the current situation, so she falls back on old learnings and becomes angry at herself, equating her feelings and the event itself with being a bad person who deserves punishment.

b. Concealment. The multiple is unable to discuss the self-abusive feelings and thoughts with the therapist. She projects onto the therapist her own belief that she must maintain a positive appearance (please the therapist) or be rejected. Fear of rejection causes her to withdraw, to deny the feelings, and intellectualize. Internal blaming and abusive messages escalate, some of which are also directed at the therapist. The client begins to lose contact; feeling isolated, she begins to believe the negative internal messages about herself and the therapist.

   c. Feelings of isolation intensify. She begins to question the therapist's behaviors and those of a spouse or friends. She imagines secrets are being kept from her. Her own withdrawal and loss of contact are experienced as rejection from others. The client feels helpless and out of control.

   d. Anxiety and instability increase. Her need to reconnect with the therapist intensifies, while at the same time she fears reconnecting. She has lost trust. Negative internal messages continue to reinforce her experience.

   e. The inner family system regains control and fights to keep the therapist "out" of the system. The client becomes blaming and abusive toward the therapist.

When the client is in this borderline phase, she projects her own thoughts and feelings onto the therapist. She was depending on the therapist to make her feel better, but the therapist can't save her, and she can't connect with the therapist, no matter how hard she tries. This lack of connectedness feels like abandonment. And with the feeling of abandonment may come anger at the therapist.

At this point of the cycle, a multiple—particularly if she has personalities with borderline traits—may feel she cannot trust the therapist. Her inner family system may even attempt to reject the therapist, to get her "out of the system" so they can return to old dissociative ways that used to work. The system tries to rebalance itself by going back to the old coping skills, because it feels as if the new ones aren't working right. The inner family members don't feel safe right now, and they want to feel safe again. So even though the multiple wants the therapist to rescue her, she may at the same time try to push the therapist away in order to rebalance the system.

The multiple reverts to the old way of thinking that saved her originally: "The only one I can trust in this world is myself." The system begins to close up again. Feeling abandoned, the multiple transfers onto the therapist the label of "the bad parent." Having done this, she then feels afraid to reconnect with her therapist, because she expects the therapist to punish her like her original bad parent did.

In an effort to protect herself, the multiple's inner system starts to close in around itself and shut others out. Unable to validate herself, and projecting her self-blame onto others, she doesn't know whom she can trust. When the client is feeling so disgusted and at war with herself, she cannot hear or believe anything good about herself. Anything the therapist says at this point may be heard as negative and rejecting, and there will be personalities who will bring this perceived rejection to the attention of all the other inner family members.

As a child, the multiple heard paradox after paradox, and double bind after double bind. When the therapist becomes the projected "bad parent" the multiple doesn't know whether she can trust and believe her or whether the therapist's reassurances may "be a trick." Having just relived a trauma from her past, she may perceive the present from the viewpoint of that past; she becomes confused and unable to discriminate what is real and not real, just as when she was a child.

However, a critically important dynamic occurs at this point in the cycle where the multiple is feeling abandoned and rejected. Because of the therapy she has already done, parts of her will be aware that she doesn't deserve to be abandoned and rejected—particularly when she is feeling so exhausted and depressed following the arduous work of abreaction. The client may begin to punish her therapist for rejecting her, placing on someone else the rage and punishment she had up to this point been turning inside on herself. All the rage she could not allow herself to show the original abuser may be displaced onto the therapist during this phase. The benefit to the multiple is that this allows her to stop punishing herself and begin to restablize and refocus on the present.

In this sense, moving into the borderline feelings allows the multiple a catharsis and a way to save herself. In phases 5 and 6 of the cycle she has been depressed and suicidal; she cannot continue to live in that state, containing within herself all those feelings. It seems her only way out is to die—*unless* she can put those rageful, depressed feelings outside of her. And the borderline part allows her to do just that, by the processes of projection and transference. She puts the rage on someone safe—the therapist.

The extent to which the multiple will transfer her feelings onto the therapist at this point will depend on whether the client has one or more personalities who are quite borderline or whether there are just borderline "traits." A client who has few borderline traits will still experience most of these painful feelings, as well as some transference during some stage of her cycle.

Phase 8: Resolution

At this point in the coping cycle, the multiple may go back into denial in order to feel safe and to put things back into some sense of order. Denial allows the restoration of order and calm, particularly if the memory just abreacted was too devastating to be completely integrated at this time. If the therapist stays with the multiple throughout the course of her cycle, then there will likely be a reconnection at this point. What the multiple's inner family has learned will be absorbed into the system. In other words, what happens is that the system begins to reclose, but fails to close up as far as before. Each time the multiple experiences the cycle of memory retrieval and abreaction, the system remains open just a bit further. The maintenance of the therapist as part of the system—even though the multiple has felt rejected and may have tried to reject her therapist in return—helps keep the inner family open and able to begin again with the work of remembering.

> JUDY: *"Each time I went through this cycle, Doris and Lynda hung in there with me. I was able to trust a little more, cope with less denial each time around, and it became easier to redevelop a trusting relationship with my therapists after doing this demanding work. This cycle occurred for me every time I processed a memory or the feelings that came with it."*

Intervention Using the Cycle

Developing a schematic of your client's coping cycle is like mapping: it gives you a generalized look at your client's behavior. As a therapist, knowing the client's cycle can help you prepare for an intervention; it allows you to predict in advance where the client's feelings and behavior are headed. You can say, "My client is going to withdraw here, and this is the reason she is afraid; therefore, when she does this, maybe I need to do that."

> DORIS: *"Judy and I figured out her cycle together; we talked about it and where she was in this cycle throughout the time she was doing memory work. Our talking about this helped Judy feel that we were working together; seeing the difference this made while she*

was in the cycle helped her feel that she had more control of herself during her coping cycle, which is what she wanted."

Knowing her cycle and how it works will in itself help the client to alleviate some of the old coping behaviors revealed in its process. You and your client may find that different individual personalities may be involved in different phases of the cycle. For example, there may be a personality who usually reports headaches or other body aches, or who visits a doctor about physical symptoms; another personality may emerge to be busy during the manic phase; one or two personalities may manifest the depression; others may carry the borderline feelings or the denial. Just becoming aware of how she copes within her inner family system and how she processes new memories and feelings will demystify herself to herself and bring meaning to her feelings and behaviors.

Headaches, for example, come to mean that memories or personalities are emerging, while the multiple is trying to keep them down. When the multiple's helper personalities discover this, they pass the information around the system, and the struggle to repress the emerging memories or personalities can lessen. The multiple can begin to aid her own process.

During the manic phase, the client can lose a sense of reality about her self-punishing behavior. The therapist can show the client how her need to clean the house or work until midnight is punishing; she can be a connection to reality. Reframing these self-punishing or manic behaviors as efforts to protect herself is helpful; in this case, the therapist must work with the individual personalities who are being (protectively) abusive.

As a therapist, realize that the multiple must have something to distract herself from the intensity of feelings. Instead of saying to the client, "Don't clean house, you shouldn't be overworking yourself like that," you can point out the behaviors, so the multiple begins to recognize what she does, understand it, and *gradually* learn other things to do. If you ask the client to simply stop doing whatever she does to distract, or to stop punishing herself in ways that make her feel better, she will need something else to take care of all those overwhelming feelings. And whatever you suggest as a replacement behavior may not be possible for the client to do—especially during those first difficult years of therapy. The client may not have a personality who can successfully govern those "destructive" behaviors.

Withdrawal may be a major characteristic of phases 5–7, and feelings of agoraphobia, paranoia, or depression may precipitate a crisis. The multiple may spiral in, closing up the inner family system as she retreats farther and farther inward. During times of abreaction and ensuing withdrawal, using physical touch may help the client stay in contact with you. Physical contact maintains the connection between the client's inner world and the outside; the therapist can touch her hand or hold her as she cries, becoming a conduit to the outside world and preventing the client from barricading herself against the world. The more a multiple can stay in touch with the outside world during the depression phases, the less likely she will be to close up the inner system afterward.

Talking about how unworthy or ashamed she feels about the memory will help lower the intensity of those feelings. The personalities who come out during the abreaction and depression need to talk, and need the reframing in order to see themselves as positive rather than negative while they are reliving or remembering the abuse. The cycle may be played out by different personalities, but the whole system of the multiple becomes involved in it.

During the suicidal phase, having a plan already thought out ahead of time helps to defuse an emergency. Having a way out of the suicidal thoughts and feelings, such as permission to telephone the therapist or a plan for hospitalization, allows the client to feel rescued and may alleviate some of the transference onto the therapist for "not being there." However, this will work only if the plan and the criteria for hospitalization are very clear and well-defined and mutually agreed upon prior to going through the cycle. If there is no prearranged plan, and the therapist puts her client in the hospital, the multiple may say, "You are punishing me by putting me in the hospital," or "You are abandoning me and trying to get rid of me." If in addition the client happens to be misunderstood and revictimized by the hospital system itself after she is admitted, the therapist can expect more blame.

If the multiple has personalities with borderline traits, the feelings of abandonment that occur in phase 7 of the cycle may be especially likely to occur. The borderline part may become abusive, rejecting, or punishing toward the therapist. When this happens, it is important for the therapist *not* to take this blaming behavior personally. To avoid the complications that will result from countertransference, the therapist must realize that the client is doing what she needs to do in order to get through the painful experiences of remembering and feeling abuse. As therapist, you may not have done anything to cause the client to blame you, except to be the recipient of transference. While the therapist may wish to always be seen as the "good" parent, allowing the transference can be good policy—not only because it is unavoidable but also because it can be useful in helping the multiple learn to vent her anger without being punished, and discover how her old feelings about the bad parent/good parent get mixed up with the therapist.

However, it does not work to try to show a client who is in the throes of the borderline phase of her coping cycle that she is projecting onto the therapist. These borderline feelings allow the multiple to dare to be angry, even if in doing so she puts those angry feelings onto the therapist instead of the abusers. It is important during this borderline phase to validate the client's angry feelings. If you try to say, "You are not mad at me, you are mad at your abusers," the multiple *when she is in this phase* will think, "That's just great; then everything I am feeling has no basis in fact, I'm making this up. I have no right to feel these feelings right now. What am I doing wrong?"

First, allow the client to express the rage, even if it is being transferred onto you in the process. Let her know, "Yes, it's OK to be angry, and the feelings you are having are very appropriate considering what happened to you." You may even be able to add, "I'm glad you're expressing your anger to me." Remember that the personalities who are borderline, like other clients with this diagnosis, are totally immersed in their feelings when they are in a borderline state. If you try to say "I know what's really going on here, and so should you," you will only give the client the message that it is not OK for her to be angry with you. You will become the punisher and she will hear, "It's OK to be mad at someone else, but not at the therapist."

If you, as a therapist, become defensive about the client's transference, you are moving into countertransference. It can happen before you've even realized it; but once you perceive your defensiveness, you can change it. Even if the client blames you, you don't have to own blame if it's not yours. However, it may be worth examining your own feelings and behaviors carefully to make sure there is not something you do need to own.

Examining your own part in the therapeutic interaction is something you can do that will be helpful when the client is in this stage of the cycle. Within all the interactions that occur between you and the client as she twists and turns through her cycle, there may be a little piece—

something you said, a tone of voice, a look on your face, a movement of your body—some little piece of behavior that may have looked to the multiple remarkably like the original abuser. Find out what the little piece is and validate it for your client. You can own that little piece as something you did do. You don't have to own abusiveness or intent to abuse, but you can acknowledge that a little piece of your behavior may have been a trigger for the multiple. You can say, "I must have sounded very much like your abuser when I said XYZ. No wonder you're feeling angry." As a therapist, you cannot possibly know what all your client's triggers are; you are human, and you don't need to punish yourself either. If you become stuck in trying to be a perfect therapist, or in having your client see you as perfect, trouble will follow.

If you allow the client in her borderline state to transfer her feelings onto you, validating whatever piece of the current client-therapist interaction that may be involved in her feelings, you will enable the client to begin to reconnect with you at this stage of the cycle. Paradoxically, the borderline phase is where the client is actually beginning to reconnect; she feels abandoned and angry, but her projection onto the therapist is a form of connection, of moving from her inside world to the outside world. In the previous depressed and suicidal phases she wished to leave; in the borderline state she behaves in a rejecting manner, but may truly wish to make contact.

During the phase of borderline feelings, know that you cannot save the client from these intensely conflicting and turbulent feelings—they are her feelings of shame, guilt, rage, and abandonment. She must experience them rather than dissociate them, as has been her old pattern. For more information on dealing with transference and borderline traits in a multiple, see Chapter 8.

In the resolution phase of the client's coping cycle, she and the therapist begin to reconnect. The denial that often accompanies this last stage, at least initially, allows the multiple to regain some distance from the overpowering force of the regained memory or feelings. "Hanging in there" with the client at this stage allows her inner family system to remain open—because of the therapist's foot in the door, so to speak. Because the therapist continues to offer validation and support of the memory and the feelings, the client gradually accepts them too.

This is also the time when the therapist may more successfully talk with the client about the transference that occurred at phase 7, when the borderline feelings were rampant. By the final phase of the cycle, the client has obtained enough distance from her feelings to look back and reassess them, with the therapist's help. Here you can encourage the multiple to begin to see that the anger she is expressing toward you, her therapist, belongs to someone else. She is expressing it at you precisely because she cannot express it toward the person she is really angry at—her abuser. During the middle stages of treatment, the client can begin to learn safe ways to express some of those feelings toward her abusers, e.g., through art or journaling.

Intensity and Duration of the Cycle

The completion of one individual cycle may take anywhere from a few days to a few months. Early in treatment, the cycle may be short; a dominant personality may come out to end the chaos of feeling and prevent a memory from completely surfacing, for example. By the middle stages of treatment there is more cooperation among the personalities in the system to allow abreaction to occur.

The intensity of feelings that a multiple experiences during the abreactive phase may not lessen over time. This doesn't mean the client or therapist is doing anything wrong. Abreaction is hellishly painful. Awareness and understanding of how she copes with the rejoining of memory and feelings will help the process, but it may not diminish the feelings. However, the intensity of other feelings or behaviors expressed in the multiple's cycle may decrease with time and learning. Manic behavior, for example, can be channelled into more constructive coping; the length of time spent in depression and the amount of denial will decrease over time.

As the multiple becomes more aware of her own coping cycle, she will become more skillful at observing her current place in that cycle. This in itself will help her in doing the work. Over time, the intensity of some of the feelings and behaviors she cycles through will lessen with increased understanding, and the multiple will be able to change or soften some of the more dysfunctional behaviors she normally uses. However, softening or shortening the cycle is a process that may take years. A multiple has so many, many memories and feelings to process, and even after integration environmental reminders of trauma may still trigger the familiar coping cycle. It is possible and perhaps likely that the client's particular cycle may continue throughout her life, but without the intensity that it held during the abreactive stages of therapy.

Even with increased awareness and understanding, it may be impossible for the client to stop the cycle from occurring; it has a momentum of its own. The client may blame herself for not being able to stop the cycle. She may think, "If only I could do better, if only I could stop these behaviors, then I could save myself this pain." A personality who is especially fearful of abandonment may make a herculean effort to avert some of the more painful parts of the cycle with the rationale, "My therapist will be pleased if I don't get so depressed or so withdrawn; she won't want to abandon me if I've done great." However, when the client cannot stop herself from coping the way she does cope, these hopeful thoughts turn against her: "If I can't accomplish (what I tried to do), I've failed again. I've failed my therapist, I'm bad, so she'll probably leave me." Here the client goes right on into the next phase of her cycle anyway, with the addition of more self-blame and the potential for more feelings of betrayal from the therapist than before.

A therapist, too, may wish she could stop the client's cycle or at least move the client quickly from trigger to abreaction to acceptance and integration without all the parts in between. *The point is not to stop the cycle but to use it therapeutically.*

If you try to stop the cycle, you may stop the work of therapy or at the least contribute to a setback. The work of therapy, of reclaiming memories and abreacting, must be done, and the client must retain and use enough of her dissociative skills to get her through this while she is learning new skills. Recognizing and understanding the client's pattern of coping makes a difference when she's going through it. Being aware of her own different phases in this dissociative coping cycle helps the client and the therapist stay connected with each other throughout, rather than feeling disconnected. Staying positively connected with the therapist while she reclaims the memories and feelings gives the multiple a healing experience and in itself teaches her a different way to cope beside detaching from herself or others, as has been her lifetime pattern.

You can begin to search for the multiple's individual cycle during the very beginning stages of therapy, realizing that she will have a coping pattern that may repeat itself again and again over time. Each multiple's style will be different from another's in some ways, but there will be a pattern. Every multiple will be torn at times between maintaining the balance of the original system she has created for herself versus bringing the therapist and new ideas into the system; each client will want to kick the therapist out of the system and go back to the old familiar ways, and yet want to reclaim her many parts and become whole. This opening and closing, reassociating and dissociating will form a pattern of coping that she uses throughout her therapeutic journey.

> DORIS: *"As we look at this cycle it's easy to see why multiples may be frequently misdiagnosed. Each of the behaviors exhibited at some point of the cycle would fit quite nicely into some category of the DMS-III-R. Knowing there is a cycle will enable you and your client to use her particular cycle as a schematic for managed treatment. By "managed" I don't mean controlled, but rather that both therapist and client will be better prepared to deal with behaviors when they are found to follow a fairly prescribed course. This rescues such behavior from a seemingly chaotic state to one that makes sense and enables therapist and client to incorporate such behavior into a positive therapeutic dynamic."*

Retrieval of memories, abreaction of feelings, and integration of both within the system are the main events of the middle stages of therapy. By this time, the therapist will have developed a strong, caring relationship with some of the dominant personalities. This is very important in order to have the cooperation that you, the therapist, will need from them. A few of the dominant personalities will help you do therapy with other personalities, participating in reconnecting the memories, and preparing others for integration. These co-therapist personalities begin to understand and accept that they will at some point no longer exist separately as they were, but will become part of the whole person. And they are willing to do this out of love and caring for the Essence and the original core child. By the end of this middle stage, the Essence personality takes on more and more of the memories and feelings being shared by others inside, and she begins to become more of a dominant personality herself, if she wasn't before. She is preparing herself for integration with the other personalities.

chapter 8

Difficult Issues in Treatment

T HIS CHAPTER WILL address issues in working with multiples that are particularly difficult. These issues include personalities often seen as negative, therapist-client problems such as transference and countertransference, and the client's fear of abandonment.

Abusive Personalities

Abusive personalities may take the role of self-destructive, verbally abusive, violent or angry personalities. These are often perceived as "bad personalities" by the therapist and/or client. We want to reiterate that the multiple's inner family system is modeled after the family of origin, so there are bound to be personalities who are abusive. Some of these personalities may resemble someone in the family of origin. They may use the same words as the original abusers or copy their behaviors; they may threaten and demean. However, unlike the original abusers, these personalities are usually using abusive behavior to keep the inner system going and to ensure the survival of the multiple. (For the exceptions to this, see the section on negative introjects later in this chapter.)

The main function of abusive personalities is to maintain the family system. Secrecy was a major rule in that original family of origin. The child was often told that if she disclosed the secret, death or terrible abuse would follow. And in most multiples' lives it did. The multiple still believes in dire consequences of disclosure, because of what she witnessed or experienced as a child.

While these personalities may be disturbing or frightening to the multiple or to the therapist, it is important to realize that they are trying to help and protect the multiple by maintaining the inner system; they use abuse to keep the other personalities in line and to maintain the status quo. Preservation of the secrets and the familiar dissociative ways of coping are all these personalities know of survival—and survival is their underlying purpose.

Abusive personalities are often experienced as voices saying such things as, "You're stupid, you don't know what you are talking about; you're lying." These, of course, are the milder forms. Abusive personalities may use profanity to put down another inner family member. They may say the opposite of what the therapist says in an attempt to discredit the therapist, for example, "Don't trust what she tells you." They may attempt to sabotage therapy by threatening bodily harm to the multiple, so that other personalities will not tell of the abuses.

> JUDY: *"I had a teenaged personality named Gerri who could be very, very abusive to the inner family. She used a voice similar to what I had heard growing up: 'Don't you dare tell about anything you little bitch; otherwise I will do this or that.' The inner family didn't know that Gerri was designed to help keep the secrets and that she was only doing her job."*

Some personalities are abusive not only verbally but also physically; there are several types of these. Some personalities become so depressed that they become suicidal; they may swallow too many pills or cut themselves. Sometimes depressed personalities want to end the whole exhausting struggle that the inner family suffers, especially after enough inner communication develops that these depressed ones become aware of other parts' suffering, as well as their own. These depressed ones are really saying, "I need help—help me."

Other abusive personalities become self-destructive and punish the body in an attempt to deal with overwhelming anxiety or tension. When someone tells a secret or begins to remember abuse, the client may have obsessive thoughts of hurting herself by cutting or mutilation. Punishment is part of the original abusive cycle that is continued in the inner family's cycle. In therapy, when memories or feelings are stirred up or a secret is told, the message to the multiple is, "If you tell, something awful is going to happen." This message is as powerful in the present as it was in the past. When anxiety builds up, the multiple waits for the "something awful." Anxiety increases if something awful *doesn't* happen, so the multiple makes it happen to end the suspense. The tension is relieved by hurting the body. Physical punishment can take the form of cutting or self-mutilation, using drugs or alcohol, damaging sexual organs, burns, bruising, or "accidents." Some punisher parts may take the multiple out to do drugs, or to a bar where she can get "picked up" by abusive people and be injured. These forms of self-punishment mirror how tension was relieved in the original family. The multiple internalizes the abusive cycle and does it to herself: she creates the same tension for herself when she does something "wrong," e.g., remembering or disclosing, and she relieves the tension in the ways she learned in the past.

An extremely punishing personality may try to destroy another personality she perceives as weak or bad, saying, "I am going to kill her; she deserves to die," not comprehending that she inhabits the same body. Again, this type of destructive behavior reflects the internalization and personalization of what the multiple learned as a child about punishment; the survival of the abusive system depended upon the abuse being kept secret and on "bad" behaviors being punished. In the same way, the violent personalities believe the survival of the inner family depends upon keeping the secrets and threatening those who tell or otherwise break family rules.

The message the multiple received as a child was that she was bad and deserved to be punished. Punishing her, according to the abusers, would make her good. The difficulty was that she was never sure what "good" was. Much of what the punishers said was good felt very bad to her. All her *own* attempts at being good failed and the punishment to make her "good" continued. If she were to be "good" it seemed that the only avenue left open to her was through punishment, which left her feeling very bad. For the adult multiple, as she tries to reclaim and rebuild her life, this presents a real dilemma. How can she overcome the belief that she is bad? How can she find ways to be good and feel good that don't involve punishment? It is important to realize that the destructive, violent personalities the therapist sees are mixed up by the messages they received as children; they are really confused and often feel crazy. Their thoughts about themselves are based on the destructive crazy-making messages they received as children. They have to be destructive to feel better.

How can a therapist work with these abusive, sometimes violent personalities? Many destructive personalities don't realize that they are a part of the same physical body as those they hate. How can they hear and believe what the therapist tells them when they have no concept of "body"? The therapist must find some way to help orient these destructive personalities *to* the body. For instance, during a therapy session, when working with a female client and a destructive male personality who is out, the therapist can point out a number of conflicting factors: e.g., that the body of this personality is definitely feminine, the clothing, jewelry, etc., are clearly designed for a female and not for a male. This can be a startling discovery and the reality that this is indeed a "shared" body may help motivate the punisher part to find another way to punish (or to protect) the system without killing or harming the body.

The therapist can also teach the abusive personalities ways to relieve tension or obsessive thoughts without harming the body, using creative ways to help decrease the intensity of the obsession. She can suggest that the destructive personality draw, paint, or use clay to express what she wants to do. If another personality is seeing or hearing instructions to harm herself from an abusive personality, the therapist can ask the nonabusive one to express what she hears in nondestructive ways. Venting feelings without acting upon them in a destructive manner will be a new experience for a multiple and add to her coping skills. Journaling about the feeling or obsessive thoughts may also help. Completing the abusive cycle in a safe way, through journaling or art, can provide some relief from the tension. It is particularly important for the therapist to remain in contact with the client during these times.

Finally, as therapist you must accept and form an alliance with these destructive personalities, just as you do with other personalities. Accept their importance in the inner family and the fact that they are integral parts who are trying to protect the system. You must help these personalities understand their positive functions in the inner family. When you start reframing them to themselves, these punishers begin to see themselves differently; you may be the first person to perceive them as "good," and this in itself helps to build a therapeutic bond. They will begin to trust and to listen to you. To reframe these personalities, look at the positive intention behind the abusiveness. Tell them that what they are actually doing is trying to preserve the inner family; these abusive parts have never seen themselves as saviors before. Then, help these personalities find other ways to protect the system without punishing.

The therapist must also examine how she feels about these abusive parts. It can be very difficult when working with some of the more dedicated personalities, who want to get on with the business of therapy, to have destructive parts put your client in serious danger. So it is important for the therapist to keep remembering the design and purpose of that inner family system. Make friends with these parts and stay in contact with them, so you can reframe and teach these destructive personalities. Good contact between the destructive personalities and the therapist is very important.

Just as the therapist will need to reframe abusive personalities to themselves, she will also need to reframe them to other inner family members. And the other inner family members will pick up on what the therapist feels about the destructive personalities. If the therapist thinks they are bad, that reinforces what the others already think. Change cannot happen if this negative belief system remains. So the therapist must examine carefully how she feels about and treats these types of personalities.

An example of reframing destructive personalities using Judy's inner family system follows. Gerri, as mentioned earlier, was one of Judy's personalities who was very destructive in physical ways. Other inner family members saw Gerri as negative; she was a personality who got them in trouble or put them in situations where they would be hurt. They would say, "We hate her, we don't want her in the inner family." They tried to ignore her and set her apart from themselves. It took a lot of reframing to the other family members for them to accept her as positive.

DORIS: *"Gerri also had to learn to accept herself. It was a matter of building her self-esteem; she didn't like herself for the things she did. She couldn't forgive herself for the things she did any more than the other inner family members could. While helping her see what her role was, I reframed that role. Gerri was a fighter and she was expressing the anger and rage toward men that the others felt but were afraid to express. She wanted to get something back for all that painful abuse. Gerri also wanted something pretty for herself—she was sick of ugly things. The way she got what she wanted was by using men. Afterward, because Gerri also believed she didn't deserve nice things, she would have to be punished for her behavior and anything she received; she was caught in a double bind. In reframing, I helped her see that it was OK to want something pretty, that she deserved pretty things, and that she had a right to be angry about being used by men. The reframe took her out of the double bind. She didn't deserve to be hurt; Gerri needed to express that anger, but without putting herself in a situation where her anger would get her hurt again.*

"I helped Gerri to accept herself positively by using a belief that was already in place in the inner system and was currently being used by another personality, Judith. Gerri needed to believe that someone could give her forgiveness for her behavior; Judith's religious faith gave Gerri spiritual support and love. In Judith's Christian belief system, a spiritual figure could take on Gerri's pain and suffering so that Gerri no longer had to do that for the inner family. As a teenage personality who was at a developmental stage where one normally searches for meaning in life and beyond, this spiritual connection was something Gerri reached out for."

What we have learned is that the therapist can use a belief that is already in place within the system to help destructive personalities reframe whatever they feel is negative about themselves. Once there is some acceptance of positive intent for negative behaviors, then those personalities can discover other ways to accomplish that intent without harming themselves or other personalities. When they see abusive personalities stop doing the things that hurt them, trust grows between inner family members. In Gerri's case, she learned to carry out her protective or revengeful feelings in a way that was not harmful and gave up sacrificing herself as perpetuator and recipient of system punishment.

Working with Anger

Personalities who are angry may scare the therapist, especially if the client herself is scared of the angry part or believes she will do something harmful to the office or to the therapist. The realization that a rageful child is sitting in front of you in the body of an adult can arouse concern about violence for a therapist. However, angry parts need to be validated and affirmed. If they have opportunities to express the anger in safe ways, they will usually not act out destructively. If the angry part is angry at you, the therapist, it is important to validate the anger and what she is angry with you about. Let her know that she does have a right to be angry, and that you want to hear what the anger has to say and where it is coming from.

> JUDY: *"In my own experience, anger was often either punished or sedated, for example, in a hospital. When that happened, the anger grew and grew. But when Lynda and Doris validated the anger it didn't explode; rather, it could be expressed in a safe way, a way that didn't hurt myself or others or destroy property."*

Anger may be directed at the therapist when transference occurs. For example, if the client has transferred the mother figure onto you, the therapist, you may do something that reminds the client of mother, something that makes her angry; but the client may be angry at *you* instead of mother. When this happens it is important to validate the piece the client is seeing in you right now. But that can be hard for a therapist.

First of all, you must look at how you feel about anger yourself, as a therapist and as a person. When people are angry toward you, what do you do with that? Does anger frighten you; does it make you feel rejected? Is anger within a therapeutic setting inappropriate unless it is contained? Is it all right for your client to scream? What is OK for an angry client to do in your office? These are questions you must ask yourself. You will react to your client's anger; when you do, what is going on inside you? Remember that anger has never been acceptable in the multiple's life; anger was ruled "bad" at a very early age, and she has had to repress it for years. An ability to express anger in the office shows healthy growth. But it can't happen unless the therapist gives permission for anger expression and offers appropriate modeling of ways to express it safely.

If the multiple feels safe enough with the therapist she will risk expressing those feelings of anger. The therapeutic bond will increase the safety factor. When the multiple has a good relationship with you, many personalities will let you know that they don't want to be hurt and don't want you to be hurt. Although some personalities may threaten violence, they don't want to break that bond — it would be too scary and too much of a loss. If you give them a safe way to vent, they can put it to use.

Find out how old the angry personality is. A teenage part who is really angry may make threats but may not really want to act on them; she may be testing the therapist, just wanting to talk about the anger. An angry child personality may secretly be hoping for boundaries and containment. Angry personalities will need to express their anger in ways appropriate to the developmental stage they are in; a four-year-old's way will be different from a teenager's way. When an angry personality threatens to be violent, tell her that you understand, that she has a right to be angry. Tell that personality, "Let's talk about it," or "Let's draw about it." Volunteer to get out the foam bats or a pillow if she needs to hit something. Be creative. When you get to know your client well, you will be able to predict what the various angry parts will or won't be likely to do and to respond as needed.

Protecting the Client from Abusive Personalities

At what point is hospitalization necessary for the protection of a client who is self-destructive? Several factors can help a therapist assess this.

1. Is the destructive personality only attempting to relieve tension without the intent to kill? If so, you probably won't need to hospitalize.
2. How cooperative are the dominant personalities at this point in

therapy? Are they able to exert control over the destructive or threatening personality? They may be able to work together to protect the multiple and prevent other personalities from doing real harm. Some helper personalities may be willing to make verbal contracts to be watchful of the destructive personalities; when they believe a destructive personality might actually try to seriously harm the body, they can agree to telephone the therapist.

3. You may be able to make a no-harm contract with a personality who wants to do destructive things, if you have successfully built a trustful, cooperative alliance with this abusive personality. This will probably be possible only if some reframing has already been done.

It is important here for the therapist to remember that the multiple is someone who has dedicated her whole life to survival; she really wants to survive or she wouldn't be sitting in your office. However, after opening up memories and feelings that she has spent her whole life dissociating from, the client enters a period of vulnerability, which is something a therapist must be sensitive to. The therapist must be there to maintain the balance during times of crisis when the familiar balance is changed and the multiple's system enters unfamiliar chaos. The therapist (and possibly other friends or a spouse) gives the multiple the support she needs in order to go through the chaos during change. Because the therapist has joined the inner family system, she becomes a powerful part of that system.

In addition, the multiple's own defensive skills will serve her well in surviving crisis. During chaotic times when all the multiple's amnestic barriers are breaking down, when she is hearing voices, uncovering the past, switching, etc., some personalities will want to restabilize and protect the inner system with familiar self-destructive behaviors. During crises, a multiple still has all her personalities and their dissociative skills to protect her, even from her own destruction.

The therapist needs to do what makes herself feel secure when the client is in crisis. Although it may be uncomfortable, it may help to learn to tolerate some of the multiple's tension-reducing and relatively minor self-destructive behavior. However, if you are not feeling secure, go ahead and hospitalize.

Working with Negative Introjects

We have already defined and described negative introjects in Chapter 4. Your goal as therapist is to help negative introjects transform to positives, just as you would other abusive, violent, or destructive personalities. Always, always try transformation. Reframing negative introjects is a process that can take many months, even a year or more. With reframing, this personality may be willing to join with the family, to take that negative energy and turn it into positive energy for the good of the inner family.

A negative introject personality as a rule will be one whose specific purpose is to be hurtful. It is an introject of an extremely abusive, destructive person in the multiple's childhood. If this particular negative introject personality refuses to be transformed, then it may be that the maintenance of that introject in the inner family will only perpetuate the original abuse. In that case, the introject personality can be asked by the inner family members to leave, with the support of the therapist.

Virginia Satir (1986) taught that we can let go of what no longer fits. The multiple's inner system, modeled after the family of origin system, operates on fear. When the multiple no longer needs that fear and abuse to function, the abuser personalities will consent to being reframed and transformed into positive parts of the inner family or they will leave. For more information about our theories on why some negative introject personalities transform and some don't, see Chapter 4. A lengthy process is involved in the departure of a negative introject personality. We will describe below some of the interventions we used with Judy.

> DORIS: *"I began by preparing the inner family to understand the negative introject personality. Other family members had fears that this personality had so much power that it would be around forever. One of the ways introjects stayed powerful was by keeping the inner family in a state of fear. It was very helpful to the other personalities to realize that the introject was different from the other personalities, that it might not belong in the inner family circle. Once the inner family knew this, the introject's power began to weaken. Once*

I was sure, I told all the personalities, as well as the negative introject, that it didn't belong. The words, "You don't belong" seemed to have great impact, and also seemed to be nonthreatening to the inner family."

As the inner family members begin to disconnect from the introject, the introject personality weakens and becomes aware of losing power; it then becomes even more verbally abusive. The abusive introject may try harder and harder to get the multiple to act self-destructively. It may call the therapist nasty names or berate the therapist to her face and to the other personalities. When this abusiveness escalates, you know that the negative introject is fighting to hold onto its power over the others.

DORIS: *"I found in Judy's case personalities that were true nega-tive introjects could personally do nothing destructive; they used other personalities to do abusive acts. They threatened, they mobi-lized the others; but introjects had no power unless they could get another personality to act for them. This is why they do their best to use fear (there may be variations on this theme with other multiples).*

"I made the other family members aware of when the negative introject was weakening, and I began to use them to help the intro-ject leave. When I began to separate the introject from the inner family, I could also begin to separate it away from the body. The introject personality had to use Judy's body—her hands, her feet, etc.—in order to do destructive things. When the introject began to separate from the inner family and began to talk about the separa-tion from the body, Judy realized that the introject couldn't use the body to hurt her without using her own hands. And soon, her hands wished to do something different from what the introject wanted."

The metaphor you use to frame the negative introject as weakening should be one that is not frightening to the other personalities. If the phrase "it has no hands" sounds scary, use a different metaphor to talk about separation from the body, such as "it's just a picture," or "it's just a face that talks, a talking picture." Play around with it until you can find the right wording that clicks for your client and is not scary. It is important to remember that each multiple is a very unique individual;

each person's ways of creating an inner family and using information will be different. Find a way that fits for her. The point is to weaken the negative introject personality.

The negative introject personality will not be able to leave in a short time, and with good reason. It takes time to determine the existence of a negative introject that absolutely cannot be reframed and changed, time for that introject to weaken, and time for the inner family to understand the introject's purpose and the limitations of its power. To the therapist who says, "I am really concerned about my client; I see this introject as a dangerous part. I don't have the time to spend on this, and I want to get it done now"—we say, "Relax!" It isn't going to work. These wishes are out of concern for one's client, but they won't work. Timing is important; readiness among the inner family members is important. The therapist acts as the helper, but only if the process is allowed to happen in the client's own time will she be able to help.

DORIS: "*Once the abusive introject personality is sufficiently weakened, it is time for it to leave. During the leaving process, there may be an attempt by the introject to physically injure the body, reenacting previous methods the original abusers used to stop the child from resisting. Just as dominant personalities are able to draw energy from other personalities, it would seem that negative introjects are able to do the same. However, once the inner family has begun to reject the introject, those energy resources begin to dry up. The negative introject weakens, and its last effort to retain or regain control uses any residual energy. It may try to use the body to do one last destructive act on its way out. (It is helpful to have two therapists present to prevent the client from injury.) The inner system closes and shuts out the negative introject, leaving it without resources, and since it is not a part of the whole, it is gone.*

"*Once the negative introject is gone, the effect is obvious. The client's whole body will relax when the introject has left the body. The multiple will report that she doesn't hear that voice inside any longer. Judy reported experiencing a quietness inside that she could tell me about; the destructive voice of that introject was gone.*

"*What I have found that works is a form of Ericksonian hypnosis called 'pacing.' Although the process is very simple, it is helpful to have two therapists present. Do not under any circumstances attempt this process if you do not have training in using hypnosis.*"

Working with Resistance

Walter Kempler (1983), an eminent Gestalt therapist, believes that resistance on the part of the client only means that the client isn't doing what the therapist wants that client to do. A resistant client may simply reflect a therapist who wants to be in control and who has an agenda for his/her client.

We have already talked about the importance of the therapist's *not* having an agenda when working with a multiple. A multiple will have personalities who very much want to please the therapist and who will try to do everything they are told to do. The therapist may like these personalities better than others, giving her client the nonverbal message that some parts are better than others, or more deserving, etc. These personalities will become the "good guys." Resistant parts, personalities who will not "cooperate," may be perceived as the "bad guys."

As the therapist, you must remember that there is always a very good reason for resistance. Resistance may be something as simple as a child personality coming out and wanting to play, interrupting the flow of the session. A therapist may want to get rid of that child personality and say "I need to speak to so-and-so." However, the interruption may signal that the multiple has done enough work on a particular issue and needs a break; or, if the therapist follows the child personality's lead, she may find that the child has come to show her something that pertains to the previous work. As another example, one personality may be drawing a sketch of a memory when the client switches; the next personality tears up the picture and throws it away. When the work becomes scary, a protective personality will often do something to intervene, distract, or "undo" the work. It is just as important to meet the personalities whose roles are protectively resistant as to meet those whose roles are to please. Validate those who appear to be resistant personalities, just as you would validate the other parts.

The therapist must recognize the fear behind the resistance and learn to trust the multiple's own timing for doing her work. Your client is going to be opening up parts of herself that she has never exposed to any living being before. There may be a real fear that moving into deeper work will cause a break between herself and the therapist. The multiple realizes that she is taking the therapist into those areas that are deeply shameful to her and she is terrified of being abandoned as she was in the past. So if there is resistance, pay attention to it; resistance means you have run into an issue or a piece of work that is extremely important. It may mean you are getting close to something very scary, and you need to do the work a little at a time. There is no need to push; let it be.

There is a time to go with the client's flow or follow her lead, and a time to put up a boundary for her to bounce against. To determine what you need to do at a certain point in time, draw from the knowledge you have gained about this particular client during your work with her, as well as your intuition. A resistant personality can be a representative "tester" for the inner family system. Her job may be to test the therapist on trust issues, while the inner family watches. Will this issue become a battle? How far will the therapist let a certain situation go? How safe is the therapist?

There are times when a multiple asks for some control by the therapist. When things are too scary and she wants to do things that aren't good for her, she needs a parent figure to say "no." So multiples will ask both these things of you, the therapist: for you to allow them control, and for you to take control at times. And they will test to see if you will put up a boundary when it's needed and whether you will go along with them when it isn't.

Working with Denial

Denial personalities are the ones who refuse to believe that anything bad ever happened to them in their lives. They may not believe they are multiples. And if the client is still in contact with the abusers, it will more than likely be through a denial personality. A denial part will believe that her abusers were wonderful and are still wonderful; she may report that she doesn't hear voices, she does not lose time, and she doesn't want to be in therapy. If there are child denial personalities, the little ones will say (if the mother was an abuser), "I had a wonderful mother," or "that wasn't my mother, my mother didn't do that," etc. (See Figure 8.1.)

Introduce these denial parts to other inner family members who can begin to invalidate the denial. Remind them of clothing differences,

FIGURE 8.1: Drawing by a child denial personality, Little Judy. She would often draw "pretty" pictures of her home after an abusive event was disclosed.

misplaced household objects, situations they have found themselves in that are unlike them. Show them that the handwriting in the journal is different from theirs, that entries are signed in different names, and that others are writing about abuses. Remind them that they forget things or lose time. Show them drawings that other personalities have made in session about past traumatic events.

Denial personalities can be difficult for the therapist to deal with, because they can feel like major roadblocks to treatment. In addition, denial personalities, like abusive ones, can put the multiple at risk sometimes by staying in contact with the abusers or ignoring obvious danger signs. However, these denial parts exist to protect the system and keep it going. When the work of therapy gets scary, the multiple wants to retreat into denial again (see Chapter 7).

It may be harder for a denial personality to give up her position than for other personalities to do so. To give up denial means taking on awarenesses and feelings she has never had to deal with before; it means knowing about memories or current behaviors she doesn't want to know about. The denial personality may never have had to experience feelings before. Denial keeps this personality and others in the inner family from having terrifying, devastating feelings and memories.

So be sensitive to the personalities who carry the denial. Sensitivity comes from doing your best to understand what it must to like to relive the memories and feel those feelings of pain and terror. It takes courage for your client to remove the amnestic barriers that have served as protection for herself and other members of the inner family. When this does occur the reality of their situation begins to vibrate throughout the whole inner system. Don't expect denial personalities to relinquish control easily; but it can happen over time with the support of the therapist and other inner family members. To ask *anyone* to give up their defenses immediately would certainly not be therapeutic, and might possibly even be destructive; to expect a multiple to do so is to court disaster.

As frustrating as this resistance may be for you, the therapist, trust the multiple's timing. Her resistance is protection from memories and feelings that if released all at once would be overwhelming. Even as the work progresses and she is better able to accept the reality of her life, expect her to retreat into denial on a somewhat regular basis. Therapists constantly work with these paradoxes. The multiple wants to be healed, wants to be whole. She wants to know, and she doesn't want to know; she wants to change yet she resists change. It takes time for the multiple, and especially her protective denial parts, to trust the therapist and the process of healing—to believe that she won't be abused.

Therapy removes a major defense system. As we remove that defense of denial, we need to help the multiple build another defense mechanism so she can tolerate the horrible memories and feelings she will be experiencing in therapy. And what is a good replacement? One of the multiple's new defenses will be support from the therapist; another will be support from other personalities within her own system, ones who can comfort, encourage and understand. As trust and cooperation grow within the inner family, the inside support that results will help the denial personalities to gradually give up denial and begin to use other forms of protection.

Borderline Traits in Personalities

According to the *DSM-III-R*, a client who has borderline personality disorder is characterized as someone who can be extremely impulsive or unpredictable in self-damaging ways, has pronounced shifts in mood, and may suddenly switch anger on and off. A borderline client often has difficulty with issues of identity, fears abandonment, and may be extremely dependent but apt to deny that. Research has shown that people with borderline personality disorder are highly dissociative (Ross, 1989).

In clients who have MPD, you will see borderline traits in some personalities. As discussed in Chapter 3, characteristics of personality disorders can become encapsulated in separate personalities during the multiple's teenage years. Adult multiples may easily be misdiagnosed as borderlines if one or more of the dominant personalities has borderline characteristics.

What does a personality with borderline traits look like? A borderline personality will probably bring the therapist a present. While this personality can be very giving, she will probably expect a lot in return. She will want and expect you to be available for her whenever she needs you — even if it is three o'clock in the morning. A personality with borderline traits may get angry with the therapist and cancel appointments — then just as suddenly reschedule the appointment in a panic.

A multiple's borderline personalities can be very manipulative. But the manipulativeness arises from the belief, as well as the past experience, that nobody will give them anything unless they give first. Having been used by others in the past, they expect others to use them. Borderline personalities will have extremely low self-esteem or none at all. These parts personify the child who wants the therapist to give her something she never had: a sense of self, a sense of worthiness, and a sense of well-being.

A borderline part may also be the container for the pain of other personalities. This part who expresses the pain of the baby who was abandoned may act out that pain for everyone in the inner family; she is the expression of that terrible need to have a parent. Because she holds the key to those early intense feelings, this is a very important personality to work with.

For multiples, the fear of abandonment is huge because they were

abandoned so often in so many ways—physically, emotionally, spiritual-
ly. The borderline personality wants someone to hang onto; there was
no one she could count on as a child. And when she finds you, this
wonderful therapist, she "falls in love." Finally someone listens to her,
someone seems to care for her. She will try to attach herself to you in a
symbiotic kind of mother-baby relationship. The baby wants the mother to nurture her the way she never was before. Because of this, any
unmet need from the therapist may be perceived as abandonment and
rejection. To these borderline parts, this feels extremely painful. Any
time these personalities have a wish for something from the therapist
and are unable to have that wish fulfilled, the old pain the very young
child felt is triggered. This happens whether the wish is realistic or
unrealistic, and whether they think they deserve to have it or not. The
old pain, "There is no one here for me," comes right up to the surface.
Dealing with this kind of transference can be difficult for the therapist
(see the next section).

Transference/Countertransference

A personality with borderline traits will always transfer heavily onto the
therapist. When that much transference occurs it is easy for the therapist to countertransfer onto the client. As the therapist, you will again
have to take a clear look at your own issues, because, if any personality
is going to stir them up, it will be the borderline part.

The borderline part's expectation from her therapist is for the therapist to be there for her like mother (or father) never was; the therapist
has become the parent. Now she expects that all of her wants, all of her
unmet needs are going to be met in this wonderful person, the therapist. It is unnecessary and unhelpful to try to block transference with a
statement such as, "I'm not your mother." Transference will happen,
even if you don't want it and try very hard not to foster it; however, if
handled well, transference can be very therapeutic for a multiple. As
the therapist, you can view the borderline part's expectation of you as
something that is very traumatic for yourself, or you can see it as a
challenge. Working with the borderline personality is an opportunity to
get to the core of the deepest issues other personalities are afraid to talk
about, and it is a chance for real healing.

A borderline part is intelligent and has feelings, but lacks a connection between the intelligence and the feelings. What a therapist works to do is help her make that connection. The borderline part of the multiple missed out on the first and second developmental stages most children process. She is unable to trust and therefore unable to separate from mother without a secure mother to come back to. The intellect went on developing, but the feelings didn't. As the therapist, you can give this personality some of the nurturing she should have had, while also putting up the boundaries she should have had as well. From the outset, you will have to set up boundaries that allow your client and yourself some safety. You will have to teach a borderline part about boundaries, but not in a hurtful way. Recognizing the different developmental stages that she has missed is important.

As the therapist you are teaching the multiple both about bonding and about separation — stage 2 development. Any person has to have a significant "other" to bond with before she can go on to separate from that person. First comes the bonding, then comes the individuation. What the therapist does is accept the parent transference, allowing the bonding to occur, and then become an enabler for the individuation. The better part of this work will occur with the borderline parts of the multiple, if they are present in the inner family system.

Unlike many clients who are diagnosed with simply borderline personality disorder, multiples who have borderline parts are teachable. Personalities that are fixated at early developmental stages can be walked through the later stages step by step, month by month, and year by year. Therapists may worry that because the work with a multiple spans such a long time, the multiple will stay "stuck" in a borderline pattern forever. But multiples fight to grow and become whole. Every multiple we have met in therapy has fervently desired to be adult and independent. However, they do need a therapist who can handle transference.

Working with the borderline parts can indeed be very demanding. As therapist, you will soon become aware of the many needs of personalities of all ages. If you are not clear about your own boundaries, if you are rather confluent yourself with the client, you will soon feel overwhelmed by the borderline parts' wants and needs. If you cannot provide adequate self-care, you will feel swallowed up by your client. What happens when the therapist gets scared or exhausted is countertransference.

Most of us grew up in a family system that was at least somewhat dysfunctional. If you have abandonment issues from your own childhood, if you have fears about being a parent, if you yourself were abused as a child, these old issues will come roaring up to meet you when the multiple begins to project her wants and demands. If the therapist begins to put herself in the victim role with the client, feeling taken advantage of, then suddenly the client looms "bigger" than the therapist and a role reversal has occurred. A therapist will feel victimized if she has not learned good boundaries and how to use them with clients. A multiple often perceives at some point that her therapist feels burdened by her; she then experiences anger at the therapist and guilt about having wants and needs.

As the therapist, if you withdraw in frustration, the ever-sensitive multiple will be aware of your withdrawal and will react strongly. A borderline part may well hang on even harder, feeling abandoned again. Other parts may feel at fault. You have just recapitulated the multiple's abandonment at stage 2 — and to a multiple, the new pain, although it has happened for a different reason, feels the same as the old one.

Other countertransference traps can occur as well. Many multiples have a part that is very nurturing and understanding; a therapist can hook into that, particularly if the therapist has a history of child abuse and still has unmet needs for nurturing. Again, what happens is a role reversal, where the multiple becomes the nurturer taking care of her therapist. This position is also extremely confusing for the multiple, who in many ways had to "take care of" her original parents in order to survive.

> JUDY: *"In looking back on my own experience, the issues created from the transference caused me to work on issues from my past — issues about the abuser, abandonment, etc. I put my feelings onto my therapists, got them outside myself and then I could see them as my issues. It wasn't until I transferred onto Doris that I was even aware that I had those issues to work on."*

A therapist who is feeling abused by a client has a difficult time staying in the here-and-now and responding rather than reacting. Multiples are very bright and they remember almost verbatim what a therapist has said three or four weeks ago, or even a year ago. A borderline personality might be very concrete and tend to hear a therapist's words quite literally. Arguments can arise from such misunderstandings, especially when transference complicates the client's interpretations. In reacting to a borderline part's anger, the therapist can easily get lost in countertransference, feeling abused, misunderstood, rejected, and unappreciated. The moment you feel a victim or feel the need for some appreciation, you have crossed the line and gotten your own feelings mixed up in your work. However, rather than being a catastrophe, countertransference simply shows that you are a human being. You can say to yourself, "Something is going on here" and ask yourself "How am I going to deal with this without allowing my own feelings to create a problem for my client?"

A co-therapist can save you from much of this struggle. The client's primary therapist inevitably receives more transference than a co-therapist does. A second therapist can often be more objective, because fewer countertransference issues become triggered for him or her. A co-therapist can help clarify the transference and countertransference issues in the session for both the multiple and the primary therapist.

> DORIS: *"At this point let me interject one of my own experiences with countertransference. Judy and I had begun our work in 1985. Lynda had joined us two years later and had become an integral part of our working triad. Vacation time came around and Lynda left for a week of much needed rest and recreation. We both thought we had carefully prepared Judy for Lynda's absence, knowing even changes in scheduling were difficult for her.*
>
> *"As a separate issue, I was also struggling at that time with some anxiety relative to Judy's environmental safety and well-being. Our work over the past three years had required a committed investment in her therapy, and the fear that all of our hard-won progress was being threatened created chaos in me. I expressed my fears to Judy and at the same time realized that there was a certain point beyond which I could not go without invading her right to make choices for herself even though I felt they might cause her harm. It was difficult for me to let these feelings go, and in fact, as I later realized, I entered this session in a depressed state, angry at my inability to control Judy's environment. My parental self, my own "part that knows what's best for everyone," contaminated the therapist in me.*

When we entered the session, my anxiety about controlling Judy's safety blocked my awareness that Judy was still working on her own issues about Lynda's absence. I thought that had been resolved.

"As I was to know later, feelings of abandonment, of not being good enough, of distrust—all the feelings the child parts had about separation and what that meant—were churning around in Judy. When she came into session she mentioned that she believed that Lynda's absence proved that Lynda didn't care enough to be there. I had had no indication that this was a problem for Judy; I thought we had discussed Lynda's need to be gone that week and that everything was OK. I overreacted. The concerns and frustration that I felt about what was happening with Judy's environment magnified the frustration I felt when I heard Judy's words that Lynda did not care about her. Judy seemed to discount not only the feelings I knew Lynda had for her, but also herself as a lovable and valued person. It was at this point that the therapy session turned into a conflict. In my own attempt to prove my point, which was basically that how Judy felt was important, I discounted her feelings. When Judy questioned the therapeutic process and asked me if there was something going on inside me that was contributing to this conflict, I stopped to reflect. What I came up with was that my concerns for Judy's welfare and my emotional connection to her were getting in the way of therapy. I did not have the detachment at that moment that would sharpen the therapeutic process. The paradox and the conflict for me was that the connection between Judy and me was what made Judy's growth possible, and at the same time that connection was making therapy impossible, at least at that moment. I felt very stuck.

"In retrospect, I realized that I wasn't listening to Judy, but was trying to prove my point, which was that she was lovable and valuable. This seemed extremely parental (and therefore negative) to Judy and was certainly not therapeutic. The lesson I 're-learned' was that I needed to be very clear about where I was and what my issues were when I worked with any client, but particularly with a multiple."

JUDY: "During sessions which seemed controlling, I always felt attacked. I felt as though my feelings, thoughts or observations were wrong or bad. Confrontation always left me believing I shouldn't *have certain feelings, and meant that I was not seeing, experiencing and feeling the way I should, and that I should know better. I really felt mixed up and my trust was shaken badly. At times when I felt either controlled or confronted I would immediately withdraw or switch personalities; I certainly could not trust my therapist or the process at those moments. I could not trust someone who at that moment did not accept my feelings or thoughts. I began to feel cornered; I felt the fears of my childhood surround me and they began to smother me. I felt isolated, afraid to move. As soon as I felt that I could not come up with the right answer, I could feel myself drifting backwards, dissociating. My body felt terrorized and my mind began to escape. I was no longer in the room with Doris. That feeling of being controlled caused me to feel overwhelmed and return immediately to my old protective mechanisms. I blocked out much of the conversation."*

The therapist must validate his or her own feelings too. Being a therapist doesn't qualify you for sainthood. We challenge anyone who works with a multiple to say truthfully, "I don't ever have feelings of being abused," or "I never feel like crying or leaving the room," or "I have never felt like saying, 'Damn it—after all I have done.'" In such an intimate relationship, client and therapist get to know each other very well. The multiple comes to know some of the therapist's vulnerabilities while the therapist is getting acquainted with the client's.

What do you do when faced with an angry, or demanding, or extremely needy borderline part who is confusing you with an abusive person from her past? Using Rogerian active listening, reflecting back to the client what she has said and what she may be feeling underneath what she has said, often helps. For a multiple, hearing herself talk, just listening to herself through you, begins to put her back in touch with reality. As she hears, she begins to make a connection between her feelings and what she is thinking; she begins to make her *own* connection. When a multiple is in a borderline place, it is impossible for a therapist to make that connection for her; logic and reasoning don't work. If you try to show that borderline part *your* point, you keep yourself in the parent role, and she will be unable to stop transferring *her* parent onto you, because she has been triggered into an old feeling experience from the past. Using Rogerian techniques allows you to let the client make a connection for herself.

LYNDA: *"The borderline personality is the personification of the egocentric child, whose needs were never met at an appropriate developmental age. You can't expect that personality to act at an older, non-egocentric age; expect that she will be age-appropriate, stage-appropriate. When this particular personality becomes angry at you, work with it. Nurture when you can, and put up boundaries when you need to; reflect the multiple's painful feelings back to her. And as much as possible, stay non-egocentric yourself."*

DORIS: *"I think the problem comes when a therapist gets into a control and power struggle with a multiple's borderline part. The part that is borderline in the* therapist *responds. You don't dare tell your client you are exhausted because she will say, 'I make you tired, you really don't want to work with me,' and turn it around so it feels like your fault. Even the therapist can get caught in being very egocentric."*

LYNDA: *"It is all right for the client and therapist to have these difficulties with transference — they are part of the therapy. You can't have separation without the attachment first, so you have to let that happen. A borderline part may feel rejected when the therapist cannot make a lengthy phone call or step into a parenting role outside of the therapy session. When you must refuse this personality a request, to her it feels like the first time she has needed or wanted; it feels like the hardest rejection, no matter how often you have had ice cream together or how many hours you have already talked to her on the phone. A borderline part lives very much in the moment, but her present may be fixated in past experience."*

DORIS: *"A multiple may have little awareness of time; if she is switching a lot, the fact that last week you spent an extra hour on the phone with one personality won't count to another. When a client is in her borderline part, she may have no concern for the therapist who has to work with six other clients that day. She feels, 'If you don't give me what I want, when I want it, then you are abandoning me.'"*

You cannot expect your multiple's borderline part to be anything but egocentric. That is how she is supposed to be, according to her developmental level. Give her permission to be angry with you when she feels abandoned and to come back when she needs to attach. You are getting into the meat of therapy when transference begins to occur. Much of therapy occurs within the client/therapist relationship itself. In the beginning a multiple may not feel safe enough to expose herself to this degree; when these issues do come up, it can be taken as a good sign that the therapist and multiple now have a good enough relationship for the multiple to show her borderline part.

Many therapists give up and bail out when this work with the borderline part begins, because they become too exhausted, lack adequate boundaries, or allow countertransference issues to interfere. Self-care is a must for the therapist. When you are working with a multiple, you will need a good support system—someone you can talk to, preferably another colleague who also works with dissociative clients. Make sure you set aside adequate time and personal space for yourself. Be consistent in your contacts with the client (see Chapter 6). Consistency not only will help alleviate the borderline part's abandonment fears, but will also help you maintain your boundaries. Learn what your personal limitations are so that you don't push yourself or allow yourself to be pressured to step over your own boundaries. And remember, the multiple is, and will continue to be, a survivor.

If it seems, in this section, that we have spent a great deal of time on borderline personality traits in multiples, it is because the borderline parts more nearly encompass the wide range of emotions, beliefs, and behaviors the therapist encounters in working with multiples. Frequently the most difficult, they play a major role in reconnecting feelings and intellect.

Paranoid Personalities

Just as there are personalities who are borderline or have borderline traits, there may also be personalities who are paranoid or who have paranoid traits. This seems rather normal considering the multiple's childhood experiences. It is true that people really *were* "out to get her" and the fear that this is going to recur reverberates throughout the entire system. The therapist needs to validate for her client that this fear has a very sound basis in fact. What the client doesn't need to hear from her therapist is that this "happened a long time ago" and that it's inappropriate for her to think it can happen now that she is big or adult. These kind of statements reflect the therapist's attempt to help her client reduce the intensity of those feelings through a process of intellectualization. However, those feelings are a result of actual experiences which are exacerbated by the many triggers around her. What the therapist is actually asking the multiple to do here is continue the very process she is trying to change: continue dissociating from the feelings. The client may feel controlled and discounted, very much as she did in her family of origin. Being able to trust the therapist is crucial for these personalities, who will be very sensitive to anything that they experience as an alignment with abusive elements. Just as when working with the borderline parts, it is important for the therapist to help these personalities connect the feelings with the intellect, discounting neither. It is then possible to explore their origin, and begin to re-associate the memories and feelings of the original frightening trauma.

In working with a paranoid part, assessing the age of that particular personality helps in designing an intervention. Many paranoid personalities are child parts who need reassurance and safe containment. Their fears may contaminate other personalities who may then express those fears in a variety of ways, ranging from extreme anxiety, to "hiding out" in her home, to belligerence and loss of trust in the therapist and in others around her. To be able to work with these frightened personalities the therapist needs to keep in mind that they are a part of the "protection," the ones who must remain ever-vigilant if the multiple is to survive. Building trust between these personalities and the therapist is an important piece of the work. If the therapist fears the more belligerent ones, she can make a plan with her client to hospitalize as necessary and continue the work in safer surroundings.

Fixated Personalities

The multiple may have some child personalities who are fixated in the past to the degree that they believe they are living in the same town, the same house they grew up in, etc., and that the abusers are coming to get them at any moment. It is extremely difficult for the therapist to bring these child personalities into the here-and-now, for they have no sense of the present. What the therapist *can* do is to bond with them by creating a safe place in therapy and using herself as a bridge to connect these children with some of the caretaker personalities inside. There are bound to be some adult personalities who "hear children crying" or who know one or two of the children. They can help the therapist by learning to nurture and comfort these children and in this way parent parts of themselves. The children will connect more readily with an inner family member, although paradoxically the therapist may be the initial connector.

Personalities Who Are Substance Abusers

It is not unusual to find a personality (or personalities) who use drugs of some kind. Drugs are one way to reduce physical and emotional pain and maintain denial. This personality may be difficult for the therapist for the simple reason that she may have an entirely different "social" life from the others, one she enjoys and doesn't want to give up. It may seem a very poor trade-off to her to give up pleasure for pain. The work required here is to find out how much co-consciousness she shares with other personalities and who she is most closely connected to in the inside family. Only after much work and strengthening of those relationships can she join her inner family enough to leave her drug-using social group behind. Her own awareness as to why she uses drugs and how this is affecting those she cares about is essential to any change. To understand her role, let go of her own denial, and experience pain require that she feel a powerful caring commitment to those other inner family members.

A therapist may send this personality to AA meetings and/or NA meetings in the hope that drug related behaviors may cease. What might happen instead is that there will be a switch and another personality will emerge to "work the program" and be quite successful, since she didn't have the problem in the first place. The therapist must remember the dynamics of the system and keep in mind that trust, connection, and cooperation among the inner family members are essential to creating change.

Separating the Multiple from
the Abusers

Many multiples who come into therapy will still have connections to
the original abusers. Sometimes they may even be living with them.
Others may have married or be living with a similarly abusive partner.

It is important to assess whether the childhood abusers are still
involved in abuse of your client. You may find that the abusers, who
have aged, are no longer overtly physically or sexually abusive. However,
they will most likely be in denial about former abuse and about the
nature of their relationship with the multiple. You may find that they
are making telephone calls to your client, or sending letters. While
these contacts may not appear abusive on the surface, they may contain embedded messages from the original family system. If there has
been ritualistic abuse, they may still be making connections to attempt
to keep your client involved in cult activities or, at the very least, to
keep her in a state of fear; their contacts may contain embedded programmed messages. The abusers will continue to be very powerful
influences in your adult client's life and the abuse will continue whether it is overt or covert. Through their interactions and contacts with the
client, they will attempt to continue the power and control they had in
the original family system, along with the secrets of the abuse.

Conflicted feelings will arise for the multiple when she is in therapy
and still in touch with the abusers. While many personalities are remembering and validating childhood abuse, a denial personality will
contact the abusers and negate the truth, backing up her view with
"how nice they are now," and the underlying wish to be loved by the
abusers. Although you, the therapist, may never meet the abusers personally, you may feel as if you're in a battle with them for the truth.

At times the client will have difficulty knowing just what the truth is.
If there is generational MPD in the client's family of origin, an abusive
parent may have a nonabusive personality who now wants a relationship with the grown-up child. Abusers will have a vested interest in
portraying themselves currently as nonabusers in order to keep the old
secrets. We have known abusers who wanted to be actively involved in
the multiple's therapy, ostensibly to help their child; abusers may try to
delude a therapist into believing they did not abuse and that the multiple has always had "serious emotional problems."

JUDY: *"It is hard to believe the memories of abuse when you visit people who abused when they were younger, but seem different now that they are older. I struggled to believe that the stories my personalities told were true, because when I was around the abusers, they denied it, and acted so differently from the way I portrayed them in therapy. It was crazy-making."*

Multiples, like all of us, have a basic need and desire to "belong," to be a part of a family. What we are asking them to do is to not belong, and to accept not belonging. So where do they belong? A multiple may have no one to replace her family of origin, especially if she has no current marital partner or nuclear family of her own. Losing her family of origin, such as it is, means grief. She will only be able to deal with this loss little by little, over time.

It may not be possible for a multiple to completely disengage from her family of origin. If ritual abuse was involved, complete separation from the abusers may not be possible prior to deprogramming. The therapist works with the client to accept the reality of the abuse; however, the relationship the client has with the abusers will remain with the client. In other words, as the therapist, don't become embroiled in conflict with your client over whether or not she has contact with the abusers. Don't demand that she confront the abusers. Work with the multiple on becoming clear about the reality of what the abusers did or may still be doing and on protecting herself should one or more personalities decide to have contact.

There is another therapy issue here. The association between the multiple and the abusers may still be symbiotic. When the therapist says, "Your abusers were wrong/bad," the multiple may hear "I am bad/I am my abusers." A multiple may not be able to see the abusers clearly (at least many personalities may not) until she has completed some stage 2 developmental work. Abusers who are still in contact with her make this developmental growth more difficult, because they, too, are "stuck" in the past, wanting their adult child to remain symbiotically attached to them for the preservation of the old family system. This is why working through attachment and separation with the therapist is so crucial, and why it is so demanding at times. A multiple may not even be able to attempt separation from the abusers unless she has done it successfully with her therapist; she has to have a place to learn how to do it. With individual therapy, each personality can be a part of the learning, and that in turn becomes part of the integration. The more personal growth each personality has, the more it brings to the whole, too. Even so, when the multiple is integrated she will have individuation issues yet to work through, since she has never done it "herself" before. The previous learnings, however, give her strength and show her that she has the ability to tackle the job.

Keep your expectations realistic. You can't expect your client, who has many, many parts that are individually working on attaching to you and being separate from *you*, to be clear about their collective relationship with the abusers. There may be personalities who are ready to separate, but certainly not the whole inner family. The client will use her multiplicity to keep her safe, as she always has.

Revictimization

Revictimization can take many forms. A therapist who refuses to believe the client's childhood stories of abuse will revictimize her. The multiple will begin to wonder if what she is saying is true; the therapist's doubt will mirror the abusers' message that she was lying, that abuse never happened. When you work with a multiple, you will hear stories that are bizarre, that will stretch the limits of your imagination. Many forms of abuse, particularly ritualistic abuse, involve using hypnosis or drugs with child victims in order to disorient them further. The child may have been told and believed she was in a boat or an airplane, even when that was physically impossible. The child's perception is her belief, and it is honest and real. A therapist who works with a multiple must be a child advocate; if you cannot believe and support the victim inside, it is not a good idea to work with multiples.

A multiple will be revictimized if she stays in contact with the abusers; the abusers will be invested in maintaining the old family system. If the therapist colludes with the abusers, she can become part of that revictimization. Do not ask the abusers to sit in a therapy session with the multiple, even if a former family member professes to want to help his or her adult child. This is the most certain way to end up colluding with the abuser in revictimizing your client. If former abusers come to session, one truth will be pitted against the other. It is not wise to ask the client to confront her abuser; even if some personalities feel up to this, the child personalities inside who were victimized by this person will feel frightened. Such a session will turn into a display of the multiple's vulnerability, in full view of the abuser, as the client falters in her words, loses her place or train of thought, or makes a visible switch to a frightened or younger personality. The result will be that trust in the safety of the therapy setting and in you will be greatly damaged. It is the therapist's job—not the client's—to be the guardian of safe boundaries within the therapy setting.

Revictimization also occurs when a therapist puts too high an expectation on a child personality or on any personality, for that matter. When the therapist gives a message that the client isn't doing something right, this sounds like the same message she heard in childhood. The client may sense that she has displeased the therapist, although she may not know how, and the disapproval of the therapist will feel like rejection, particularly to a borderline part. It is unrealistic to expect your client to stay in the intellect and act logically and sensibly—particularly at times when she is being triggered by your own behavior or expectations.

The issues we have discussed in this chapter are particularly challenging ones, for both therapist and client. Yet these issues—dealing with abusive and angry personalities; denial, borderline traits and abandonment fears; recognizing and using transference to the best advantage—are often the crucial parts of therapy upon which the success of the journey hinges. Each of these issues involves the *relationship* between the multiple and her therapist. When these difficult issues are resolved in healing ways, the multiple's inner family learns from the therapeutic system how to grow and change.

chapter 9

Integration

T HE CLIENT'S OWN timing is extremely important in the integration process. Some multiples will need very little structure from the therapist as to how and when to integrate; however, in most cases the therapist and the client can work together as a team. When trust and understanding between client and therapist have been growing and thriving for a period of years, the therapist's timing may be in sync with the client's, and the client may feel quite safe with an offer of structure and assistance from the therapist. Some clients may want and need a method for integration, and the therapist can be of help. If the multiple experiences safety and success with the first integration, that will help her to undertake the second and third, and so on.

It is important for the therapist to know that she cannot force integration. The therapist helps the multiple prepare for integration, may help structure the process, and certainly can help by being present and supportive, but the actual integration is something the client will do herself, inside herself. If the therapist does encourage and assist an integration when the client's inner family system is not ready, the integration may appear to "take" for a while, and then disintegrate later. If the therapist is pushy to the point of coercion, the client may have to

218

dissociate to handle the anxiety this will cause. In such a situation, the client may try to please the therapist and feign an integration, or she may hide the personality who was supposed to integrate inside where she will be safe from the therapist. There are many ways to accomplish integration, and they can all work. Take your cues from the client, find out what she wants and what feels comfortable to her; don't try to force her to do it a certain way.

A Safe Inner Place for Integration

DORIS: *"Judy's child personalities told me there was a place inside they could go, a place that they knew and had already been to from time to time called 'the shining place.' The dominant personalities also seemed to have some knowledge of what the 'shining place' was like; it was a place that everyone in the inner family knew about. 'The shining place' was Judy's metaphor for a gathering place where personalities could join together. Many adult multiples may have a specific place where their different personalities are able to meet and make some kind of contact, a place inside themselves where integration or joining can take place."*

JUDY: *"Many times in my childhood I almost died. At those times I had what are called 'near death' or 'out-of-body experiences.' But for multiples they are inner-body experiences. For me, a near death experience was a dissociation, but also a time of connection with the spiritual part of myself."*

DORIS: *"Judy's picture of the 'shining place' fits well with what we know as near death experiences. Many people who have such experiences report a supreme feeling of safety and peace, and moving toward a light. A child who survives an extreme trauma experiences a spiritual journey out of her body; the near-death experience takes her in essence outside herself and into the spiritual world. This initial contact with the spiritual world is internalized and becomes a part of the whole inner system; now the multiple no longer has to go outside herself for her spiritual experience, but inside herself to her own safe place."*

JUDY: *"This is something a multiple has done her whole life—she finds a place within herself to survive and be safe. Other people reach beyond themselves, but the multiple always reaches within herself. She learns to turn inward for safety because there never was a place outside herself for safety. Spirituality was an important aspect of creating the safety of the 'shining place.' I had to create a place as separate and different as I could from the violence and ritual abuse I was involved in as a child. So I created a place of light.*

"During the process of integration my personalities used that place, which was connected to the spiritual personality, as a place to go for the joining of the whole. A feeling of safety for the child personalities was essential for integration. 'The shining place' was a place they could live in forever, a place of safety they had not had in real life as children. It was important that they believed they had an opportunity to feel that safety for the rest of their lives. During the process of integrating, every personality in my inner family connected to that spiritual part. This was the one part of my self that no one could get to, the one part that could never be touched or destroyed by all the abuse. The spiritual part is and was much stronger than life itself, and it gave me the ability to continue surviving. In my integration process, the 'shining place' was one of life and hope and joy."

The inside safe place may contain running water, green grass, bright yellow light, living trees, golden feelings. A safe place is a place of life, and it lends to the integration process a life-giving experience. This is a beautiful reframing of life for the child personalities who have been so terribly abused. They can look forward to leaving and integrating when they can be in a place that feels wonderful and alive, a place where they can live forever and never have to be alone again. They will be with the rest of the inner family in the 'shining place.'

Judy's experience of an inner safe place for integration can be generalized to fit other clients. The factor that is important is safety, whether the multiple describes her inner sanctum as a safe room, a place under a tree, or a place beyond a golden gate. It doesn't matter, as long as it is a safe place created by the multiple inside of herself.

Some multiples may not be aware of their own inner sanctum. It is important for the therapist to help the multiple discover or create her own 'shining place' inside. If possible, it is helpful to have the client decide and describe for herself what her inner safe place is like, rather the therapist creating that description for her. It has to be her own. If she is already aware of having such a place inside, the multiple will not talk about that inner safe place until she feels trusting enough of the therapist, which might be a year or two into therapy. The spiritual is at the very center of the being and that is a very protected place.

Fusion of the Essence and the Core Personality

The sequence of integration for the personalities may be a bit different for each multiple. For example, one client may integrate some non-dominant personalities with the Essence or with another dominant personality following a completed piece of memory work and abreaction; others may join one dominant personality with another if those two are ready first. No matter how it gets started, we believe that the joining of the Essence personality and the original child allows the process of integration to begin in earnest. When the Essence and the Core child join together, the Essence is no longer considered just the essence or shadow of the original child; she is now the "Core person."

How does this happen? The therapist will most likely meet the Essence personality first, and spend time getting to know her, just as the whole inner family will do. As trust and cooperation grow within the system, the Essence spends more and more time "out" in the body. At some point in therapy, the Core or original child will emerge to meet the inner family system that was created to protect her. This will not happen until many dominant personalities have built cooperative alliances among themselves and some of the nondominant personalities, as well as between each other. When the inner family has enough confidence in the therapist as someone they can trust, they will allow the Core child to emerge and to connect with the therapist. The meeting between the Core and the therapist is important; it creates a connection for the Core part with the outside world. She has been so well hidden and protected under layers and layers of personalities that it takes a certain amount of time and trust to allow her awakening within the inner family.

After the therapist and the Core child have connected, then that original child can begin to connect with the Essence personality, the one who has in a sense represented her into adulthood. For some multiples like Judy, the Core child and the Essence personality may merge right away. This can happen if the Essence is strong enough and has spent enough time out in the world to begin to play a larger role in the multiple's life in the outside world at the time the Core child emerges. If the Essence is not yet ready for joining when the Core child emerges, then the two will remain separate until the Essence is able to begin her new role as the connector.

How will you know when these two important personalities have merged? One clue is that the Essence, who has always been dissociated from her childhood, will begin to talk about a childhood. She may also begin to report some memory of childhood, perhaps the few experiences the Core child still carried with her. This connection between the Essence and the Core child may be what allows the other personalities to begin to do their integration. This fusion of the Essence and the Core child may not need to take place in the therapist's office. It is a natural joining that may occur rather spontaneously if both parts are ready.

Integration of Nondominant Personalities

The integration experience can be very different for nondominant and dominant personalities. For the nondominant personalities, who are often child parts, integration seems a gain; joining with others may be just what they wish to do after they have released the old memories and feelings they were created to hold. For the dominant personalities, however, integration involves many losses and feelings of fear and grief. We will discuss integration of the nondominant personalities first, since they may be the first ones ready to join permanently with others.

A lot of work precedes integration, even of nondominant personalities. In a sense, all the work of therapy is integration work. Each personality inside, no matter how small, must be validated, and validation makes it possible for the part to integrate. Each of these younger personalities needs recognition of the fact that she exists. Personalities cannot integrate until they have first been present separately; they cannot merge into the background of the whole until they have been noticed as separate and equal in the foreground.

All the personalities need to have a bond with the therapist, no matter how small a part they are, so they can separate from the inner family enough to emerge fully and tell their individual stories. This "individuation" process precedes the later merging of integration. The experience of their outside contact with the therapist is something each personality also takes back to the whole. Each individual personality needs that outside contact, some way of connecting with the outside world that is different from the abuse she experienced. When the personalities experience a positive outside contact with the therapist, they each internalize it and make it their own. This adds to the personalities, allowing them to integrate with greater health than they would have had without the experience.

The child parts emerge to tell their stories, to abreact, and to give their information about abusive situations and their feelings to the larger system. When abreaction happens the therapist reframes the traumatic experience by providing safety, reassurance, validation, and comfort. Paradoxically, while the child part is in session talking about a terrible unsafe experience, she feels safe enough to tell about that unsafeness, which changes the experience. Safety and validation help bring the child into the here-and-now, which is also preparation for integration with the whole. The safety the therapist creates in session is something the parts can take back with them to the entire family system; it is a gift, given back to the multiple.

Every positive experience that happens for each personality in therapy adds a different dimension to the inner family; every little piece of work is important. In the therapy session, each child part can have an experience of feeling good, feeling safe, feeling somewhat normal. Those positive feelings remain as new learnings for each little personality, even after they have returned to the inside world. And they also give the multiple a little more to work with as an integrated person later.

Touch is a form of therapist contact that is especially valuable to these child personalities. Being held or even feeling the touch of a hand gives them a positive experience of human contact. Nondemanding touch is a gift to parts of a human being who never felt comfort in their lives before. Not all of the little frightened personalities or personality fragments may be physically touched before they integrate, but they get touched with your words, your listening, or by your presence and your feeling for them. These are contacts that are different from the outside contact they received when they were created; these child personalities were created precisely because the contact was so abusive. We believe the major child personalities will benefit tremendously from the experience of positive touch, even if it is just once.

Integration of Dominant Personalities

The dominant personalities' experience of integration is different, because they have had important roles in the multiple's everyday life. Judy provides an example. One of her personalities named Judith had the role of housekeeper and mother, and was the personality involved in a socially appropriate way with her community and her family. When it came time for Judith to integrate, her leaving meant that Judy no longer would have someone separate to take over that role. The dominant personalities actually live their roles; they have real lives in the outside world.

The dominant parts are of major importance in keeping the inner family system going. Because of this, they have fears about giving up themselves and their roles to integration. One fear is that the system will collapse when a dominant personality is no longer available to fulfill a role, and that something awful will happen to the family system. The inner system was originally set up in order to allow the multiple to dissociate the pain in her life; each personality who integrates takes the multiple — and the original child — one step closer to that pain. As the barricades against the pain come down more and more, the dominant personality has to believe that the person she was protecting will be able to handle the pain when she integrates.

Another fear dominant personalities have is for themselves and what will happen to their lives. They wonder, "What happens to me when I give up my role? Where do I go? I am me — I am Judith; I have feelings, I have thoughts, I have likes and dislikes. What will happen to those things which are 'me'?" Although integration means joining and becoming a part of something whole, the dominant personalities *feel* as if they will be leaving their lives behind or dying. At one time in her existence, each dominant personality may have truly believed she was a whole human being, that she was "it." She had hopes and dreams about a future for herself. In the realization that she is only a part of someone, that she is not a whole human being, pain becomes very real.

Recognizing that her life must be not separate but conjoined, she feels a great loss. Her dream of being someone herself is lost. "If I melt into the whole, will my hopes still remain, or will I lose those, too?" That is what the dominant personalities, who may be the mother, the wife, or the career woman, ask themselves.

How as a therapist do you help the dominant personalities prepare for integration? The entire journey of therapy has been groundwork for integration. The first step involves making every personality aware that all the others exist. The next task for the therapist is to find out which of the personalities will be able to be the connector or the bridge for integration; this is the Essence personality. She, in particular must become more aware of those personalities she doesn't know about. The next step is to help the inner family members to become acquainted with one another. As they begin to form working relationships with one another, the therapist reframes each personality's behaviors one to another. Behaviors that seem negative, inappropriate, or restrictive must be reframed as you help the dominant personalities become aware of their roles and their importance in the inner family system. Teach them about systems, how systems and families work; it is important to educate the dominant personalities. Dominant personalities need to know as much about their system's process as possible, and about how and why they exist. Help them to become aware that their reason for being created was to protect the original child.

Next, teach each dominant personality to relate to one another in a way that is caring, rather than competitive. Everyone is working for the same goal, and that goal goes back to protecting the original child. With the awareness of the original child comes the next step. What do they want to do about that child they have been protecting all this time? Is it time for that child to emerge and to come into being once again? If so, how can these personalities help?

Now we are at the cooperation stage of the journey. And this is an especially difficult part for the dominant personalities. They do not want to cooperate with each other at first; because they have their individuality and because they have so much invested in being who they are, cooperative living in itself means a loss. If the dominant personalities don't learn to care about each other, and if they don't believe in the common cause, they will not become willing to cooperate with the others. This is a stage that can take years—learning to help each other, learning to care for one another, to share time and make allowances for each other. Cooperation and caring are major preparatory tasks of the journey.

Meanwhile abreaction will have begun, as memories are being retrieved. The less dominant personalities, the ones who experienced the traumatic events, may abreact the memories and the feelings, and begin to release them to the Essence personality as well as to others in the system. The Essence has been growing in breadth and dominance during this time; if she is ready to receive the abreacted memories and feelings right away, then many nondominant personalities, having finished their work, will be ready to integrate with her at that point. However, if the connector is not ready, the abreactive process may recur until the memories and feelings can be released to the Essence.

So at this point in the road, abreaction may be followed by small integrations of the nondominant personalities who experienced specific abuses or traumatic events. The dominant personalities, who have lives, dreams, and feelings, and who have carved out a place for themselves in the world, will now begin to think about integration — and that process will take more time for them.

The therapist may need to work with each personality who realizes she is only a part, to accept, understand, and process her feelings. This is where some individual therapy comes in. This is also an opportunity for encouraging communication and caring among the dominant personalities, teaching each one why she evolved or was created, what her purpose was for being. It is important to help each personality find the caring part of herself; the caring is there or she wouldn't be a part of that system. This is work that needs to be done over and over before the dominant personalities are willing to join. It is very hard to give oneself up, which is what we are asking the personalities to do when they integrate. It is a loving thing to do.

DORIS: *"What happened in Judy's case was that, over time, each dominant personality became her champion to 'become.' Each one learned to care for her, the Essence. What I saw was that the dominant personalities finally accepted that Judy indeed existed as the major figure, the one for whom they had all taken on these roles. Once they accepted that, they began caring for Judy, wanting her to 'be.' The possibility of integration came out of that caring. They were willing to give up whatever they had built for themselves, because they wanted Judy to be. It was a loving act."*

> JUDY: *"At first, there was an intellectual realization that a multiple is made up of fragments of a self; each personality realized they were only a part of something. Then they searched to find what that original self was, and they were willing to join together in that search. They had discovered what their broader purpose was as a part. A transformation occurred, from investing in separateness, to giving what they had in their lives back to the Essence, who they finally realized was the person they were a part of."*

The inner family system has just so much energy as a whole, and this energy is allocated to each separate personality. As integration begins to take place, many of the less dominant personalities will join with the Essence, who receives their energy. The Essence will as a result become more powerful, and have more and more energy of her own. The other dominant personalities, as they become more aware of the others and of the Essence, will find in turn that they begin to have less and less energy and are unable to be out in the body as long as they used to be. The system's energy, while it remains the same, is being redistributed.

Loss of energy plays a major role in being able to integrate. Loss of individual energy enables the dominant personalities to be more in touch with the reality that they are not the "only one," that they are parts of a whole. Having less will and energy to fight it, as well as more and more reason to join, the dominant personalities move even closer to integration. However, what happens for those who give themselves up for the Essence and for the whole is grief. Much grief work will have to be done before these personalities can integrate, as well as afterward.

> DORIS: *"My experience with Judy was that each dominant personality knew ahead of time that she was going to integrate, and each one prepared herself. We talked a lot about integration and about loss; we talked about what integration meant, that they would be joining, rather than dying. Each one needed to know that she would not be lost, that she would remain an important part of the whole; each one would still be "there," would always exist, but in a different way. Without exception, each of these personalities told me 'good-bye'; then they integrated, when the time was right for them."*

Grief Work and Loss Issues

In doing grief work with the dominant personalities, it is important to help them separate and identify their feelings. They will have a number of losses. During the middle stages of therapy, the dominant personalities will have been receiving memories and feelings in much the same way the Essence has. Becoming aware of the abuse will bring up for them the loss of childhood for the first time. As the nondominant personalities abreact and give up their memories and feelings to the Essence, they will integrate; many of the dominant personalities will then be saying "good-bye" to others in the inner family as they go. Some of the dominant ones have nurtured and taken care of these child personalities inside for years, and the integration of the little ones will be a loss for them.

In addition, the dominant personalities mourn the loss they feel personally when they give themselves up for the good of the whole to integrate. Some personalities will be fighting against integration because of this loss. For instance, the particular personality who married a husband may not want to give up that relationship. The personality who is the wife may experience a real loss in giving up the man she loves to another.

> JUDY: *"Jane, one of my personalities, wrote in her diary how she felt when she married my husband, and how she felt as part of birthing my son. And she wrote that she realized she was not going to have the opportunity to be there in the future after integration because she was not real, she was only part of someone else. She deeply mourned the losses of her husband and her son. And it is part of the loss of being integrated, that although you have all your memories back, you yourself never had the experiences of marriage or birthing when they happened."*

In order to integrate, the multiple has to go back through her pain and accept her childhood as it was. Plus she will trade away the intimate relationships she has developed between her many parts for a different kind of inside relationship. This also causes her pain. A multiple has to trust that the therapist will be there for her not only as she forges ahead through pain, but also as she breaks unfamiliar ground in integration. As the therapist, you must realize that you are asking the client to go through hell. And somehow it has to be worth it for her. She has already been through hell in the past, and now you are asking her to go through it again. However, a multiple wouldn't be sitting in the chair in your office if she didn't believe the pain was worth it; she wants to be whole — and she needs you to be there for her through the integration process.

With all the different kinds of losses the multiple will be weathering during integration, you will have to help her sort them out so she knows which loss she is grieving at the moment — because she will not know. She may become confused about where the pain is coming from, because the pain that she has known prior to integration has always been equated with what happened to her as a child. She has never been in the position that she now finds herself in during and following integration: the position of having to experience her own pain. Pain has always been experienced from a distance or through "someone else," another personality, because that is where the multiple kept it. An integrating multiple must learn about her own pain, what it means, and how to grieve it.

> JUDY: *"It helped me to have my therapists encourage the realization of my losses and encourage me to cry. I needed them to support me in expressing the pain I was feeling through tears, through art or poems, or through talking. My therapists taught me about loss and grief, that it was okay to feel that pain. I know that I minimized my own feelings; I dissociated the loss and grief to some degree while I was going through it so that it would not be overwhelming. On a scale of one to ten my losses were at about a twelve. Grieving also became more intense as the feelings became more a part of me. So I used my dissociative skills to lessen the grief and my feelings of loss at first. It was also okay to feel it over a period of time, to take my time grieving, and not be overwhelmed by those feelings."*

As the therapist, it is not helpful to minimize the extent of the pain or the losses the multiple is experiencing. Accept the multiple's perspective of her sadness and encourage grieving. The client may tend to minimize her own grief, especially at first, and will need much permission and support to go ahead and grieve to the full extent she may need.

For example, many multiples may not even let themselves cry, because crying was something punishable too. While you are encouraging grief work, be sensitive to the multiple's need to *not* grieve as fully as you think she should at the moment; follow her lead, encourage her without rushing her. The multiple can begin to use her ability to dissociate from pain in a positive way. Allow this pain to come out in the way a pressure cooker vents—a little at a time, little by little. Help your client do it her way, in the best way she knows, learning as she goes along. She will know better than anyone else how much grief she can handle. Remember also that the client is doing her grief work right along with the rest of her therapy work, which will include continuing abreaction and integration. These also demand energy from her.

> JUDY: *"In my own case, I also had other responsibilities, such as a family to take care of. I couldn't often just sit down and grieve; I had to be in the real world and function. I couldn't let my grief paralyze me. I had to let it out slowly, at a pace that was comfortable to me and that would allow me to keep going in other areas of my life."*

Grief work will involve many other feelings besides sadness and loss. Anger will surface, as will shame, embarrassment, and depression. Remember that the multiple will be working within her coping cycle during integration. To a multiple, it may seem that once she gets going, memory follows memory and one abreaction leads to another, each stage of the cycle flooding on top of another. It is easy for the client during this stage to snowball into a crisis. The feelings may be so overwhelming that the client feels saturated with pain, sadness, depression, and memories. Be prepared to offer support and interventions throughout the cycle (see Chapter 7).

Developing New Coping Skills and Maximizing the Old Skills

Multiples will continue to dissociate while they are learning new skills. Having new feelings and memories will cause the multiple a lot of anxiety; her first instinct in coping with these memories and feelings and body sensations may be to dissociate from them again. When she finds herself dissociating from what she has worked so hard to obtain, she may then feel shame and guilt. She thinks, "Here I am integrating and I should do better than this. Why am I dissociating?"

When we say multiples may continue to use dissociation, we don't mean they are busy creating new personalities. They are just distancing inside, using the skill they know best. There is some good in that, because when the feelings become overwhelming, it is just not possible to carry and face them all at once. We all use dissociation to some degree to avoid being swallowed up by feelings, e.g., when a loved one dies, when going through divorce, or even while recovering from a car accident. We all have ways of dissociating ourselves from very intense pain. Rather than creating new personalities, multiples may learn to use their dissociative skills in a healthy way.

So if your client seems to be moving along on the road to integration and still does some dissociating, don't let that be a negative for her. Help her understand that dissociation is her way of taking care of herself and that it can be useful in protecting herself from pian that is too hard to handle in the moment. It does not mean that she is going to split off a new personality or that she is not moving toward integration.

Other old coping skills will also remain in use throughout the process of integration. The multiple will continue to use her coping cycle to deal with the new memories and feelings that she gains with each integration, and to deal with the feelings of loss and grief. The Essence, now joined with the Core, has become the new Core person. She will gradually learn how to handle new memories and feelings with each abreaction she observes and participates in, and with each integration of other personalities.

The multiple learns new coping skills throughout her journey in therapy. The therapist will be encouraging her to face, feel, and express her memories and feelings through art, journaling, play, and talking. The important thing is for a multiple to learn to get what is being held inside out where it can be acknowledged, expressed, explored, clarified, and gradually dissipated. Rather than holding feelings captive and encapsulated inside, she learns to share them with the inner family and with trusted people in her outside world. These are the same coping skills she will be perfecting as she works through integration and beyond.

At the point where many major integrations have taken place, *posttraumatic stress* will remain. A newly created person—that person who is the joining of the Essence, the Core child, and all the other personalities — now takes on all the memories and feelings she has received from the others. Prior to integrating, each personality had dealt with a share of the memories and feelings on his/her own, separately. Now the integrated person must cope on her own; for this new person, it may feel like starting over. It is up to her alone to do something with these memories, feelings, and body sensations that are now hers. She can no longer simply make a new personality to deal with these things. As a multiple, she always had someone "else" available to deal with life, and now she can no longer call upon other personalities for help. There is no one watching from the inside, no one to protect her; she is truly on her own. More than one multiple has noted that to have someone else, i.e., another personality, take the job is easier than to handle it herself.

The multiple must now learn milder, gentler ways of putting off feelings until she can deal with them. The therapist can also reassure her client that she already has ways to cope at her disposal. Despite her integration, she will continue to use some old coping skills like manic behaviors and milder dissociation when memories and feelings are intense. The cycle we talked about will still be very much in use, although the behaviors may appear in milder forms. Just as she has learned to use and modify her cycle during other phases of her therapy, the client can continue to use and intervene in her old cycle. Using the old cycle in new ways becomes part of her new coping skills. It is important for the integrated client to know that it is perfectly all right to do what she does; everyone has to have defensive coping skills.

Far from being a paradise, she will find her new life still full of triggers that can cause anxiety, fear, and remembered pain. The integrated client must learn to deal with these recurring triggers over time. She will practice her new coping skills and modify the old ones for better use along the way. It is important for the integrated client to remain in therapy. Therapy continues to be a setting where the client can express and vent the many feelings she is experiencing and finding a place for inside.

The Multiple's Post-Integration Experience

Many multiples, as well as therapists, have misconceptions about life after integration. One myth is that integration means that therapy is finished, and now you can get on with your life. Another myth is that an integrated multiple will no longer have problems, or have a hard time with the childhood memories, or have feelings about them. This kind of thinking leaves no room for being a normal human being following integration.

Although the integrated client is no longer a multiple, she is still a person who has been terribly abused and who will have residual effects from that abuse. She now begins a class called "Real Life 101." This new person will be learning to experience life outside of therapy, a life that may include a husband, friends, and a career.

What does integration feel like to a multiple?

> JUDY: *"There was an awareness that a part of myself had been filled and wasn't empty anymore. There was an awareness of the self, of being more full as a human being. I filled myself up, with my inside parts connecting to create a complete inner person that I had never been before. Sometimes I had physical sensations when I did integration work; sometimes I felt the pain the other personalities had carried with them when they integrated with me. But to be filled, to feel whole as a human being—that in itself was new."*

Other multiples may report feeling "thicker," fuller or taller. They may find that visual clarity improves, or hearing is better. With many integrations, the inner silence that results may allow more awareness of the outside world and its sights and sounds. The experience of integration will be a bit different for each multiple.

> JUDY: *"For me, integration means that I am a whole human being. It means that I learn to use my whole self in living, something I had never done before. The whole self includes all the stuff each former part brought to integration. I still have my memories and pain; I will carry it with me every day for the rest of my life. I thought at first that integration meant not having memories or feelings anymore about the past abuse, not even thinking about them; but they didn't go away when I integrated. Integration is not the great cure-all. It doesn't mean you will thank your therapist, leave therapy, and have a happy life. You will still have problems to deal with. Integration doesn't make the memories of abuse go away, it doesn't stop the pain from hurting. What I had to deal with was how to feel my feelings without letting them overwhelm me. Now that I am integrated, I am*

learning how to cope with my past—not a part of myself, not another personality, but me—I am learning it.

"In therapy, I learned that real people do have "stuff"; other people are no more or less than I am in my struggle with life. As a multiple, I learned how to disguise my pain, and that's really a good skill at times to have in the world. So as therapy continued I learned to use my old coping skills in a positive way. I learned that whatever works, whatever is comfortable, is OK. A certain way of coping is not good or bad; what's important is what is comfortable for me. I learned that I get to choose."

Is integration worth the work? And if so what makes it worth it? We believe it is worth the work; the client still has the memories of what happened, but now she has the opportunity to live.

JUDY: *"I think anything less than integration is only a superficial bandage on a large deep wound. I believe that integration is worth the effort. Finally, after being subjected to abuse, never feeling good about myself, and hiding inside all these years, I am able to experience the good things in life. For the first time the child inside can see that there is another side to life other than the horrible things she experienced.*

"The pain and memories of the abuse are still there; no matter how hard you try to put it away, it stays with you. I will always remember what happened to me. But I am learning to make something of what I've got—the best possible life for myself. Now I can enjoy all the little things in life. I have such a deep appreciation for just waking up in the morning, seeing the day, knowing I'm still alive. I think my experiences of being abused and going through the healing process have enabled me to value life even more. Life is much fuller for me now than I could have ever dreamed. It seems like a treasure, that my life is now my life. After the loss of all those years, I don't want to waste any more time. I hate feeling depressed, or having issues still to work on in therapy!

"To other multiples I would say that it's going to be a tough road— but go for it. Go for the gold! Because the child who suffered all those atrocities finally has the chance to just stop and smell the flowers. She won't get that chance if she stays in parts. It is only through integration that the child will have the fullness of a human being to experience life for herself."

Lost Developmental Stages and the
Integrated Multiple

Integrated multiples will be learning skills from missed developmental stages, just as their many personalities have done throughout the therapeutic journey. Although she gains much experience from the integrated experiences of her many parts, the integrated client is a new creation; she has never had a chance to have life experiences *herself* until now. Remember, after a certain point in time the child who became a multiple was "gone," and the other personalities did her living for her; their experiences were the multiple's experiences—but not the reintegrated client's experiences. What the client has after integration are the memories and the feelings, but not the actual experiences. So she will be learning many new skills for herself, as the new person that she is.

> DORIS: *"Therapists may not realize that once a multiple is integrated, she still has not had the actual experiences of living. Memories are not the same as living through day-to-day processes. Following integration, the client is again a very intelligent person who has done all this work—and yet has some confusion about the how-to's of life. I believe this comes from not ever really having experienced life, and never having been allowed to grow through developmental stages."*

We will discuss briefly some of the developmental learnings that take place with integration, following along with the first five developmental stages. One learning involves trust versus mistrust. Trust is something multiples will be assessing and learning as a risk-taking experience throughout their lives, even after integration. After so much abuse, it is only natural to be slow to trust others. However, the relationship with the therapist that has been built on trust, along with the resultant healing, is a good beginning.

> JUDY: *"I have learned over time that I can trust a few people in my life. Let me say, I have some trust for some people; I still do not and probably will not ever completely trust again. I won't let people ever again have total power over me. I still see power and trust as connected, and I would expect people to misuse their power over me if I trusted them completely, so I don't."*

As therapy continues during and after integration, the client will learn how to make personal space for herself, how to have privacy, and how to have boundaries. She needs to know what does and doesn't feel intrusive, and how to keep her boundaries from being violated. Boundaries and control issues are part of stage 2 developmental work. The integrated client will be trying on her new independence, and struggling with the stage-appropriate fears and guilt while she does so.

> JUDY: *"I still have to have some control of a situation to feel safe. Yet I have learned to voice my opinions and state my needs and have that feel OK."*

Working with boundaries and learning to feel comfortable with more control or less control are tasks that most people have to keep working on throughout their lives, at least to some extent. It is important that a therapist have appropriate expectations for a newly integrated client. Because the client is a very intelligent person who has come such a long way, a therapist may expect that she would have these issues pretty well resolved—but this will probably not be the case. Reassure her that she does not need to feel shame or guilt when she wants to take control or when she finds herself doing that. Issues with boundaries and control are a legacy of severe abuse.

Stage 3 involves learning to take the initiative and risk new things, without feeling guilty. For a multiple it is extremely risky to take the initiative. She learned very early that her role was to obey rules set forth by others. Any independent behavior on her part was promptly negated by cruel and demeaning punishment, leaving her with feelings of shame and guilt. Reactive behavior rather than risk-taking became her way of life. In the world outside the family the different personalities, not knowing what was expected of them there, learned how to fit in by observing the behavior of others. These behaviors came as a rote experience, never assimilated as her own and therefore never allowing for the flexibility that comes from having prior knowledge. Behavior was always subject to change, depending upon the behaviors of those around her. This certainly accounts, in part, for the differences in behaviors of personalities of all ages and the difficulty they have with one another in understanding that behavior.

A multiple who has integrated will retain the ability to observe, react, and behave accordingly but she will have very few resources of her own until she has been able to risk and experience the world for herself. To do this she needs a solid and safe "home base" to return to when fears of failure and inadequacy engulf her. She will need someone to encourage her, someone to teach her, someone to support her and someone who understands how difficult her struggle is. This person will, in all probability, be her therapist. The shame and guilt that are a major part of her existence and very closely related not only to her abuse but also to the loss of this developmental stage will continue to distress her.

Stage 4 involves making relationships with peers and feeling good about physical, intellectual, and social skills. Relationships will be a particularly difficult task for a multiple, even after she is integrated. She is trying out being "herself" now, someone she may not have been for thirty years or more. Children learn by observation and experimentation. This is hard for the client, who is just beginning to develop social skills as an adult and is acutely aware that other adults will assume she already has these skills. And because of her past abusive relationships, she will have to unlearn and relearn old ways of being with people. One thing a therapist can do is talk about how other people do things. Most of us do learn by watching when it comes to dealing with our peers.

> JUDY: *"It is easy enough to learn how to laugh; it is harder to learn to cry when it is appropriate. Learning to make friends, learning to feel accepted, learning how to 'be' so that I don't feel too vulnerable—all these things are difficult. I've had to learn how much to give of myself in a friendship; for example, am I giving too much or not enough? What do others expect of me? I'm learning how to be more consciously aware of my own self when I'm with others."*

The last stage of development in childhood years is stage 5, adolescence. A multiple enters adolescence not having completed the first four developmental stages and therefore totally unprepared for this stage. To develop an ego identity, to individuate from the family—these are the tasks of the adolescent and they are foreign to the multiple. Each personality has had her own identity and each has coped with the particular set of problems she was created to take care of. Individuation was not even a consideration. How will this affect the integrated adult client? She will find herself in the midst of an identity crisis, confused about her role and with few skills to master the last of the five stages of childhood development. In the final stages of her therapy she confronts this new task by experimenting and experiencing who she is in the world. During this time the therapist serves not only as someone who validates her client's search for self and her personal growth, but also as the one who can teach the process of individuation; for it is at this stage that the client begins to assert her independence, a healthy developmental response to growing ego strength.

> JUDY: *"Because I have learned to intervene much better in my own cycle of coping with stresses, I have been able to individuate more from my therapists. I've found I can often 'do it myself,' and it feels good. Finally I have more control of my own life. It's something I never had before, and it feels powerful."*

One of the major goals of therapy is to help the multiple take back control. She will have a lot of neediness that has to be taken care of first; she will want to be independent and at the same time want to be taken care of. If the therapist can realize that the client truly wants to be a strong, independent individual and that at the same time she will have needs for nurturing, then she can help the client achieve her goal without being so fearful of the client's dependent part. As a therapist, you may find yourself in some verbal fights with the client who is learning in this developmental stage, and that is a good sign. For the client to be able to argue with her therapist, stand her ground and get her point across knowing that an argument doesn't mean death or the end of a relationship is healthy. She will use the relationship with her therapist to learn that people can disagree and still be friends. As a therapist, you need to allow the client to try out these new skills with you in therapy. You may find yourself growing right along with your client.

Reclaiming the Body

One of the ways a multiple survives horrible abuses is to dissociate from her body. Multiples may appear to have no problems with physical contact; they may be able to accept a hug or respond sexually to their mates as if they are very much in contact with their bodies. But in reality, the body will react in a manner that is behaviorally learned, which is quite different from feeling. Through integration, a multiple may connect emotions with memories of abuse; however, she may still not be connected to her body. Without the connection of body and mind there can be only partial healing, and the core person who has integrated all her personalities may still be missing some big pieces of self-esteem.

Addictive behavior involving drugs, alcohol, sugar, caffeine, etc., may be a continuation of self-abuse in an integrated multiple. Although integrated, the client may use old patterns of addiction to numb the body, soothe the pain, and control the body—thereby denying the body. This continues the punishment/addiction cycle from the family of origin. While she may no longer act out abuse, the integrated multiple, like others recovering from abuse, may still try to desensitize the body; and the body may still ask to be recognized. To heal fully, release and integration must happen in the body as well (Bass & Davis, 1988).

> JUDY: *"So much objectification occurred when I was a child that I thought of my body as a 'thing.' The 'thing' is what got abused sexually or physically, and the 'thing' was something I had to leave because I could not bear the pain that was placed on or within it. I was able to dissociate from the shame, guilt and pain by seeing my body as the thing that was abused, rather than myself. To this day it is hard not to see my body as a 'thing,' but as a part of me. Even though my awareness now is that this is my body, it's hard for me to stay in contact with it."*

It is not only the physical or sexual abuse of the body that makes dissociation necessary for the child. The body was viewed as "bad" by others and as something the abusers controlled. The child was made constantly aware of this by the behaviors and remarks that abusing adults made and by what these people showed the child about her body. If ritual abuse occurred, separation from and abuse of the body may also have been programmed. Looking at her body through other people's eyes, the child sees an ugly object; the child then believes what they tell her and internalizes these messages. So there are three different dynamics that cause the child to have an extremely negative view of her body and to dissociate from it. First, the body is used and abused, causing overwhelming pain; secondly, the abusers give the child nega-tive messages about her body and remove her personal control of her body; third, the child comes to view her body as bad, ugly, and as an object as well.

Using touch as part of therapy helps the client begin to recontact or re-associate with her body. The touch of a hand, or giving and receiving hugs teaches her that positive, nonharmful touch is possible. We are talking about nondemand touch; it is the choice and the lack of de-mand that make touch unintrusive and safe. Verbal reframing also helps. The body must be reframed from a negative to a positive, just as if it were a separate personality—because it, too, has been split off and rejected. One of the hardest things for a multiple to hear and accept is that others view her positively. She must come to believe that she did not bring the abuse on herself, that it didn't happen because she was ugly or unlovable. Constant reframing is needed for the client to begin to see herself as a lovely person and to believe that others also see her that way. The whole process of therapy involves giving the multiple new messages about herself with which she can replace the old nega-tive ones, and providing a setting in which she can internalize those positive messages.

Reclaiming her sexuality will be a difficult task. Anyone who has been sexually traumatized to the degree that multiples have may con-tinue to feel unsafe with sexuality. A female client may want to remain somewhat unfeminine in her looks and style; to be female can mean being used. The less feminine she is, the less desirable she looks, the safer she may feel. In essence she may wish to be androgynous, neither male nor female. A therapist must be sensitive to the client's funda-mental and continuing need to protect herself. Reclaiming the body is a slow process that extends past integration. A client may never totally reown her body—and that should be all right. It is important to allow people to maintain the protective barriers they need to keep surviving; when the wound has been very deep, some protection may have to remain.

Body work with multiples, as well as with other clients, is a relatively new field. However, we have found that the work to reclaim the body and all the physical feelings may be best done following the reclaiming of memory and emotions. Doing the body work first may bring up the memories, but it will also open up vulnerabilities that may be too difficult for the first few stages of therapy. In addition, if client and therapist cannot achieve the results they are hoping for, feelings of failure or a renewed need to dissociate from the body may follow.

DORIS: *"I think we as therapists need to be realistic when we work with terribly traumatized people. We cannot expect miraculous results in a short period of time, and we must be patient. Adult multiples have taken care of themselves through dissociation for years, and will be unable to make changes overnight. I use this simple theory with all my clients. I do not expect my clients to be today where they would like to be tomorrow, because that just isn't possible. Today is where they are, so I go with that. Multiples are often anxious to work so rapidly that they get ahead of themselves. As a therapist, your worry will be not that the client isn't moving fast enough, but that she is trying to move too fast. A multiple in therapy wants so much to become a whole person; she needs to be reassured over and over that where she is now is OK, and that she is doing fine in working toward where she wants to be."*

In reclaiming the body, the client learns to use her body in positive ways. When she experiences emotional pain or high anxiety from triggering or remembering, she finds a means of working through that pain without harming her body. Even after integration is complete, she will have negative energy that needs to be dissipated when memories and feelings tumble around inside. The client needs to know that she will probably turn to her old cycle, but that she can trade the extremely harmful behaviors of the past for something less harmful, e.g., cleaning one room instead of the whole house. She needs to be reassured that she does not have to be disappointed in herself for doing so.

JUDY: *"During the process of having memories, abreacting, and having the pain of those memories in my body, I thought of the pain as happening to this body, this 'thing' I didn't like anyway. Learning to reverse those thoughts and make the container of that pain into a positive was very difficult for me. One of the few things I could do to punish myself during my cycle was to take it out on my body by abuse or to use alcohol or drugs. Not only did I have to learn other ways to punish myself that caused less harm, but when it came to reclaiming and owning my body, I also had to find other ways to deal with my emotional pain without punishing. The work of a multiple is so all-encompassing, involving so many levels. It takes a lot of effort to become healthy when you've been so badly abused. Hard work remains even after integration."*

Continuation of Memories Following Integration

After integration, multiples—like other human beings—do not have complete memory of every event that occurred in their lives. This is particularly true of negative events. Although a multiple has worked through the very major traumas and all the known personalities are now integrated, that does not mean that every piece of every memory has been retrieved; there may still be bits and pieces that remain hidden. It is important for the therapist to be aware that multiples, like most people, will have triggers in current life that will suddenly loosen unclaimed memories they have forgotten and which still exist. If the client has been ritually abused, there may very well be some programming which is deeply embedded in the unconscious, and is yet to be uncovered. For some clients, the ego strength gained in integration provides enough safety to now begin that work.

We have found that, even at the point where integration seems complete, a multiple may continue to call up and process the remaining bits and pieces of memories though dissociated personality fragments. These fragments are smaller than the former nondominant personalities were, and much less complete. When and if new personality fragments appear with still-to-be-reclaimed memories, the newly integrated multiple may feel as if she has failed at integration; she "should" be finished with all the memories, she "shouldn't" be using dissociation to remember old stuff anymore. You can reassure her that having bits and pieces to process does not in any way negate or invalidate the integrations she has already completed. Both client and therapist must be aware of creating false expectations of integration and of being "finished." Continuing to have memories surface, even in the form of personality fragments, does not negate the integration she has already achieved; what she has done is done. It only means that dissociation may continue to be her method of choice in processing the remaining memories.

> DORIS: *"During Judy's post-integration work, she was more and more able to use her cognitive skills to have control over her work. I have watched her learn to design her own treatment program, to say 'Well, OK—something is coming up for me. I'm not sure what it is. . . . Let's go do some art work. I think I'll work in clay, or maybe I'll paint.' And out of her own ideas, and with her own control, she has been able to bring out from the inside what was surfacing and talk about it."*

Finally, after all the bits of memories and all the personality fragments have been reclaimed, and after all the deprogramming has been completed, some symptoms of post-traumatic stress will probably remain. Environmental triggers may no longer cause dissociation, but will churn up anxiety, as well as old memories and feelings—all of which is normal.

> JUDY: *"Since integration, my relationship with my therapists has changed, because I have changed and my needs have changed. I'm doing OK. I'm learning how to make decisions about things, I am learning how to be on my own. I am still dealing with post-traumatic stress because I am still a person who was terribly abused; I still deal with issues about abuse, with triggers, and I still work on self-esteem. I don't think the rest of my life will be void of the old abuse issues, but it will be under the surface, instead of on the surface all the time. The abuse has left a big scar, but it doesn't take up all my energy trying to keep those memories of abuse away. I feel really lucky."*

> DORIS: *"I like to think of post integration as having a photograph album in which all your history is in pictures. When you first take a picture it is very clear and easy to see; over time the picture begins to fade and turn a little yellow. The images are not as clear and distinct, but they are still there. There may always be feelings and thoughts from time to time about those old pictures."*

FIGURE 9.1: This drawing shows Judy's exultant child in charge of her own power.

JUDY: *"One of the things I was so frightened of was the pain of remembering. I thought I would die from it. But you know, I can live with the pain of remembering now. Just recognizing it as painful deflates some of the anxiety about feeling it. Being integrated, I now have the means to fight my own battles. I use my anger to fight child abuse as well, making people realize what abuse does, and why people abuse. I don't want society to dissociate this information, so I have made it my job to help other people become sensitive to it. This helps me feel my own power.*

"In closing, I want to teach multiples that through the process of integration, you can become everything you were meant to be, as best you can. And this is a great gift you can give that terribly hurt child you once were. You can take back your power and your own life." (See Figure 9.1.)

chapter 10

Ritualistic Abuse

Ritualistic abuse (also called "ritual abuse") is any kind of abuse done in a ceremonial or systematic form by a specific group. The group can be described as a cult or any organized (usually religious) group that performs purposeful rituals that have specific meaning to that organization. Although a child may be abused by one individual in a ritualistic manner, for our purposes we are talking about abuse that occurs in groups. We believe that satanic abuse does occur, and that when you encounter ritual abuse you will more than likely be working with multiples who were involved in satanic cults or their offshoots.

Our own experience indicates that there may be a very high rate of ritual abuse among multiples. Of the population we are most familiar with, which includes our clients and those of our colleagues, two-thirds have been involved in ritual abuse as children. Some adult multiples in therapy have personalities who remain in contact with the cults, making the work in therapy more difficult. We believe it is very important for therapists to be aware of the fact that ritual abuse does exist and has a tremendous impact on their clients. Our goal is not to alarm therapists but to aid them in finding ways to work with their clients who have been ritually abused.

The Credibility Factor

JUDY: *"I speak not only for myself but also for other multiples when I say that the stories we tell about just physical and sexual abuse are often extraordinary. The memories of ritual abuse sound even more bizarre, and telling feels very risky. The fear you have, and the fear you grow up with, is that such stories will never be believed. In fact, as a child I was told that no one would believe me, so I might as well not tell. The incredulity that such atrocities actually happened to a child and that the child or adult could truly remember it makes the telling more difficult."*

Multiples themselves have great difficulty believing that ritual abuse could have happened to them. They may have a very different relationship with the abusers as adults than they did as children. Such abusers make sure they protect themselves from being found out, and may present a very different aspect of themselves to the grown-up child, particularly when she is in therapy. They want to be seen as good, helpful people by the therapist. This can be confusing for the multiple as she looks at these people who appear now to be kind and caring. But the multiple is faced with more than the denial of her personal abusers; the denial in our culture is so powerful that the reality of ritual abuse remains hidden.

JUDY: *"As an adult I went to church, I was well-read, I watched the nightly news. Although I stayed informed, there wasn't a clue in any of this that ritual abuse was a part of the world I lived in. So how could I believe that such a thing had happened to me? The life experience I saw and heard around me was so different from what had actually happened to me that I doubted myself. I thought, how could this be true?"*

Ritual abuse seems so out of the ordinary, so outrageous, so dark, that it is set off in a category by itself. Yet people are intrigued by that darkness. For example, when the motion picture "Silence of the Lambs" came out, people were shocked—but they flocked to see it. People are not prepared for the outrageous to happen in real life, nor are they prepared to believe that something like ritualistic abuse can happen on a large scale. They can believe that it happens in one or two isolated cases, but not that it occurs in an organized, systematic manner. However, the truth is that what are now called religious cults have been in existence for centuries.

In our culture, we have a difficult time believing that child abuse in general is widespread. The laws against sexual abuse in this country were not adopted in most states until the 1970s, and it took years longer for the possibility of incest to become a routine part of psychological assessments by therapists in the field. Ritualistic abuse, seen as one step beyond other types of abuse, seems to exceed the believable. The fact that an entire society can scarcely believe that such activities occur makes it even more difficult for a multiple who has been ritually abused to believe that it happened to her. Other than in the make-believe realm of television and movies, there is little in our culture that we can point to and say, "See — ritual abuse does happen."

> JUDY: *"In my own case, much of the ritual abuse was set up to make it look as if what happened during the activity wasn't true or couldn't have happened. The element of unreality helps to disorient the child and ensure that she won't disclose or be believed. It was one more way the abusers confused me and kept me in denial. I felt crazy telling these stories of abuse as an adult. Stories in the news media or on talk shows about individuals involved in "bizarre satanic rites" seemed to discredit those telling about the abuse and were presented as isolated instances. When I began to understand that even the mental health field had skepticism about ritual abuse, I really felt defeated. I wondered if there would be anyone I could tell, or anyone who would understand and believe me. There are so many therapists who still don't believe multiple personality exists, let alone ritual abuse."*

In 1992 our profession has just begun to believe and to accept that multiple personality is not the rare condition it was once thought to be. It will probably take much more time for therapists to accept the prevalence of ritualistic abuse. Meanwhile those multiples who have suffered this type of abuse must maintain their own system of denial in order to fit in with the larger society. Therapists who have knowledge of and believe in the actuality of ritual abuse are in a position to lead the multiple out of her denial, to face the reality of the abuse, and so begin the road to healing.

Indicators of Ritualistic Abuse

Most multiples who were or are involved in ritual abuse will at some point during therapy begin to divulge information to the therapist if an atmosphere of safety has been established. Be aware that you may not hear about ritual abuse from the client until years after she begins therapy, although there may be signs much sooner. If you know what to look for, you can spot a history of ritual abuse early in treatment. However, it is important to trust the client's timing in bringing up this issue; if she has been ritually abused, it will be the most frightening of all her traumatic experiences. While some clients do bring up ritual abuse information early in treatment, many wait until a great deal of trust has been built with the therapist.

What are some of the signs of ritual abuse? The client may show extreme fear around Christian holidays that coincide with satanic holidays, such as Halloween, Easter, or Christmas. Birthdays may contain special dread. Drawings may contain pictures or symbols of ritual abuse (see Figure 10.1); poems and journals may suggest cult involvement by the content or use of unusual symbols or handwriting. You may notice specific hand movements or responses to environmental triggers that suggest the client may have been programmed.

Triggers from outside stimuli such as photographs, movies, television, books or magazines may cause switching and chaos for many multiples, but if the client has been ritually abused, the triggers may be much more subtle. For such a client, a common word or phrase, a hand or body motion from a stranger, certain colors or styles of clothing may trigger switching or programmed responses. Some cults use brainwashing, programming, hypnosis, and drugs to accomplish their goals with child victims. Many multiples who were ritually abused were programmed during the rituals to stay in contact with the cult, to report back about disclosure, or to return to participation in the cult. This is the way that the cult and the abusers stay in control. Some excellent information about ritualistic abuse and programming is available in the field. Some resources for information on ritual abuse are *Combatting Cult Mind Control* (Hassan, 1988), *Cults That Kill* (Kahaner, 1988), *Ritual Abuse: Definitions, Glossary, the Use of Mind Control* (Los Angeles County Commission for Women, 1991), *Michelle Remembers* (Smith & Pazder, 1980), and *Suffer the Child* (Spenser, 1989).

FIGURE 10.1: A drawing of ritual abuse made by an older personality.

From a systemic point of view, it makes sense that a multiple who was ritually abused will have one or more personalities who were created to carry out assigned roles in the cult. These personalities will continue to be a part of the inner family system, even if the adult is no longer involved in the cult. The inner system will be set up *as if* the cult still existed in her life. And if the multiple was programmed at one time as part of the ritual abuse (which is almost a certainty), the program may still be actively working to either keep the client in contact with the cult or to keep the client feeling as if she were still in contact with the cult even when she is not. She will have the same fears and responses to programmed stimuli, even if she is not actively involved with the cult at present. Active involvement can range from current participation in rituals, to physical contact with cult persons, to being the victim of subtle forms of harassment by active or nonactive cult members. Former abusers may keep the multiple oppressed by telephone calls and letters containing words or symbols used in the initial programming.

Therapist Fears

Many therapists worry that there is danger in working with clients who have been ritually abused. One fear is that the cult will harm the therapist. We know of therapists who have worked with many, many ritually abused clients, both children and adults. While these therapists have on rare occasions received a letter from a nonclient cult member, none that we know of has been threatened personally at their homes or offices. Cults have no reason to risk exposure by threatening a therapist. Our intent as therapists is not to challenge or expose cults. Our intent as writers is to help therapists who work with clients who have been ritually abused, so those clients may become whole persons.

Another fear is that a client who is or was involved with a cult may harm the therapist. Our experience has been that multiples who come in for therapy and stay for this arduous journey really want to be whole, want to be well. A client who is in therapy may have one or more personalities who because of programming are still interacting with the cult or with cult members; however, other personalities will be extremely frightened by cult involvement, by the pull of programming, or by the memory of past ritual abuse. The inner family system as a whole, when bonded by trust to the therapist, will work very hard to separate from this kind of abuse. They do not want to harm the therapist or to be harmed themselves; they want out. The participating personalities act out of the need to survive.

Both multiples and therapists may have misconceptions about the power of the cult versus the power of the client. A cult may deliberately use hypnosis and programming to cause the child to split off personalities that can be used as victims or victimizers during the rituals. The child may come away from the experience believing that the cult "made" certain personalities and that the cult therefore owns her and is in charge of her. However, the truth is that all of the multiple's personalities *were created by the multiple herself* — to cope with trauma and to allow her to survive. *She* created her own personalities.

The client may have a personality who is programmed to do destructive things to someone else during a ritual. However, even though this may be the case, the therapist can let her know that she is not going to do that in the therapist's office: there is no point in doing it in the office, because she is not in the cult at the moment. Nor does the cult have that kind of power over her. What the cult does have the power to do to the client is terrify her, and thereby frighten the therapist as well. The child who is victimized by a cult has almost all her power removed by her abusers; further, they induce her to believe that they still have total control over her for the rest of her life. However, even during the most tormenting abuses, the child retained power: the power to dissociate, to split, and to keep her innermost self protected. She has that power still, as an adult. The reality is that the child created her own personalities, and she can, with the therapist's help, reframe them, deprogram them, and heal.

> JUDY: *"Cults use not only physical and sexual torture but also spiritual abuse; they try to rape your very soul. They coax you, rape you, drug you, and beat you into believing you belong to them, that you are their 'thing' to use in any way they desire. I believed my abusers, of course; I was only a child. It was a wonderful reframing to hear my personalities were not owned or even made by the cult. It helped me take back some of my own power."*

As a therapist, you will first come up against your own fear and your own denial. You will need a strong spiritual foundation of your own in order to undertake the therapeutic journey with a client who has been ritually abused. You will need to be grounded in whatever spiritual belief you have and you will need to stay centered in order to help the multiple weather the storm of remembering. A child personality may need a very concrete answer to a very specific spiritual question; unless you believe in something yourself, you will find yourself at a loss.

Working with Ritually Abused Multiples

Working with multiples who have been ritually abused does not require a therapist to have a different mind set or a whole different set of skills in order to be competent. However, we do suggest that any therapist who works with a multiple read and attend workshops about ritual abuse. Use the acquired information naturally, as it pertains to what *your* client is bringing up in session. The therapist must believe that ritualistic abuse does exist, or she will become a part of the multiple's denial system. Let yourself be open to what the client shows you, and she will teach you. Even after informing yourself as much as possible, it is important to keep in mind the client's uniqueness, her timing, what you know about her and what she knows about herself.

Child victims of ritualistic abuse did not choose to participate in such events; they were forced. The personalities that were created during ritual abuse allowed the child to survive specific events. What you may see is an abusive personality, or a self-destructive personality who acts upon the belief that the cult still has power over her. This personality may be one who endured the actual abuse, one who participated in order to live, or a personality who was programmed to maintain the abusers' control by reporting on or punishing other personalities who disclose the secrets.

The stories of ritual abuse may be told through the eyes of a terrified observer personality, by those who endured the abuse, or by a personality who was created to hold the memories but was dissociated from the emotions and physical pain of the trauma. The therapist must move slowly with these parts who have seen and experienced such abuse; they are usually the most severely damaged personalities within the multiple.

We use the same techniques in working with multiples who have been ritually abused as we use with any multiple. Affirm the different personalities as they appear. Listen to the stories they have to tell and help them accept as truth the horrors of their lives. Each personality has a place and a function within the inner family system, and will need to work through feelings of shame and pain, as well as feelings of being "different." A multiple who has survived ritual abuse may need to know that the abusers and the ritual acts could not and did not remove her soul from her, that she never lost her spiritual part. In fact, survivors of such spiritual abuse may have an enhanced spirituality about them.

Personalities who are angry or destructive will need the same acceptance, respect and reframing that any other such personality would (see Chapter 8). Allow them to express and diffuse their rage safely, realizing that such feelings exist with good reason. Some personalities will suffer guilt for their participation in cult practices and guilt for surviving when others didn't. It is important to reinforce the fact that when a personality participated in abuse, it was to enable the child to survive, or to gain approval, or to satisfy other needs for belonging or personal power in a world where the child had so little. Acceptance of any participation in cult rituals is extremely difficult for multiples, even when they were brutally victimized, because they equate themselves with the abusers and with the bad feelings they have. Multiples blame themselves for what took place; they must be told again and again that they were only children and that participatory personalities allowed them to survive. The child was not given a choice to perform or not perform an act. Teenage or adult personalities who participated in cult rituals will need help sorting out what part of their feelings of guilt they need to own and what belongs to the abusers. These personalities must also be reminded again and again of the life-threatening aspects of the situations they were in, and of the effects of drugs, hypnosis, and programming.

As the personalities involved in ritual abuse recall the events and abreact, deprogramming takes place. Programming may be one of the last pieces to be resolved in treatment—and deprogramming takes time. Although you may get acquainted early on with a personality who has been programmed, this doesn't mean it is possible or timely to immediately deprogram that personality. In our experience, deprogramming can take place only when the multiple's inner family system has enough trust in the therapist, and enough trust and cooperation among its parts, to support the telling of each and every detail of the abusive ritual. Without all the information, deprogramming doesn't work. If you attempt deprogramming too soon, you may force a crisis or cause the programmed material to be further dissociated. Like all memory work, retrieving memories and feelings from ritualistic trauma is a long, slow process; bits and pieces will be found, only to be lost again temporarily. With patience, each piece can be reclaimed and integrated.

We live in a society in which, paradoxically, violence is rampant, yet disbelieved. We are bombarded with violence in the news, in entertainment, and in the common everyday language we use with one another. Placing the abuse of human beings in the realm of the amusing or the bizarre is a way of saying, "That's really horrible," and then breathing a sigh of relief that it is not true, not real. It is our way of making such violence seem less powerful and frightening, of keeping the awareness of evil unconscious. As we become desensitized to the violence around us, that violence continues to grow, an ever-present shadow within each one who participates in the denial.

> JUDY: *"The ultimate reality is that many, many children are being used and abused by cults today. We must begin to believe these victims; otherwise their numbers will continue to grow. The ultimate price of our choosing not to believe that ritualistic abuse exists will be paid by the children who die. We as a culture must begin to believe, protect, and nurture the children who have been so terribly abused. For the survivors to face disbelief is a recapitulation of the abuse. I beg the mental health communities to believe that ritual abuse does exist and to help those who have survived."*

References

Allison, R. (1974). A new treatment approach for multiple personalities. *American Journal of Clinical Hypnosis, 17*:15–32.

American Psychiatric Association (1987). *Diagnostic and statistical manual of mental disorders (3rd edition, revised)*. Washington, DC.

Bass, E., & Davis, L. (1988). *The courage to heal: A guide for woman survivors of child sexual abuse*. New York: Harper & Row.

Beahrs, J. (1982). *Unity and multiplicity*. New York: Brunner/Mazel.

Bliss, E. (1983). Multiple personalities, related disorders and hypnosis. *American Journal of Clinical Hypnosis, 26*:114–123.

Bloch, J. (1991). *Assessment and treatment of multiple personality and dissociative disorders*. Sarasota, FL: Professional Resource Press.

Blume, E. S. (1990). *Secret survivors: Uncovering incest and its aftereffects in women*. New York: John Wiley and Sons.

Braun, B. (1985). The transgenerational incidence of dissociation and multiple personality disorder: A preliminary report. In R. Kluft (Ed.), *Childhood antecedents of multiple personality disorder* (pp. 127–150). Washington, DC: American Psychiatric Press.

Braun, B., & Sachs, R. (1985). The development of multiple personality disorder: Predisposing, precipitating, and perpetuating factors. In R. Kluft (Ed.), *Childhood antecedents of multiple personality disorder* (pp. 37–64). Washington, DC: American Psychiatric Press.

Chase, T. (1987). *When rabbit howls*. New York: E. P. Dutton.

Clarke, J. (1978). *Self-esteem: A family affair*. Minneapolis, MN: Winston Press.

Dell, P. (1988). Professional skepticism about multiple personality. *Journal of Nervous & Mental Disease, 176*:528–538.

Duvall, E. (1971). *Family development, fourth edition.* Philadelphia: Lippincott.

Erikson, E. (1950). *Childhood and society.* New York: Norton.

Frischholz, E. (1985). The relationship among dissociation, hypnosis, and child abuse in the development of multiple personality disorder. In R. Kluft (Ed.), *Childhood antecedents of multiple personality disorder* (pp. 99–126). Washington, DC: American Psychiatric Press.

Goodwin, J. (1985). Credibility problems in multiple personality disorder patients and abused children. In R. Kluft (Ed.), *Childhood antecedents of multiple personality disorder* (pp. 1–20). Washington, DC: American Psychiatric Press.

Hassan, S. (1988). *Combatting cult mind control.* Rochester, VT: Park Street Press.

Kahaner, L. (1988). *Cults that kill: Probing the underworld of occult crime.* New York: Warner Books.

Kempler, W. (1983). *The myth of resistance.* Costa Mesa, CA: The Kempler Institute.

Kluft, R. (1982). Varieties of hypnotic interventions in the treatment of multiple personality. *American Journal of Clinical Hypnosis, 24*:230–240.

Kluft, R. (1984). An introduction to multiple personality disorder. *Psychiatric Annals, 14*:19–24.

Kluft, R. (1985). The natural history of multiple personality disorder. In R. Kluft (Ed.), *Childhood antecedents of multiple personality disorder* (pp. 197–238). Washington, DC: American Psychiatric Press.

Kluft, R. (1986). Treating children who have multiple personality disorder. In B. Braun (Ed.), *Treatment of multiple personality disorder* (pp. 81–105). Washington, DC: American Psychiatric Press.

Kohlberg, L. (1969). Stage and sequence: The cognitive-developmental approach to socialization. In D. Goslin (Ed.), *Handbook of socialization and research.* Chicago: Rand McNally.

Los Angeles County Commission for Women (1991). *Ritual abuse: Definitions, glossary, the use of mind control.* Report of the Ritual Abuse Task Force.

Miller, A. (1981). *The drama of the gifted child: The search for the true self.* New York: Basic Books.

O'Regan, B. (Ed.). (1985). *Investigations, 1:*3/4, 1–23.

Pruyser, P. (1981). *The psychological examination: A guide for clinicians.* New York: International Universities Press.

Putnam, F., Guroff, J., Silberman, E., Barban, L., & Post, R. (1986). The clinical phenomenology of multiple personality disorder: Review of 100 cases. *Journal of Clinical Psychiatry, 47*:285–293.

Putnam, F. (1989). *Diagnosis and treatment of multiple personality disorder.* New York: Guilford.

Ross, C. (1989). *Multiple personality disorder: Diagnosis, clinical features and treatment.* New York: John Wiley and Sons.

Satir, V. (1978). *Your many faces: The first step to being loved.* Berkeley, CA: Celestial Arts.

Satir, V. (1986). Lecture at the International Training Institute, Crested Butte, CO.

Satir, V. (1988). *The new peoplemaking.* Mountain View, CA: Science and Behavior Books, Inc.

Shengold, L. (1979). Child abuse and deprivation: Soul murder. *Journal of the American Psychoanalytic Association, 29*:533–599.

Smith, M., & Pazder, L. (1980). *Michelle remembers.* New York: Congden and Lattes.

Spenser, J. (1989). *Suffer the child.* New York: Pocket Books.

Spiegel, D. (1986). Dissociation, double binds, and posttraumatic stress in multiple personality disorder. In B. Braun (Ed.), *Treatment of multiple personality disorder* (pp. 61–78). Washington, DC: American Psychiatric Press.

Summit, R. (1983). The child sexual abuse accommodation syndrome. *Child Abuse and Neglect,* 7:177–193.

Index